"For those tired of the old arguments, welcome to the new arguments. No matter what your position, *Contemporary Nuclear Debates* is a treasure trove of informed analysis and new thinking on some of today's most critical issues."

> —Joseph Cirincione, Director,
> Carnegie Endowment Non-Proliferation Project

"Over the last decade the United States and the Russian Federation, through the Cooperative Threat Reduction initiative, have deactivated nearly 6,000 nuclear warheads. Yet the weapons of the Cold War continue to threaten peace and stability. One of the tremendous ironies of the post-Cold War world—and an important focus of this book—is that our countries may face a greater threat today than we did at the height of the Cold War."

> —U.S. Senator Richard Lugar

"Could missile defense and arms control advance the U.S. and international security in the new century? *Contemporary Nuclear Debates* is a remarkable contribution to the current deliberation."

> —Dingli Shen, Professor and Deputy Director,
> Center for American Studies, Fudan University, China

"*Contemporary Nuclear Debates* succeeds admirably in presenting a wide range of views on traditional nuclear questions recast in the current international environment. Especially noteworthy is its treatment of the potential impact of a limited U.S. national missile defense."

> —Dean A. Wilkening,
> Center for International Security and Cooperation,
> Stanford University

A WASHINGTON QUARTERLY READER

Contemporary Nuclear Debates

MISSILE DEFENSE, ARMS CONTROL, AND ARMS RACES IN THE TWENTY-FIRST CENTURY

EDITED BY
ALEXANDER T. J. LENNON

THE MIT PRESS
Cambridge, Massachusetts
London, England

Michael Nacht, "The Politics: How Did We Get Here?" *TWQ* 23, No. 3 (Summer 2000); Stephen J. Hadley, "A Call to Deploy," *TWQ* 23, No. 3 (Summer 2000); Richard L. Garwin, "A Defense That Will Not Defend," *TWQ* 23, No. 3 (Summer 2000); Hans Binnendijk and George Stewart, "Toward Missile Defenses from the Sea," *TWQ* 25, No. 3 (Summer 2002); Kevin McLaughlin, "Would Space-Based Defenses Improve Security?" *TWQ* 25, No. 3 (Summer 2002); James M. Lindsay and Michael E. O'Hanlon, "Missile Defense after the ABM Treaty," *TWQ* 25, No. 3 (Summer 2002); Francois Heisbourg, "Brussels's Burden," *TWQ* 23, No. 3 (Summer 2000); Yoichi Funabashi, "Tokyo's Temperance," *TWQ* 23, No. 3 (Summer 2000); Brahma Chellaney, "New Delhi's Dilemma," *TWQ* 23, No. 3 (Summer 2000); Efraim Karsh, "Israel's Imperative," *TWQ* 23, No. 3 (Summer 2000); Scott Snyder, "Pyongyang's Pressure," *TWQ* 23, No. 3 (Summer 2000); Anoushiravan Ehteshami, "Tehran's Tocsin," *TWQ* 23, No. 3 (Summer 2000); Michael McDevitt, "Beijing's Bind," *TWQ* 23, No. 3 (Summer 2000); Alexander A. Pikayev, "Moscow's Matrix," *TWQ* 23, No. 3 (Summer 2000); Leon Fuerth, "Return of the Nuclear Debate," *TWQ* 24, No. 4 (Autumn 2001); Keith B. Payne, "Action-Reaction Metaphysics and Negligence," *TWQ* 24, No. 4 (Autumn 2001); Bruno Tertrais, "Do Arms Races Matter?" *TWQ* 24, No. 4 (Autumn 2001); Leon Sloss, "The New Arms Race," *TWQ* 24, No. 4 (Autumn 2001); Harold Brown, "Is Arms Control Dead?" *TWQ* 23, No. 2 (Spring 2000); James Schlesinger, "The Demise of Arms Control?" *TWQ* 23, No. 2 (Spring 2000); Brad Roberts, "The Road Ahead," *TWQ* 23, No. 2 (Spring 2000); Thomas Graham, "Strengthening Arms Control," *TWQ* 23, No. 2 (Spring 2000); Stephen Cambone, "An Inherent Lesson," *TWQ* 23, No. 2 (Spring 2000); Rose Gottemoeller, "Arms Control in a New Era," *TWQ* 24, No. 3 (Summer 2001); John Steinbruner, "Renovation through Reassurance," *TWQ* 23, No. 2 (Spring 2000).

Library of Congress Cataloging-in-Publication Data

Contemporary nuclear debates: missile defense, arms control, and arms races in the twenty-first century / edited by Alexander T.J. Lennon
     p.   cm. — (A Washington quarterly reader)
   Includes bibliographical references.
   ISBN 0-262-62166-5 (pbk. : alk. paper)
     1. Ballistic missile defenses—United States 2. Nuclear weapons. 3. Arms race.
   4. Nuclear arms control. 5. World politics—21st century. I. Lennon, Alexander T.
   II. Series.

   UG743.C65 2002
   358.1'74'0973—dc21

                                                                    2002026437

CONTENTS

vii Introduction: Modernizing Strategic Nuclear Debates ▪
Alexander T. J. Lennon

PART I: U.S. NATIONAL MISSILE DEFENSE: WHEN AND HOW?

3 The Politics: How Did We Get Here? ▪ Michael Nacht

12 A Call to Deploy ▪ Stephen J. Hadley

29 A Defense That Will Not Defend ▪ Richard L. Garwin

48 Toward Missile Defenses from the Sea ▪ Hans Binnendijk
and George Stewart

65 Would Space-Based Defenses Improve Security? ▪
Kevin McLaughlin

83 Missile Defense after the ABM Treaty ▪ James M. Lindsay
and Michael E. O'Hanlon

PART II: GLOBAL PERCEPTIONS OF MISSILE DEFENSE

101 Brussels's Burden ▪ François Heisbourg

110 Tokyo's Temperance ▪ Yoichi Funabashi

122 New Delhi's Dilemma ▪ Brahma Chellaney

133 Israel's Imperative ▪ Efraim Karsh

141 Pyongyang's Pressure ▪ Scott Snyder

151 Tehran's Tocsin ▪ Anoushiravan Ehteshami

158 Beijing's Bind ▪ Michael McDevitt

171 Moscow's Matrix ▪ Alexander A. Pikayev

PART III: DO ARMS RACES MATTER ANYMORE?

183 Return of the Nuclear Debate ▪ Leon Fuerth

197 Action-Reaction Metaphysics and Negligence ▪ Keith B. Payne

213   **Do Arms Races Matter?** ▪ *Bruno Tertrais*

226   **The New Arms Race** ▪ *Leon Sloss*

PART IV: IS ARMS CONTROL DEAD?

245   **Is Arms Control Dead?** ▪ *Harold Brown*

251   **The Demise of Arms Control?** ▪ *James Schlesinger*

256   **The Road Ahead** ▪ *Brad Roberts*

273   **Strengthening Arms Control** ▪ *Thomas Graham*

290   **An Inherent Lesson** ▪ *Stephen Cambone*

304   **Arms Control in a New Era** ▪ *Rose Gottemoeller*

321   **Renovation through Reassurance** ▪ *John Steinbruner*

Alexander T. J. Lennon

Introduction: Modernizing Strategic Nuclear Debates

D o nuclear weapons matter anymore? By opening this book, you
have already acknowledged that the answer is "yes"; but the reasons
why nuclear weapons raise concern and the terms of debate about their
future have changed dramatically during the last ten to fifteen years.
Contemporary threats derive primarily from smaller states or terrorists
getting access to nuclear weapons and other weapons of mass destruction. Yet, ironically, many of the same debates that have taken place in
the past continue: Should the United States build a national (or strategic) missile defense system? How would our friends and former, or even
current, adversaries react? Are arms races still a concern? Can arms control help? One may wonder if these debates are still relevant or if inertia drives them.

This book turns to some of the world's most prominent defense and
nuclear experts to update these strategic nuclear controversies. Although the questions may remain the same and their salience is undi-
minished, the answers are dramatically different.

Part I asks: How should the United States build national (or strategic) missile defense? This section does not address in great detail
whether a national missile defense should be built. Michael Nacht explains some of the political reasons that made missile defense inevitable
at the turn of the twenty-first century, tracing the debate as far back as

Alexander T. J. Lennon is editor-in-chief of *The Washington Quarterly*, and is
pursuing his Ph.D. in policy studies, part-time, at the University of Maryland's
School of Public Affairs.

the Johnson administration in the 1960s. Steven J. Hadley, who has since become deputy national security adviser in George W. Bush's administration, introduces some of the threats and concerns about deploying national missile defense. Concluding this section, James M. Lindsay and Michael E. O'Hanlon argue that the September 11 terrorist attacks have entrenched the consensus in favor of missile defense, but that the Bush administration has not yet decided what system to deploy.

The other three chapters in Part I examine this next, and even more contentious, discussion: How should the United States deploy national, or strategic, missile defense? This question will dominate the future policy debate. At what stage should a missile defense attempt to intercept a missile? Where should the United States base a missile defense system? Muddling these separate questions is extremely easy but distinguishing them is critical.

Richard L. Garwin outlines arguments for a boost-phase missile defense, which many of the other authors in this section subsequently evaluate. The first questions to ask are whether a missile defense system should provide a boost-phase capability—or the ability to intercept a missile early while it is accelerating into the atmosphere, generally within three to five minutes of its launch—and when such a system might be technologically deployable.

The other issue discussed within Part I focuses on where to base such a defense system. Although Bill Clinton's administration proposed a ground-based system, Hans Binnendijk and George Stewart sketch the arguments for sea-based systems, and Kevin McLaughlin addresses space basing. The choices about whether to base systems on the ground, at sea, or in space are not mutually exclusive, nor does this book intend to imply that dilemma. For one thing, different elements of a system may be located in different places. Where one bases a system's "eyes" (radars and sensors) may not be where one bases the interceptors themselves. Although even this introduction may lead some readers to fear getting lost in a sea of technological jargon, these articles concentrate on *strategic* arguments to inform readers not well versed in the terminology of missile defense, while also providing the framework for those otherwise immersed in the technical debate.

Beyond the domestic debate, international reactions will frame a crucial criterion for missile defense's future. Against what size of an arsenal should a defense system be built? What is the geographic direction from which Washington most fears missiles? Should allies and even former adversaries be included in a defense umbrella? All of these questions revolve around international considerations. Although national missile defense has its advantages, it is also the technology that can enable the greatest fears of other countries to come true. Some worry that the United States might retreat behind its defenses, disengaging from the world. Conversely, others dread a bolder United States, able to throw its weight around, confident in the protection missile defense would provide. In either case, deploying a workable defense system without due consideration to international reactions, among other concerns, could create potentially avoidable global tensions.

Part II presents the initial reactions of eight key countries to a potential U.S. deployment. This section's purpose is not to advocate giving any country veto power over U.S. decisions, just as no other country would allow countries outside their own borders to make their national security decisions. Ignoring the likely reactions of allies, adversaries, and former adversaries, however, risks stubbornly overlooking potential compromises on architectures and the timing of their deployment that can more easily secure international stability as well as U.S. national security. As with the other articles in this section, readers should keep in mind that the authors are individuals whose national perspectives shape their arguments. The authors' arguments should not be interpreted as government, or consensus, opinions.

Francois Heisbourg and Yoichi Funabashi begin Part II by delineating the initial considerations for NATO and Japan, respectively. Brahma Chellaney elaborates on the potential benefits of national missile defense for India's bilateral relationship with the United States. Similar to NATO and Japan, however, India may also have concerns about negative reactions from Russia or China. From Israel, Efraim

Karsh foreshadows the political benefit that a U.S. national or strategic missile defense debate and deployment may bring Tel Aviv in addition to the potential benefit to Israel's bilateral relationship with the United States.

Part II then turns to current and former adversaries. Both North Korea and Iran have limited military means to overwhelm any missile defense system, but Scott Snyder and Anoushiravan Ehteshami evaluate the potential political as well as military responses those countries could employ. The final perspectives Part II considers are those of China and Russia. Michael McDevitt contends that Beijing initially relied on the Anti-Ballistic Missile (ABM) Treaty to constrain U.S. deployment, leaving itself no contingency plans for the end of that agreement. Alexander Pikayev, meanwhile, catalogs a range of potential incentives that could be used to solicit Russian agreement beyond the progress made to date. One specific feared consequence of U.S. national or strategic missile defense deployment is that it would provoke China and/or Russia to ignite an arms race, the subject of the next section of this book.

Leon Fuerth begins Part III by elaborating concerns that national missile defense might set off an arms race with Russia. He effectively sets up a debate with Keith Payne who, in the next chapter, disputes the arms race argument. Bruno Tertrais advocates discarding "arms race" as a term from contemporary security debates altogether, while Leon Sloss concludes the section by responding that arms races may occur, but in an unfamiliar way—with many different countries in many different weapons systems.

Whatever one's conclusion, the objective of this section is to make the reader think about exactly what the term "arms race" means. Which countries or organizations have the capability to conduct an arms race with the United States in the contemporary international system? Even if the capability exists, who would choose to challenge the United States in this manner? What weapons might they choose to build? Which capabilities of a missile defense system might provoke an arms race? Which systems could avoid provoking one?

Part IV asks one other contemporary nuclear question: Is arms control dead? In the early summer of 2002, signals conflicted. On the one hand, after initial and public hesitation by the Bush administration, the United States and Russia signed a binding treaty in May 2002 to drastically reduce strategic nuclear forces. On the other hand, just a few weeks later, the ABM Treaty, which many believe was the cornerstone of arms control, expired when U.S. withdrawal became official.

The previous decade saw similar mixed signals. Successes such as the 1995 indefinite extension of the Nuclear Non-Proliferation Treaty (NPT) heralded the continuing relevance of arms control to some. Thomas Graham, who led the U.S. government efforts extending the NPT, makes the case in his chapter for the enduring importance of arms control to future nonproliferation. In contrast, perceived failures such as the U.S. Senate's rejection of the Comprehensive Test Ban Treaty (CTBT), a case that Stephen Cambone details within Part IV, marked the death of arms control to others.

Former secretaries of defense Harold Brown and James Schlesinger project arms control's role for contemporary international security. Other chapters look at specific, potential future arms control roles. Brad Roberts distinguishes among three forks of the arms control path: future strategic force reductions, nonproliferation, and current treaty implementation. Rose Gottemoeller argues that relying on unilateral reductions in U.S. and Russian strategic nuclear forces could damage future bilateral relations. Finally, John Steinbruner proposes reassurance as the principle around which arms control can be restructured and forecasts what such agreements might look like.

Together, the goal of compiling these diverse perspectives is to add new muscle and flesh to the old skeleton of strategic nuclear debates. In the 1980s missile defense was envisioned as a "Star Wars" system, but more limited roles to address different threats currently animate political dialogue. International reactions are framed not by the Cold War but by a more flexible and complex international system. Invoking the danger of arms races means something entirely different than in the past. Ultimately, the role of arms control, and the treaties and norms that make up the arms-control regime, aim to assuage different concerns and combat different threats.

Although the questions posed in each part of this book may seem familiar at first glance, the answers in these pages compel a closer look. These chapters aim to stimulate you, as a reader, to learn from the authors' insight, challenge their thoughts, and continue the debates (whether in halls of power, in a classroom, online, or elsewhere) to reshape the ideas of others. The goal of the chapters that follow is modernization—not of nuclear forces themselves, but of the debates that shape their future....

Part I

U.S. National Missile Defense: When and How?

Michael Nacht

The Politics:
How Did We Get Here?

Aftter many years of being on the "back burner," it is increasingly apparent that a broad consensus is building among Washington policymakers to authorize the initial deployment of a national missile defense (NMD) system. This political turnaround is surprising given the decades-long debate about the wisdom of sustaining the Anti-Ballistic Missile (ABM) Treaty and the unwillingness of Presidents Ronald Reagan or George Bush to seek withdrawal from this treaty. What has led to this pronounced shift in attitudes? It is instructive to understand the historical evolution of the political debate to appreciate both where we are and where we might be headed.

Historical Perspectives

It is a completely natural instinct to protect oneself against potential adversaries. The dynamic of measure, countermeasure, and counter-countermeasure has always been at the heart of military affairs. Anti-submarine warfare capabilities and anti-aircraft systems have been central elements of modern military arsenals for more than a half-cen-

Michael Nacht is dean and professor of public policy in the Goldman School of Public Policy at the University of California, Berkeley. From 1994 to 1997 he served as assistant director of the U.S. Arms Control and Disarmament Agency.

Copyright © 2000 by The Center for Strategic and International Studies and the Massachusetts Institute of Technology
The Washington Quarterly • 23:3 pp. 87–94.

tury. After the United States and the Soviet Union began to deploy nuclear-armed ballistic missiles in the late 1950s and 1960s, it was not at all surprising that each side would in turn seek to acquire missile defenses against these nuclear threats. Indeed, it was the Soviet Union that first deployed an active ABM system around Moscow in the 1960s.

THE JOHNSON-NIXON YEARS

Strategic writings in the 1960s pointing out that deployment of ABM systems could be "destabilizing" were embraced by Secretary of Defense Robert McNamara during the Johnson administration. McNamara's basic argument, in rational and apolitical terms, was that if both Moscow and Washington deployed large numbers of nuclear-armed missiles, each side would be deterred from attacking the other as long as neither side believed it had an ability to disarm the other in a first strike. But if one side then began to deploy extensive ABM systems, in the name of its own defense, the other side could believe it was a provocative act. The reasoning goes as follows: A and B each have extensive offensive nuclear forces. Then A begins to deploy ABM systems. B believes that A plans to launch a first strike against B's nuclear forces and would then use its ABM systems to destroy B's residual retaliatory forces, thereby prevailing in a nuclear exchange.

McNamara believed, and argued to Soviet president Aleksey Kosygin at a U.S.-Soviet summit meeting in 1967 in Glassboro, New Jersey, that ABM system deployment was "destabilizing" in two respects: first, it would stimulate arms racing by each side to overcome the defenses of the other, and second, in a crisis, it could provoke a first strike by the side that did not have ABM systems. McNamara argued that "arms race stability" and "crisis stability" could both be preserved, ironically, if both sides were defenseless against nuclear attack. This reasoning gave birth to the notion of "mutual assured destruction" as the bedrock of deterrence in the nuclear age.

Although Kosygin rejected this reasoning at Glassboro, U.S.-Soviet negotiations in the Strategic Arms Limitations Talks (SALT) led in

1972 to the signing of the ABM Treaty that limited both sides to modest missile defenses.

It is worth recalling this experience because it lies at the root of the current debate on missile defense. In the late 1960s, and through the ratification debate on the ABM Treaty, there was deep division within the U.S. strategic community (perhaps no more than a few hundred civilians and military leaders who paid attention to this issue) on whether this logic made sense. Senator Henry Jackson and his aide Richard Perle (later a high-ranking defense official in the Reagan administration) rejected McNamara's strategic logic. They argued that the United States should exploit its technological edge to protect U.S. cities and military targets from Soviet attack. They also doubted that Soviet officials would respect the treaty.

The ABM Treaty entered into force in October 1972 after a heated debate in the U.S. Senate, but the political wounds from these doctrinal differences never healed. There was then—and remains today—a large cadre of specialists who believe the entire notion of being defenseless in the nuclear age is totally misguided and highly dangerous. When the Soviet Union built up extensive nuclear forces in the 1970s and early 1980s, with the ABM Treaty in force, critics pointed to this evidence to support their case. Arms race stability, they argued, was in no way assured by being defenseless. Moreover, Paul Nitze and others claimed that the United States was in mortal danger of a "window of vulnerability" in which the Soviet Union might launch a "disarming first strike" against U.S. intercontinental ballistic missiles (ICBMs), long-range aircraft, and submarine-launched ballistic missiles. Being defenseless did not promote crisis stability either, it was argued.

THE REAGAN YEARS

When Reagan became president in 1981, he was committed to overturning this policy and launched the famous Strategic Defense Initiative (SDI) in 1983. The nuclear weapons laboratories, important segments of the aerospace industry, and senior civilian and military officials were mobilized around the Strategic Defense Initiative Office (SDIO). The SDIO was to develop and deploy a space-based system that could destroy as many as several thousand Soviet ballistic missiles by striking them upon launch (in the "boost phase"), attacking those that survived in mid-course, and destroying what was left before they reached their targets (terminal phase). Critics of the ABM Treaty, on the one hand, applauded this hard-headed approach to dealing with the Soviet threat. On the other hand, supporters of the ABM Treaty were deeply alarmed that this initiative could even precipitate a Soviet-U.S. nuclear exchange with disastrous consequences.

Despite a tremendous budgetary, technological, and organizational effort, by the end of Reagan's second term, it was deemed not technically feasible to deploy such a system. Critics of SDI breathed a great sigh of relief and noted that Reagan did not exercise the supreme national interest clause to remove the United States from its obligations under the treaty. Despite much heated debate, the ABM Treaty survived the Reagan two-term presidency. Nonetheless, supporters of SDI claimed, and still claim today, that the defense initiative stimulated such a budgetary response in Moscow that it contributed greatly to their economic problems and was a key cause of the collapse of the Soviet Union.[1]

THE BUSH YEARS

When Bush replaced Reagan in 1989, and especially after the collapse of Soviet influence in Eastern Europe, Secretary of Defense Dick Cheney downgraded the SDIO to the Ballistic Missile Defense Office (BMDO). Its budget and political profile were greatly reduced and its mission changed to primarily research. Bush, however, in fact *advanced* Reagan's ideas of Strategic Arms Reduction Talks (START) and reached the START I agreement with President Mikhail Gorbachev in 1991 that promised major reductions in the deployed number of strategic nuclear warheads. There was no talk of ABM Treaty withdrawal or abrogation. Indeed, with the waning of the Cold War, military attention shifted away from nuclear forces and related systems. Each military service needed budgetary support for enhanced conventional forces to wage several major regional conflicts simultaneously. Therefore, enthusiasm for missile defense programs declined within the military services.

What was unanticipated was the effect of the Persian Gulf War on the logic of missile defense. Saddam Hussein used Scud B missiles to attack U.S. forces and allies in Saudia Arabia and Israeli civilian targets. As a result, it became widely accepted across the political spectrum that what was needed was not space-based defenses against a Soviet threat, but land and sea-based defenses against regional missile threats. With the leadership of Senator Sam Nunn, then chairman of the Senate Armed Services Committee, and Representative Les Aspin, then chairman of the House Armed Services Committee, both houses of Congress passed overwhelmingly the Missile Defense Act of 1991. Research and development began on theater missile defenses (TMD) that would protect U.S. forward-deployed forces and our allies.

In the last year of the Bush administration and throughout the two terms of the Clinton presidency, there has been widespread (although not universal) support for these TMD programs. The U.S. Army, Navy, and Air Force have all been funded to work on this problem. The Army land-based theater high-altitude area defense (THAAD) system, the Navy area-wide and theater-wide systems using Aegis cruisers, and the Air Force airborne laser programs and subsequent modifications all remain active despite some testing failures. The United States is also working with Israel on the Arrow system for Israeli defense and on European-based programs. It has further enhanced the Patriot system, originally designed for air defense and rushed into service during the Gulf War as a TMD system.

THE CLINTON YEARS

U.S. TMD initiatives triggered concern in Russia about its relationship to the ABM Treaty. President Bill Clinton, despite the criticism of primarily Republican skeptics, agreed in late 1993 to begin Russian-U.S. negotiations on missile defense "demarcation" to clarify the nature of TMD deployments and their relationship to the treaty. Because the Soviet Union (one of the two original parties to the ABM Treaty) no longer existed, the United States agreed to negotiate not only with Russia but also with the other nuclear successor states of the Soviet Union (Ukraine, Belarus, and Kazakhstan). In the fall of 1997, a demarcation agreement was reached that permitted deployment of currently planned U.S. TMD systems. Critics argued that this agreement was wholly misguided because the Clinton administration was striving to preserve a treaty that is now completely out of date with a party that no longer exists.

The Resurgence of National Missile Defense

During the first Clinton term, the executive branch was far more cautious toward NMD. Several national intelligence estimates (NIEs) prepared for the president claimed that no "rogue state"—regional powers with hostile intent toward the United States, notably North Korea, Iran, Iraq, and Libya—was likely to be able to mount an effective missile threat against the U.S. homeland for at least 15 years. The administration responded by mounting a "three plus three" program in which three years would be spent assessing the technical feasibility of an NMD program. If, after three years, it was determined that such a system could be deployed and if it was also judged that the threat warranted it, a decision could be made to deploy the system three years hence.

Buttressed by defense critics of the administration, several prominent members of Congress—including Senators Thad Cochran, Jon Kyl, Trent Lott, and John McCain, as well as Representative Curt Weldon—argued that this approach was too little and too late. Then, in 1998, these critics received two important measures of support. Former Defense Secretary Donald Rumsfeld chaired a bipartisan committee of experts that issued a report in the summer claiming that the NIEs were incorrect and that rogue states could directly threaten U.S. targets within 5 years, not 15. Right after the report was issued, North Korea launched a missile test that traversed Japanese territory. These two developments altered congressional thinking on this issue and eventually led to a change in Clinton's position. He has now agreed to authorize deployment of an NMD system against rogue states as soon as it is technologically feasible.

Major Considerations in the Current Debate

Supporters of NMD deployment argue:
1. The rogue state threat is real. The United States will have limited warning time once North Korea or Iran tests a missile system. We should put in the field whatever we have as soon as we have it; a partial defense is better than none.
2. The costs (several billions of dollars) are a tiny fraction of the defense budget and a small price to protect U.S. lives, property, and military assets from such attacks.
3. By deploying such systems quickly, the United States will maximize its freedom of action in regional crises or conflict situations. The United States would then not be deterred from conventional military involvement for fear of being vulnerable to missile attack from a rogue state.
4. The systems are not designed for use against either Russia or China, and we have told them so in great detail. If Russia cannot accept this pledge and is unwilling to renegotiate the ABM Treaty, it is no great loss because the treaty was never more than an illusion of security. As for China, the leadership has already decided to modernize its nuclear forces and is not responding to U.S. NMD programs. Eventually, we may need an anti-Chinese NMD system anyway as part of our efforts to defend Taiwan against Chinese attack. Our European allies may be nervous about these developments, but they are always nervous and will ultimately go along.

Critics of NMD deployment argue:
1. The systems have not proven technologically feasible. Some of the tests appear to have involved "cooperation" between target and interceptor to facilitate a successful result. Even if technologically feasible, the systems can be easily defeated by offensive saturation, by

decoys and other means of "fooling" the system, and by blinding the sensors on which the system's logic is based.

2. The several billion dollars in funding will continue to grow, robbing needed conventional-force programs of important budgetary support.

3. The United States is working to improve relations with both North Korea and Iran that would, it is hoped, lead to a moderation in their hostility toward the United States. Deployment of these systems does not serve these political purposes, especially because the systems are not likely to be effective anyway.

4. Deployment of NMD will mean the end of the ABM Treaty and a resurgence of a hostile U.S.-Russia strategic relationship that is not in either of our interests. Such a development would only retard Russian progress toward democratization and a true market economy. Deployment of NMD systems, coupled with TMD deployments in East Asia, will greatly exacerbate U.S.-China relations without enhancing U.S. security. Moreover, the Europeans will see these initiatives as a unilateralist effort to "decouple" U.S. security from its allies, stimulating European defense programs and policies taken without U.S. consultation. In sum, argue the critics, the U.S. will deploy an NMD system that does not work and in turn exacerbates relations with Russia, China, and our European allies.

Given that the presidential election campaign is in full swing, it is not surprising that this national security issue, as others, could be subject to the vicissitudes of U.S. domestic politics. Some claim that Clinton is likely to support at least initial deployment of the NMD program later this fall, in part to protect Vice President Al Gore from criticism on this issue by his Republican challenger. A few prominent Democratic senators, notably Joseph Biden, ranking minority member on the Senate Foreign Relations Committee, have urged that the decision be delayed until the next administration takes office. Others claim that the Republicans do not want to give Clinton and Gore any political cover on this issue. If the president requests funds for Phase I of the program, they predict that it will be defeated by the Republicans. The Republican majority will argue that funding for a full-scale, three-phase system is warranted immediately and that to approve Clinton's request will reduce the likelihood that what is actually needed will be supported.

The NMD issue has yet to reach the political consciousness of most Americans. Foreign and defense policy issues generally have had a minor role in the past two presidential election campaigns. But Governor George W. Bush has consistently claimed that he will raise the "rebuilding of the U.S. military" as a key element of his campaign. Surely NMD will fit squarely in this strategy.

On the industrial front, NMD programs are looming as important new funding sources for key players in the aerospace industry. One can expect support for NMD from those organizations and individuals who stand to gain financially from an effort that could rise rapidly in budgetary support in the next decade.

There are two large unknowns in the NMD political equation. First, what is the probability of a crisis during 2000 in which missile defense issues play a role? Second, in the absence of such a crisis, how will the U.S. voter respond to a debate on these issues? Neither question is easily answered.

Slowly but surely we are all trying to adjust to the complexities and uncertainties of the contemporary era. This era is marked by the information revolution, economic globalization, the resurgence of ethnic conflict, rogue states whose behavior we are trying to moderate, and relations with Russia and China that are at the same time competitive and cooperative. This is a difficult and demanding environment for the United States to assess threats and countermeasures. The collective judgment of the public—from focus groups to the national election—will play a key role in shaping the future direction of the NMD effort.

Note

1. This claim is serious and worth detailed research to determine the degree of its validity; to this author's knowledge, such research is now being undertaken as part of the Cold War History Project of the Smithsonian Institution.

Stephen J. Hadley

A Call to Deploy

The United States will soon decide whether to begin deploying a national missile defense (NMD) system designed to defend the territory of the United States against ballistic missiles. The system proposed by the Clinton administration is a far cry from the Strategic Defense Initiative (SDI), or "Star Wars," originally proposed by President Ronald Reagan in 1983. The early SDI concept envisioned an extensive system of ground-based and space-based interceptors designed to defend the U.S. homeland against a massive attack by Soviet strategic ballistic missiles.

By contrast, the system proposed by the Clinton administration would involve up to only 100 land-based interceptors located at a single site in Alaska. This system is intended to provide a very limited defense capable of shooting down 10 to 20 ballistic missile warheads launched at the United States, primarily from North Korea. Such a system would do nothing about the thousands of strategic ballistic missile warheads still deployed by Russia and relatively little about ballistic missiles that might be launched at the United States from countries such as Iraq and Iran in the Middle East. The administration has said it would seek to address the threat from Iran or Iraq in a later Phase 2 deployment, once that threat "emerges."

Stephen J. Hadley is a partner at the law firm of Shea and Gardner and a principal in the Scowcroft Group, Inc. He served as the assistant secretary of defense for international security policy from 1989 to 1993.

Copyright © 2000 by The Center for Strategic and International Studies and the Massachusetts Institute of Technology
The Washington Quarterly • 23:3 pp. 95–108.

A Critical Decision

Even the very limited defense system envisaged by the Clinton administration has caused great controversy in the United States and abroad. The stakes could not be higher. Some of its closest allies have complained that the U.S. effort to defend its territory against ballistic missiles is evidence of a new U.S. "hegemonism" that seeks to make the United States invulnerable to attack while leaving its allies undefended. Key Russian officials have threatened that they would pull out of the START I and START II arms control agreements, which provide for a dramatic reduction in the number of strategic nuclear weapons deployed by the United States and Russia. China has made clear that it would view U.S. NMD deployment as a hostile act, further taxing a U.S.-China relationship already badly strained over the Taiwan issue.

The Clinton administration has said a decision this fall to pursue even the limited system it proposes could require a six-month notice of withdrawal from the 1972 Anti-Ballistic Missile (ABM) Treaty unless Russia agreed to modify the treaty to permit deployment. The ABM Treaty, between the United States and the Soviet Union, prohibited deploying ABM systems to defend national territory against strategic ballistic missiles. A U.S. notice of withdrawal could touch off an international outcry and confront the new U.S. president in January 2001 with a major diplomatic crisis.

In view of the major consequences of a deployment decision, a number of supporters and critics of NMD have called upon President Bill Clinton to defer the deployment issue to his successor, and some have particularly pressed to defer any effort to reach an agreement with Russia on ABM Treaty modifications. Even assuming the nation needs a national missile defense, does it need to begin deployment now?

This article argues that the United States urgently needs to make a deployment decision. It may already be too late to have a system before the United States will have need to use it. But the decision needs to be the right one—a decision to deploy a system that will adequately meet the defense needs of the nation. The Clinton administration's plan fails to meet this test.

The Urgency of the Threat

Any judgment about the timing of NMD deployment must begin with an appreciation of how long it will take, with its current approach, for the United States to field a defense against the ballistic missile threat. The program proposed by the Clinton administration would not be operational until 2005 at the earliest. A more realistic schedule is probably 2007 or 2008. Any effort to provide comparably effective protection of the United States against missiles from the Middle East as well as North Korea is not likely to be completed until into the second decade of the twenty-first century.

By contrast, the most recent authoritative assessments suggest that a ballistic missile threat could materialize from North Korea or from sources in the Middle East within as few as five years. Furthermore, these assessments suggest that, in certain scenarios, the United States would have little or no warning of the emergence of these threats. This leads to the inescapable conclusion that, if the goal is to have in place a defense against these threats before they emerge, the U.S. NMD program is already well behind and likely to lose the race against the threat—if the race has not already been lost.

The unclassified and public summary of the 1999 National Intelligence Estimate (NIE) produced by the U.S. intelligence community on the ballistic missile threat confirms this assessment. Here are some excerpts:

> North Korea *could convert* its Taepo Dong-I space launch vehicle (SLV) into an ICBM [an intercontinental ballistic missile or long-range ballistic missile capable of reaching U.S. territory] that could deliver a light payload (sufficient for a biological or chemical weapon) to the United States. ... North Korea is *more likely to weaponize* the larger Taepo Dong-2 ICBM that could deliver a several-hundred-kilogram payload (sufficient for early generation nuclear weapons) to

the United States. Most analysts believe it could be tested at any time, probably initially as an SLV, unless it is delayed for political reasons.[1] [Emphasis, in each case, is in the original]

Iraq *could test* a North Korean-type ICBM that could deliver a several-hundred-kilogram payload to the United States in the last half of the next decade [the decade beginning with calendar year 2000] depending on the level of foreign assistance. Although less likely, most analysts believe it *could test* an ICBM that could deliver a lighter payload to the United States in a few years based on its failed SLV or the Taepo Dong-I, if it began development now. ... If Iraq could buy a Taepo Dong-II from North Korea it *could have a launch capability* within months of the purchase. ... If it could acquire Nodongs [a medium-range ballistic missile] from North Korea, Iraq *could test* a much more capable ICBM along the same lines within a few years of the Nodong acquisition.[2]

Iran *could test* an ICBM that could deliver a several-hundred-kilogram payload to many parts of the United States in the last half of the next decade [the decade beginning with calendar year 2000] using Russian technology and assistance. Most analysts believe that it could test an ICBM capable of delivering a lighter payload to the United States in the next few years following the North Korea pattern.[3]

Sales of ICBMs or SLVs, which have inherent ICBM capabilities and could be converted relatively quickly with little or no warning, could increase the number of countries able to threaten the United States. North Korea continues to demonstrate a willingness to sell its missiles. Although we judge that Russia or China is unlikely to sell ICBM or SLV in the next fifteen years, the consequences of even one sale would be extremely serious.[4]

Moreover, the intelligence community is not confident that it can provide much if any warning of these developments. In a 1998 report, the intelligence community stated that it had "high confidence" that it could provide warning "five years *before deployment* that a potentially hostile country was trying to *develop and deploy* an ICBM." In the 1999 report, the intelligence community was less confident:

We continue to judge that we may not be able to provide much warning if a country purchased an ICBM or if a country already had an SLV capability. ... North Korea and other countries, such as Iran and an unconstrained Iraq, could develop an SLV booster, then flight-test it as an ICBM with a re-entry vehicle (RV) [or warhead] with little or no warning.[5]

The difficulty in providing warning is underscored in a recent report of the Rumsfeld Commission, established by Congress in 1997 to assess the nature and magnitude of the existing and emerging ballistic missile threat to the United States. The Rumsfeld Commission concluded:

> A new strategic environment now gives emerging ballistic missile powers the capacity, through a combination of domestic development and foreign assistance, to acquire the means to strike the [United States] within about five years of a decision to acquire such capability (ten years in the case of Iraq). During several of those years, the United States might not be aware that such a decision had been made. Available alternative means of delivery can shorten the warning time of deployment nearly to zero.[6]

This is not to say that a ballistic missile is the only way to deliver a weapon of mass destruction. These weapons could also be delivered by aircraft, cruise missiles, shipping containers, or a suitcase carried by a terrorist—all of which are serious threats. But the United States already has committed substantial effort and resources to combating most of these threats through military programs, border controls, and counterterrorism operations. Only against ballistic missiles does the United States remain vulnerable through continued adherence to the ABM Treaty. Yet whatever NMD's critics may say about the greater ease of these other methods of delivery, the fact is that nations that do not wish the United States well are concentrating their efforts on acquiring ballistic missiles.

Is This the Way to Deal with a National Crisis?

Many NMD supporters and critics share the view that the proliferation of weapons of mass destruction (WMD)—nuclear, chemical, and biological—and the means to deliver them represent the most serious challenge to U.S. national security of this decade. Given both the imminence and potential undetectability of the ballistic missile threat, one might expect development of defenses against these missiles to have the highest national priority. One might expect a Manhattan Project approach similar to that used to develop the atomic bomb in World War II. In fact, NMD has had uneven political support and variable funding, and been a subject of deep disagreement between the Democratic-controlled White House and the Republican-controlled Congress. Only recently has this situation begun to change, as even traditional opponents are now talking about limited deployments.

The NMD that has emerged is in many ways a traditional defense program. It is highly structured and largely subject to the same testing and procurement practices that apply to most defense programs, many of which involve meeting much less urgent national requirements. Although the development schedule is compressed, with reduced testing traded off against increased program risk, the approach has largely been "business as usual."

Yet the countries that are seeking to acquire ballistic missiles—including North Korea, Iran, and probably Iraq—are using untraditional methods. These countries are not developing their own indigenous capability to produce a large number of ballistic missiles designed with a high degree of accuracy, survivability, and reliability. Rather, they appear to be seeking at least initially a more limited capability—a few missiles begged, borrowed, or stolen and declared ready for use after few if any flight tests.

Those who have watched these efforts explain this approach on the grounds that these weapons "are not envisioned at the outset as operational weapons of war, but primarily as strategic weapons of deterrence and coercive diplomacy."[7] These potential terror weapons, acquired for their political impact, are intended to blackmail or coerce neighboring states while neutralizing the ability or willingness of the United States and its allies to intervene.

A National Priority: An Emergency Response Capability

This nontraditional approach to the acquisition and use of these weapons should be met by a nontraditional approach in defeating them. A president truly committed to defending the nation against these threats would bring together, on an urgent basis, the best scientific and engineering talent in our academic institutions and defense contractor community to develop on a crash basis some interim or even experimental capabilities to defend the United States against ballistic missiles. The goal would be to give the United States at least some capability to counter these threats before 2005 (or more likely 2007 or 2008), when a more mature capability could be developed.

There is precedent for this kind of approach. The United States, concerned with the vulnerability of its land-based ballistic missiles at the height of the Cold War, demonstrated experimentally the ability to carry a long-range ballistic missile aloft in an aircraft and to launch it during flight by ejecting the missile from the aircraft and igniting it. This, albeit limited, experiment demonstrated to the Soviet Union that the United States had both the capacity and the will to deal with a serious national security problem.

Interim "quick fixes" offering even the most limited capability against the ballistic missile threat would send a similar signal to countries now seeking these weapons. Making clear that the United States will not remain vulnerable to ballistic missile attack should make those nations pause to consider whether the benefits they hope to achieve at considerable cost with these weapons will ever materialize.

Any such interim approaches should take maximum advantage of investments that the United States has already made in its ballistic missile defense programs and in such things as the Aegis air defense system being deployed on many of the nation's naval ships, offering protection against both ballistic and cruise missile attack.

For example, there are two Aegis cruisers already doing initial operational testing of the Navy's area missile defense system. Some have suggested that one or both of these ships (or a small number of other Aegis cruisers) might be outfitted with an upgrade of the Standard Missile interceptor, currently in development for the Navy theater missile defense (TMD) system (which could still fit in the existing missile launchers on these ships). These interceptor missiles would in turn carry either an adapted "missile kill" vehicle already being developed under the current NMD program or an advanced version of the kill vehicle (called LEAP) already being developed for the Navy's TMD system. A radar would be needed to track the incoming ballistic missile (the existing SPY radar on the Aegis cruisers being too limited to play this role), but this radar could be a ground-based radar, a new radar deployed on another ship, or a modified special sea-based missile tracking ship already in existence.

The result would be a limited capability, to be sure, but at least the United States would have an "emergency deployment option" in case of crisis. The system would provide a capability to intercept threatening missiles early in their flight (in the "post-boost" or "mid-course" phases). This could give the United States the chance of destroying the missile before it had deployed the "countermeasures" that many critics contend could defeat the land-based system now being developed by the Clinton administration.

Some critics might argue that such an "emergency deployment option" would still violate the ABM Treaty's ban on sea-based ABM systems. But because its capability would be so limited and so temporary in nature, this "emergency deployment option" could be considered an "ABM system" only in the loosest sense of that term. It would certainly not be the kind of ABM system that the parties had in mind when they entered into the ABM Treaty—namely, ABM systems capable of countering strategic ballistic missiles of the United States and the Soviet Union, respectively. As such, any sensible reading of the treaty would put the "emergency deployment option" outside its prohibitions and limitations."

A president serious about defending the country against this threat would establish a temporary command to focus completely on bringing some kind of interim, emergency capability into existence.

Should a Deployment Decision Be Deferred?

The search for interim "quick fix" measures need not detract from the ongoing effort to develop through traditional programs a defense against ballistic missiles. Given the threats that exist or could emerge with little or no warning, it is hard to argue for deferral of the deployment decision that the Clinton administration has scheduled for itself this fall. But, although a deployment decision should not be deferred, it is important that the deployment decision be the *right* decision. At this point, the Clinton administration is poised to make the *wrong* decision.

The *right* decision would be to immediately approve NMD deployment that would provide protection to the entire territory of the United States against limited ballistic missile threats from the Middle East as well as Asia. This system should protect U.S. allies in Europe and Asia as well. This might require, for example, deployment to at least four sites, with one site in Alaska and one in Maine, and at least one site each in Asia and Europe. Current intelligence assessments of the potential for ballistic missile threats to emerge from the Middle East and elsewhere, with little notice, make a compelling case for beginning now to deploy a system able to defend against limited threats on a global basis.

Such a deployment decision would also require a change in the approach of the Clinton administration to amending or modifying the ABM Treaty to permit limited NMD deployments. Any formal negotiations with Russia should seek Russian agreement now to amendments or modifications that would permit the ultimate deployment of the expanded system described above. Obtaining Russian agreement only to amendments permitting the more limited deployment proposed will make it harder for the Clinton administration to get Moscow to agree later to further amendments permitting more ambitious deployment.

Any amendments or modifications could be worked out with the Russians as part of a package in which a START III agreement would be reached, establishing lower levels of strategic nuclear forces that would be easier for the Russians to sustain with their limited economic resources. In addition, amendments or modifications to the ABM Treaty should eliminate restrictions on NMD research, development, and testing and their ability to use information from radar, satellites, or sensors of any sort. This will permit any NMD system actually deployed to be improved so as to meet the changing capability of potential adversaries.

The Objections to Deployment Are Unsound

A number of objections to this approach can be anticipated.

THE TECHNOLOGY IS NOT READY

The current U.S. approach to NMD involves crashing an interceptor missile at high speed into an incoming ballistic missile warhead to destroy it (so-called "hit to kill"). This concept has been tested enough in connection with the upgraded Patriot theater ballistic missile defense system of Gulf War fame (PAC-III), the Army's theater ballistic missile defense system (THAAD), and the administration's proposed NMD system to give confidence that the concept will work. It is not a problem of physics but of engineering. It is true that there have been test failures, and there will undoubtedly be more in the future. But the history of virtually every sophisticated, state-of-the-art weapons system ever deployed (from airplanes to Polaris missiles) is one of initial failures and setbacks and gradual increases in performance and effectiveness as the system matures.

Critics argue that any NMD system must be shown to be nearly 100 percent effective before it is deployed. They argue that the current design can be easily defeated by ballistic missiles equipped with various types of countermeasures and penetration aids designed to ensure that the ballistic missile and the warheads it carries will be able to avoid or confuse any interceptor missile.

Under this standard, the United States would never have deployed most of the weapon systems that its security has depended on since World War II. Countermeasures and penetration aids pose a challenge, but many of these challenges already have solutions, or solutions can be found for them. The United States will never find them if it does not "get in the business" of defending itself against ballistic missile attack.

The United States must not let the "best" be the enemy of the "good." An NMD system does not need to be perfect to significantly help the United States deal with the ballistic missile threat. Even a system of limited effectiveness may discourage countries from acquiring ballistic missiles and help to persuade a potential adversary that blackmailing or coercing the United States from aiding a friend or ally will not succeed. Even a system of limited effectiveness can supplement conventional military force and the threat of U.S. retaliation as part of a strategy to deter the use of ballistic missiles against the territory of the United States and its friends and allies. This would advance—not under-mine—other aspects of U.S. policy against the proliferation of WMD and the means to deliver it.

THE COST IS TOO GREAT

Current estimates are that the Clinton adminis-tration's program based on a single site in Alaska will require an additional expenditure of ap-proximately $12-18 billion between now and deployment. A more ex-panded deployment protecting the entire United States from threats from both Asia and the Middle East could require perhaps an addi-tional $10-15 billion. Additional sites to protect U.S. friends and allies in Europe and Asia could involve additional expenditures, although presumably those countries would bear most of this cost.

Critics argue that the United States cannot afford the cost of such a deployment. It is hard to see how this could be so in a period of increas-ing budgetary surpluses where the proliferation of WMD and the means to deliver it are widely viewed as representing the greatest threat to the security of the United States.

It is also difficult to understand this view when the United States will spend vast sums on power projection forces designed, among other things, to protect friends and allies overseas. It is hard to justify these costs in the absence of an adequate ballistic missile defense program. Without such a program, the United States significantly risks never using its power projec-tion forces. The threat of an attack by ballistic missiles—even if armed with only conventional explosives rather than WMD—may be sufficient to convince a U.S. president not to use those power projection forces in sup-port of a friend or ally. Remember that the Senate resolution supporting the Gulf War against Iraq in January 1991 passed by only five votes. One can only wonder what the vote would have been if Saddam Hussein had had a long-range ballistic missile capable of reaching the territory of the United States, or even one of its closest allies, and had threatened to use it if the United States tried to roll back his invasion of Kuwait.

THE ALLIES ARE OPPOSED

It is true that the Clinton administration has only recently begun any real consultations with friends and allies about its NMD plans. But the idea of defending the territory of the United States against ballistic missiles has had great public currency since Reagan's so-called Star Wars speech on March 23, 1983. In 1992, the Bush administration conducted intensive discussions with European and Asian allies about a limited NMD then called Global Protection Against Limited Strikes (GPALS), and the issue has been part of the U.S. political debate since then. Only someone virtually oblivious to the U.S. political scene for the past two decades could be "surprised" by the U.S. NMD effort.

The Clinton administration is right to argue that deployment of an NMD system by the United States will not undermine or "decouple" the security link between the United States and its allies. To ensure that the United States can defend itself against ballistic missiles makes it more likely, not less likely, that the United States will come to the defense of its friends and allies. But it is also true that a United States defended against ballistic missile threats, when its allies are not, invites a Saddam Hussein of the future to seek to influence the behavior of a U.S. president by threatening to use ballistic missiles against U.S. allies.

For this reason, the United States should tell its friends and allies that it will not defend itself against these threats at their expense. The United States should make clear that it is willing to work with its friends and allies to develop an approach to defending against ballistic missiles that extends to them as well.

This effort will require the United States to undertake on an urgent basis the most intensive consultations with its friends and allies. The consultations should have three elements:

1. A quiet, intensive, and systematic dialogue among the respective intelligence and policy communities to develop a common understanding about the seriousness of the threat represented by the proliferation of WMD and the means to deliver it, including but not limited to ballistic missiles.

2. Intensive discussions between the respective defense experts to develop an approach to ballistic missile defense that will protect friends and allies as well as the United States. It may be that the same architecture is not the best way to protect all of these countries. A ground-based approach may make sense for the United States. A sea-based approach—building on the Aegis air defense system—may make more sense, particularly for Asian allies such as Japan. Europe may need a mix of both approaches.

3. Intensive discussions between the respective policy officials to develop a common strategy tailored to each state that is pursuing a policy of proliferation. This strategy should bring to bear in a comprehensive and coordinated way the full array of available instruments—political, economic, diplomatic, and legal—against that state in a way that is designed to prevent, discourage, or at least delay the development of WMD and the means to deliver it.

To the extent that key U.S. friends and allies are concerned about the deployment of defenses against ballistic missiles, this may give the United States leverage to obtain their cooperation and hard work in dealing with the proliferation problem in some other way. There is still time to pursue other measures. Even the limited system envisaged by the Clinton administration cannot be deployed until 2005 at the earliest. While some deployment is essential, the size of the NMD system the United States ultimately needs to deploy—and the urgency of Europe's need to defend itself—could be dramatically affected by real progress in the effort against proliferation. An Iran, for example, that turns away from terrorism, abandons its nuclear program, gives up its pursuit of ballistic missiles, and seeks to reform its regime and open itself to the rest of the world could potentially reduce a major source of concern about missile and other forms of proliferation.

The United States should do all it can to encourage and facilitate the protection of key friends and allies from the threat of ballistic missiles, but the decision about whether these countries will ultimately be defended against this threat is theirs. Although the United States must make clear that it will respect their ultimate decision, it should make equally clear that their decision to remain undefended against these threats will not prevent the United States from protecting itself and its people.

THE CHINESE WILL BECOME OUR ADVERSARY

Critics argue that a U.S. NMD system will provoke China to increase the number, sophistication, and survivability of its force of long-range ballistic missiles capable of reaching the United States. China currently has about 20 such missiles and is actively developing a new long-range, land-based mobile missile targeted primarily against the United States and a similar missile that can be launched from submarines. The intelligence community already projects that China will have by 2015 "tens of missiles targeted against the United States."[8]

This projection should obviously concern the United States. It is a change from the past when China lived with a ballistic missile force that was small in number and highly vulnerable to attack by U.S. military forces. It seems likely that China's current effort to expand and upgrade its ballistic missile force arises out of its desire to play a more dominant role in Asia. More particularly, it may reflect Beijing's desire to have the option to use military force against Taiwan to enforce reunification.

To the extent that this picture of Chinese motivation is accurate, it presents a dilemma for U.S. policymakers. Is the United States really prepared to forgo NMD so that China will be free to use its ballistic missile forces to blackmail the United States into sitting on the sidelines so it can use military force against Taiwan? Indeed, doesn't this basis for Chinese objectors to a U.S. NMD system become reason to deploy such a system rather than reason to forgo it?

The United States should have no need to deploy an NMD system against China. But if China continues to insist that it is free to use force against Taiwan, continues to deploy more ballistic missiles aimed at Taiwan and at the United States, and continues to threaten to use those missiles against both, then the United States may simply have no choice.

THE RUSSIANS WILL RESTART THE ARMS RACE

The United States needs to engage Russia in an intensive, high-level dialogue on the issue of proliferation of WMD and the means to deliver it—particularly ballistic missile proliferation. President Bush and President Boris Yeltsin established just such a dialogue by their summit declaration of June 1992. These discussions included identifying ways in which the United States and Russia could establish a "global protection system" that would offer a way for those two countries and all other countries committed to the fight against proliferation ultimately to be protected against the ballistic missile threat.

Regrettably, the Clinton administration discontinued these high-level talks shortly after taking office in 1993. Belatedly, the administration has recently tried to revive part of these discussions. Unfortunately, seven years have passed and diplomatic relations between the United States and Russia have deteriorated considerably.

The United States should continue actively to seek to engage Russia in joining with the United States and its friends and allies in the effort against the proliferation of WMD and the means to deliver it. No such effort can succeed without Moscow because Russia is potentially the greatest source of technology relevant to these weapons. The United States should press for the same kind of intensive dialogue on NMD that the United States must have with its friends and allies. This should be an area of common interest, for the countries that are pursuing acquisition of ballistic missiles are closer to Russia than to the United States.

The United States should offer to include Russia in any cooperative programs that it has with its friends and allies to develop defenses against intermediate- and long-range ballistic missiles. This cooperation could include helping to improve early-warning systems against ballistic missile attack, pooling information from various early-warning radar, collaborating on computer simulation of antimissile defense systems, and even conducting joint exercises in battlefield missile defense. The United States could even consider making U.S. and Russian theater missile defense systems—the U.S. PAC III and the Russian S300—interoperable. This would permit these systems to be sold as a package by a U.S.-Russian joint venture company to countries that do not represent a proliferation threat but are threatened by proliferating neighbors. This would offer Russia the incentive of a role in a legitimate defense export market in exchange for eliminating support for proliferating countries.

The United States should explain its NMD plans to Russia. It should be clear that the United States feels no threat from Russian ballistic missiles, any more than Russia should feel threatened by U.S. ballistic missiles. It is time for both parties to move beyond the Cold War system of confrontation and threats of mutual annihilation. This means moving beyond the ABM Treaty, which symbolizes and codifies the old system.

If it is Russia's preference, the United States should be willing to agree to amendments to the ABM Treaty that would give Russia greater comfort about U.S. NMD. But it should do so only if those amendments permit both the United States and Russia to deploy defenses that would be adequate for their needs. For the United States, this would mean the ability adequately to defend its own territory against global threats and the freedom to provide a similar defense to its friends and allies. It must include the freedom to pursue land-based, aircraft-based, and sea-based systems, free use of sensors including space-based sensors, and freedom to research, develop, and test.

In exchange, the United States would accept quantitative limits on the size of the system it can deploy. This would help meet any residual Russian concern that the United States could rapidly expand its limited deployment to the point where it could significantly degrade the Russian nuclear deterrent. This concern is not new, but a variation of the "break out" problem that the Soviet Union and the United States confronted during the Cold War in connection with negotiating limits on the numbers of strategic nuclear forces they deployed. That problem was also addressed by treaty limits.

Although U.S. preferences would be to move forward without treaty constraints, the United States should recognize that the treaty has a political reality. The United States should make clear that unless agreement can be reached in a relatively short time on acceptable amendments, it will exercise its unarguable legal right to withdraw from the treaty as provided in Article XV of the treaty text. This action would be necessary because the United States is simply unwilling to leave its people undefended against the ballistic missile threat.

This approach gives Russia a way to limit the size of the U.S. national missile deployment. If it chooses not to do so, and responds angrily to the U.S. decision to withdraw, it is as likely to be out of pretext as out of conviction. For in the end, the Russians know that the U.S. system will have limited capability against Russia's nuclear deterrent. For support, it need only listen to U.S. critics of the system. If Russia's real motivation is to prevent the United States from defending itself against retrograde states armed with ballistic missiles, then its objections simply cannot be countenanced.

Notes

1. *Foreign Missile Developments and the Ballistic Missile Threat to the United States through 2015*, unclassified paper prepared by the National Intelligence Officer for Strategic and Nuclear Programs (September 1999), 4. (Hereafter, NIE Summary.)
2. Ibid., 4, 10.
3. Ibid., 4.
4. Ibid., 5.
5. Ibid.,12.
6. Report of the Commission to Assess the Ballistic Missile Threat to the United States, Executive Summary, July 15, 1998, 25.
7. NIE Summary, p. 8.
8. Ibid., 11.

Richard L. Garwin

A Defense That Will Not Defend

$\mathbf{M}$ost Americans are unconcerned that anthrax or nuclear weapons might be delivered to the United States by long-range missiles from North Korea. If asked, they feel protected by some kind of defense; and they are—by the U.S. nuclear deterrent. Nevertheless, U.S. leaders in Congress are determined to defend against this threat by deploying a national missile defense (NMD). Unfortunately the program as planned will not defend against even the minimal threat of four or five North Korean missiles if they are suitably equipped to penetrate the defense, which can be achieved with a fraction of the effort and skill required to build the missiles themselves.

This summer, the Department of Defense is scheduled to conduct its Deployment Readiness Review of the National Missile Defense Program, and President Bill Clinton has committed himself shortly thereafter to decide whether the United States should deploy the proposed NMD. He will do so on the basis of four criteria:[1] (1) whether the threat is materializing; (2) the status of the technology based on an initial series of rigorous flight tests, and the proposed system's operational effectiveness; (3) whether the system is affordable; and (4) the implica-

Richard L. Garwin is the Philip D. Reed Senior Fellow for Science and Technology at the Council on Foreign Relations, a member of the Rumsfeld Commission, and a consultant to the U.S. government on nuclear weapons and national security since 1950.

Copyright © 2000 by The Center for Strategic and International Studies and the Massachusetts Institute of Technology
The Washington Quarterly • 23:3 pp. 109–123.

tions that going forward with NMD deployment would hold for the overall strategic environment and our arms control objectives, including efforts to achieve further reductions in strategic nuclear arms under START II and START III.

The Long-Range Missile Threat

Since 1949, when the Soviet Union exploded its first nuclear weapon, the United States has been vulnerable to strategic attack. The Soviet Union still has more than 6,000 strategic nuclear warheads to use against the United States (and vice versa). Their use not only would destroy the United States as a nation, killing more than 200 million people, but also could imperil civilization on earth by the worldwide effects of nuclear explosions—radioactive fallout and destruction of the ozone layer.

I served from 1958 to 1973 on the Strategic Military Panel of the President's Science Advisory Committee. The Strategic Panel met for two days every month in Rooms 206-208 of the Old Executive Office Building to analyze and advise on U.S. strategic offensive and defensive missile systems.[2] Every month or so, we heard from the Army (in charge of antimissile defense) on the status of its ongoing developments and tests of defenses against ballistic missiles. We were frequently briefed by the contractors that were building test hardware and that would build a deployed system. We also heard from the national laboratories and other facilities that were carrying out sophisticated tests of radar to detect warheads and to discriminate them from the fuel tanks of ballistic missiles or from decoys that might be sent along to divert interceptors from the actual warhead.

Because the nuclear warheads of the interceptors might have an effective kill range of 10 kilometers against an incoming nuclear warhead, decoys that were close to the offensive warhead would not help its survival. Therefore, they were deployed farther away, in a long "train" that would reenter the atmosphere as if they were to land on the same target. There was no good way to distinguish decoys from warheads after the missile got up to speed and arched through space in its fall toward its target. Multiple light decoys could be deployed to resemble the warhead. This was particularly feasible when one considered the use of "antisimulation," in which the warhead was dressed to resemble an easily fabricated decoy.

Without antisimulation, a decoy would need to resemble the conical warhead, which is carefully fashioned and has a surface coating to survive the fiery heat of reentry without damaging the warhead contained within. Certainly one could make a lightweight decoy of the same shape and hope to give it the same radar cross section, but it is far easier to use as a decoy a simple balloon to resemble an inflated one around the warhead. These analyses were the daily meat of the Strategic Panel and of the reports we gave to the president. Each year, we assessed the status of our capability to defend against Soviet ballistic missiles (or against Chinese ballistic missiles) and judged that we could not mount an effective defense against nuclear warheads. The problem was not ideological; it was technical. It was far easier to add a modest amount of payload capacity for decoys (and jammers to emit radio noise to distract or to blank out the ground-based radar) than to build a system that could cope with such an attack. Large potential attacks also could be directed against the defensive system itself.

Having committed in 1969 to deployment of Sentinel—the Johnson administration's version of a defensive system—the Nixon administration was astonished to find that the U.S. populace was not standing in line, city after city, asking to be among the first to be defended. In fact, the citizenry made it perfectly clear that they did not want "bombs in the backyard," such as the nuclear warheads on the ballistic missile defense (BMD)—also called antiballistic missile (ABM) defense—interceptors. Nixon changed course and deployed the Sentinel hardware to defend our own land-based intercontinental ballistic missiles (ICBMs)— the Minuteman missiles housed in silos in North Dakota. Only the name was changed—to Safeguard. By 1974, two ABM radars and 100 interceptors were deployed there to defend a fraction of the U.S. land-based missile force.

Twenty of these interceptors were large Spartan rockets armed with 5-megaton nuclear explosives which would sweep a large region of space free of nuclear warheads and decoys. But 20 individual rockets, armed with warheads or not, could exhaust this supply of Spartans. The interceptor force was supplemented by 80 Sprint interceptors— small, fast-reacting rockets carrying kiloton-yield neutron bomb warheads. These small nuclear explosives would have an adequate kill radius within the atmosphere to destroy an incoming warhead as it fell through the atmosphere and slowed. In reality, warheads aimed at the radar that was essential to the system could have destroyed it and rendered the system impotent long before the interceptor stock had been exhausted.

This prospect of an enormous force directed against the defense itself kept us from building any kind of effective system against the Soviet Union. Against a light force such as China's, the problem was that antisimulation and decoys would prevent the intercept of these warheads in space. To catch them within the atmosphere would require country-wide deployment of interceptors and radar. Even now, the Chinese ICBM force is reputed to number approximately 20, which could in no way threaten the survival of the United States as a nation or its population, but it could destroy that many cities and, with their reputed 3-megaton warheads, could kill 25 million Americans. If one deployed a defense of successive cities with interceptors that would work within the atmosphere—where decoys would be stripped away to reveal the warheads—other cities could be targeted in their stead.

With the gradual evolution and spread of technology, with the digital revolution in which the personal computer on your desktop is capable of a billion multiplications per second—compared with a few million in a large computer in the early 1970s—and with the continued tension and warfare throughout the rest of the world, it is no wonder ballistic missiles of short and intermediate range have become commonplace articles of commerce. In particular, the Soviet Union in the 1950s built the so-called Scud missile that could carry a ton of high explosives to a range of 300 kilometers (200 miles). These missiles were gradually improved and sold to Warsaw Pact members and then to Egypt and many other countries. They found their way to North Korea and through various indigenous developments emerged as longer-range missiles of 600- or 900-kilometer range, such as those used against Israel and Saudi Arabia by Iraq in the 1991 Persian Gulf War. Hundreds had previously been used by Iraq against Iran (and vice versa) in their conflict. North Korea further developed Scud technology to make the larger No Dong missile, of 1,300-kilometer range, which it tested in 1993. North Korea has apparently sold many of these missiles to other countries and maintains that it does this to earn irreplaceable foreign exchange. Pakistan in 1998 tested the Ghauri missile—which appears to be a No Dong—with which it can threaten much of India.

After a good deal of controversy about the emerging missile threat, the Commission to Assess the Ballistic Missile Threat to the United States (the Rumsfeld Commission) was created and was to report in July 1998 after a six-month study. The commission identified three nations—North Korea, Iraq, and Iran—as enemies of the United States with an interest in building long-range missiles that could threaten the United States. I was a member of this nine-person commission, chaired by former Secretary of Defense Donald H. Rumsfeld. Our unclassified summary[3] stated that any of these nations, given a high-priority program, enough money, and technology could obtain within five years—by exchange among themselves, or from China or Russia—the abilty to build a few unreliable, inaccurate ICBMs that could carry a nuclear warhead or biological warfare agent to the United States. We did not judge whether such ICBM development programs were under way, but said that for several of those five years we might well have no hard evidence that such a program existed. We thought that at least one test would be required before such a weapon could be used.

Six weeks after our report on August 31, 1998, North Korea fired its Taep'odong 1, which U.S. intelligence agencies expected to be a test of a two-stage missile. This would have demonstrated one of the essential technologies for making a long-range missile—that of "staging." The simple understanding of rocket propulsion is based on a rocket engine that accelerates the rocket by expulsion through a nozzle of hot gas from burned rocket fuel. The momentum of the gas gives an equal and opposite momentum to the rest of the rocket. A bit of algebra shows that the ultimate speed of a rocket is determined by its initial mass and its final mass (that is, the initial mass less the expended fuel) and the speed of the exhaust gases. A typical Scud exhaust gas speed is 2.25 km/s, and that rocket has an empty weight (engine plus tankage, with no payload) of approximately 22 percent of its loaded weight. This fraction will result in a velocity gain of the empty rocket of approximately 3.4 km/s.[4] To reach intercontinental range requires some 7 km/s. (To put a payload into orbit requires approximately 8 km/s.) So a single-stage rocket of this technology cannot possibly achieve ICBM range, even without a warhead.

For more than 100 years, it has been known that the solution to this problem is to "stage" the rocket. Much of the structure, tankage, and engines are thrown away after the rocket achieves some reasonable speed and has burned all the fuel of the first stage. This can readily be done by clustering rockets in parallel or by "stacking" a rocket on top of another one. The Scud technology involves steel tankage, fuel that does not have a very high exhaust velocity, and engines that are quite heavy. At this technology level, a two-stage rocket cannot achieve ICBM speed, and a true ICBM would require three stages.

North Korea claimed that the Taep'odong 1 test put a small satellite in orbit. It was a three-stage rocket with that intent, but a malfunction during the firing of the third stage probably prevented the satellite from entering orbit. Nevertheless, North Korea demonstrated the separation not only of a first and second stage but also of a second and third stage. It also demonstrated that the United States, with all of its intelligence capability, had no idea that this would be a three-stage rocket test. It would take a much larger rocket—the Taep'odong 2, which is perhaps four times the size of the Taep'odong 1—to send a significant amount of biological warfare agent to the United States. According to the Rumsfeld Commission, a "lightweight variation" of the Taep'odong 2 would be needed to deliver a nuclear warhead to the United States. This might be a missile of high-strength aluminum alloy rather than the steel of the Scud technology, and it would require testing.

First-generation ICBMs are likely to be armed with first-generation nuclear weapons of yield on the order of 10 kilotons—similar to or somewhat less powerful than those that destroyed Hiroshima and Nagasaki. But the ICBMs are likely to be wildly inaccurate, perhaps with a 100-kilometer uncertainty along their track and 10-kilometer uncertainty right to left. They are therefore unlikely to directly hit a region with the largest population density where 100,000 people might be killed in a successful rocket flight and nuclear explosion. Perhaps 2,000 people in areas of average population density would have been likely. A few such warheads constitute the threat against which the national missile defense (NMD) would be deployed.

Technological Readiness and Operational Effectiveness

On March 18, 1999, the House of Representatives passed a bill stating "That it is the policy of the United States to deploy a national missile defense."[5] The previous day, the Senate had passed a similar bill, stating,

> It is the policy of the United States to deploy as soon as it is technologically possible an effective national missile defense system capable of defending the territory of the United States against limited ballistic missile attack (whether accidental, unauthorized, or deliberate) with funding subject to the annual authorization of appropriations and the annual appropriation of funds for national missile defense. [and] It is the policy of the United States to seek continued negotiated reductions in Russian nuclear forces.[6]

On July 23, the president signed the Senate version of the resulting legislation. The schedule set by the Ballistic Missile Defense Organization (BMDO) in the Pentagon leads to a deployment readiness review in June 2000. In late 1999, BMDO said that it would judge itself ready to deploy if it had two successful NMD interceptor flights in which the interceptor destroyed a mock warhead.

The three-stage interceptors to be deployed with the NMD are not available and will not fly for more than a year. The actual kill vehicle (KV) that is to destroy the warhead by colliding with it at a speed of typically 10 km/s is not ready either, but a functionally similar KV is to perform the hit-to-kill role in these tests. The KV contains what is essentially a fancy video camera that transmits infrared, and a focal plane—similar to the film in an ordinary camera or to the charge-coupled device sensor in a video camera—that forms an image using the heat radiated from the warhead. In October 1999, an NMD interceptor was launched from Kwajalein Atoll to intercept a mock warhead delivered by a Minuteman missile launched from Vandenberg Air Force Base in California. BMDO announced that the trial was a success. In January 2000, a similar test was conducted, but this time with additional system communications to the interceptor. The KV was unable to see the warhead (or anything), and the test was clearly a failure. It was revealed that the coolant had frozen water vapor in the system, blocking the tubing so that the infrared imager could not work. It was blinded by its own heat from the detectors that were at room temperature instead of being extremely cold.

The infrared focal plane has a modest number of detectors (perhaps 256 by 256 pixels) and observes in several bands of wavelengths ("colors" of infrared). The infrared imager is thus able, in principle, to determine the temperature of the object that it sees in a single pixel and also its area. But not every object at room temperature radiates the same amount of heat, even if it is the same area. A blackbody is one that absorbs all the light or heat falling on it and by the same token radiates the maximum amount at any given temperature. A body that is coated with aluminum foil radiates only about 4 percent as much, and one that has a thin layer of gold only approximately 3 percent as much. Furthermore, various coatings radiate a different fraction of the blackbody emission in different color bands, so that a false temperature may be inferred by the imager.

In January 2000, it was revealed that in the October intercept test, the KV did not initially see the mock warhead, but instead observed a balloon that was significantly larger and brighter than the warhead it accompanied. Only after the KV identified the balloon as the warhead and maneuvered to attack it did the mock warhead itself come into view in the infrared image and was successfully attacked.

On March 21, 2000, Lieutenant General Ronald Kadish, head of the BMDO, announced that the third interceptor test would be postponed until June 26. He also provided a life-cycle cost estimate of $38 billion for the NMD containing a single site of 100 interceptors. That price includes upgrades to five early-warning radars; deployment of an X-Band radar at Shemya, Alaska; and the communication system necessary to link satellite warning to the radars and to the interceptors.

Evidently, Clinton expects to make the deployment decision without a single test against countermeasures. Yet countermeasures are the key to the performance of a defensive system. It is natural to ask: if we can make rockets carrying hydrogen bombs, if we can have gone to the moon in the 1960s, if we can put a cruise missile through a specified window in a building, why can't we defend against long-range ballistic missiles?

The answer is that nature does not observe what we are doing and try to counter it. The moon does not hide, jump out of the way, or shoot back.

Eric Burgess's 1961 book, *Long-Range Ballistic Missiles*, contained the following:

> It certainly cannot be concluded that an attacker will merely use simple warheads, letting his ballistic missiles perform like high-altitude research vehicles. We must expect that the warhead will be protected by countermeasures against the AMM (anti-missile missiles), including decoys, missiles launched in front of the actual ICBM, and expandable radar reflectors ejected from the ICBM afterbody or from the reentry body itself. ... The reentry body itself might be super-cooled by refrigerants before reentry to upset the infrared detectors.

The key problem is that the proposed NMD system relies on intercept in the vacuum of space, where a feather follows the same path as a nuclear warhead. Even nuclear-armed interceptors are outdone by the multiple lightweight decoys in space, as evidenced by the dependence of the 1974 Safeguard defense system on intercept within the atmosphere.

We have already met the nemesis of the proposed NMD system—the hundreds of bomblets containing anthrax or other disease-producing agents that would be liberated by the missile as soon as it reached its full speed and that would fall separately through space to their targets. A nuclear warhead would be enclosed in a balloon, with similar balloons nearby.

Antisimulation is a simple but powerful tool. Rather than have all warheads identical and pose the problem for the decoy balloon to resemble the warheads so accurately as to deceive a precision sensor on the interceptor, the offense would enclose the reentry vehicle (RV) containing the nuclear warhead in a balloon chosen at random from a range of sizes, shapes, and surface treatment. A motley set of decoy balloons need not resemble one another closely, but should reasonably overlap the spread of sizes, shapes, and surface treatments chosen for balloons surrounding the warheads. Of course, the offense does not want to devote approximately 1,000 pounds of payload to each of the decoys, but in the vacuum of space, a featherweight balloon will do just as well. The heavy warhead stays warm during its flight, while an attack in which the payload is in the shadow of the earth would allow the decoy balloons to cool. The solution is unfortunately simple: wrap the warhead in multilayer aluminized plastic insulation to limit the amount of heat that it would transfer to the enclosing balloon, and provide a one-pound battery and heater to provide comparable heat to each of the decoy balloons during its half-hour flight time. Or, it turns out, that one could use a warhead wrapped in shiny silver foil inside a balloon painted white over its aluminized plastic film, which will achieve a temperature in the Earth's shadow that in no way can be distinguished from that of an empty balloon.[7]

The Rumsfeld Commission notes specifically the potential for using bomblets as a biological warfare agent, even in the absence of defenses, as a means to improve military effectiveness. Rather than a single plume of biological agent carried by the wind through the city (with lethal impact on all those within the plume), bomblets provide multiple plumes over the city and will likely increase casualties or fatalities by factors of 4 to 10. This is no minor matter, because it allows, for a given effectiveness, the use of a missile 4 to 10 times smaller or a similar economy in number of missiles.

Had the Rumsfeld Commission been given the task of evaluating a responsive threat, it would have had to evaluate countermeasures. But it would have taken our group of nine far longer to do that job than the six months we thought we needed for a responsible evaluation of the potential threat. That simple countermeasures will defeat the proposed NMD system is not difficult to assess, if one lifts one's head out of the sand. The September 1999 National Intelligence Estimate states:

> We assess that countries developing ballistic missiles would also develop various responses to U.S. theater and national defenses. Russia and China each have developed numerous countermeasures and probably are willing to sell the requisite technologies.
>
> Many countries, such as North Korea, Iran, and Iraq probably would rely initially on readily available technology—including separating RVs, spin-stabilized RVs, RV reorientation, radar absorbing material (RAM), booster fragmentation, low-power jammers, chaff, and simple (balloon) decoys—to develop penetration aids and countermeasures.
>
> These countries could develop countermeasures based on these technologies by the time they flight test their missiles.[8]

Two remarkable reports by a committee chaired by Gen. Larry D. Welch, USAF, Ret., advised BMDO on its program. The February 1998 report is generally known as "Rush To Failure" because of its characterization of the theater high-altitude area defense (THAAD) theater missile defense program. The report faulted BMDO for far too little testing and for relying excessively on simulation to the exclusion of including "hardware in the loop" to exercise and validate sensors, even in situations in which the sensor was not flown on an actual interceptor. It judged successful execution of the NMD program on the planned schedule to be "highly unlikely."

The second report of November 1999 emphasized the problems caused for the BMDO program by the reluctance to abandon the 2003 date for deployment (although Secretary of Defense William Cohen in January 1999 had postponed the initial operational capability from 2003 to 2005). The compressed nature of the NMD program (even with the 2005 deployment date) may be appreciated from the fact that THAAD is not scheduled to be operational until 2008, even though we have been working on it for five years. The report concluded that BMDO could conduct a meaningful deployment readiness review no earlier than 2003, although it might conduct a technological feasibility review in 2000.

The specific reliability goals of the NMD interceptor are classified, but it is clear that there is not sufficient testing built into the program to justify the assumed reliability. In particular, NMD designers appear to be counting on an 85 percent probability of kill from a single intercept attempt. For a series of 20 tests of the complete system against the countermeasures that could be used by an attacker, all 20 would have to be successful to provide 95 percent confidence that the kill probability was 85 percent or greater. If there were three failures in a test series, 47 tests would need to be successful to provide the same confidence in the same single-shot kill probability.

The proposed NMD may fail because the contractors cannot build reliable interceptors. But it will surely fail because it has not taken into account the feasible countermeasures that could be deployed and will be deployed by North Korea with its first ICBM.

Cost of the NMD Program

The March 2000 BMDO cost estimate of $38 billion does not include the planned expansion of the system to two sites and more interceptors and the deployment of seven additional X-Band radars, more communication systems, and a new constellation of low-altitude space-based infrared satellites (SBIRS low). I believe that the cost will also include essentially scrapping the NMD system to develop and deploy something that might be effective against the countermeasures that will defeat the proposed system. There are just no good estimates of the program cost, which is likely to exceed $100 billion. A Congressional Budget Office estimate is due soon.

Side Effects of Deployment of NMD

For the sake of discussion, let us assume that the NMD would somehow "work" against a few North Korean ICBMs armed with nuclear warheads and that it is also effective in countering "limited ballistic missile attack (whether accidental, unauthorized, or deliberate)," as stated in the legislation.

In 1972, the United States and the Soviet Union signed the ABM Treaty limiting defenses against strategic ballistic missiles to avoid expansion of the offensive missile threat, which in any case would have overcome the defensive system deployed to counter it in that era. In particular, the ABM Treaty banned a "defense of the national territory." It permitted (according to a 1974 protocol) only a single site with no more than 100 interceptors and with a few radars deployed all within a circle of 300-kilometer diameter centered either on the national capital or on a deployment field of ICBMs.

The Soviet Union chose to defend Moscow, whereas the United States declared that it would defend Minuteman missiles from a base at Grand Forks, North Dakota. The 20 high-yield nuclear-armed Spartan interceptors of the ill-fated Safeguard system had some potential for defending the national territory, but the system was vulnerable to attack on its radar, and the few interceptors had no significant impact on the Soviet strategic offensive force. The deployment of the Moscow system greatly increased the number of U.S. warheads targeted against Moscow and impelled British and French military planners to deploy penetration aids to nullify the Moscow system.

The START II Treaty ratified by the Duma in April 2000 limits deployed strategic warheads to 3,000-3,500. At the time of writing, Russia (nuclear heir to the Soviet Union) wants to adopt a START III Treaty that will limit deployed strategic warheads to 1,000-1,500, whereas the United States would like a START III in the 2,000-2,500 range.

Russia maintains that, even in the first phase of the NMD, the United States is building an infrastructure capable of handling many more interceptors and thus poses a substantial threat to Russian strategic effectiveness. There is no doubt that Russia can deploy forces sufficient to overcome and penetrate such an expanded NMD system, but it does not want to spend the money to make the changes in its armory to do so. The United States is spending a good fraction of a billion dollars annually in Russia to provide security for its material excess to the nuclear weapons program and to provide employment for its high-tech people. Otherwise they might look for employment with countries that are enemies of the United States and that want nuclear weapons, long-range missiles, or both. Russia is a member of the Missile Technology Control Regime (MTCR) and limits its transfer of missile technology to rockets with a range of more than 300 kilometers and payloads of more than 500 kilograms.

By far the biggest threat to the survival of the United States is the 6,000 or more deployed strategic warheads in Russia, many of which are on hair-trigger alert. Because there is no significant defense against such weapons, Russia, as the United States does, relies on deterrence by threat of retaliation. The United States foolishly (to my mind) in the 1970s improved the accuracy of its ICBMs and, particularly, its more numerous SLBM (submarine-launched ballistic missile) warheads, so that they have a very good chance of destroying a hardened Russian ICBM silo. Russia fears that its submarines are vulnerable to preemptive destruction by antisubmarine warfare and that their silos could be destroyed in a preemptive strike by the United States.

Accordingly, Russia maintains a warning system so that in case of massive attack by the United States that might constitute a disarming strike, Russian missiles would be launched before they could be destroyed. This launch would be massive, constituting most of the Russian deterrent. I have maintained for decades that U.S. security would be improved if our missiles were too inaccurate to hold Russian silos at risk, and I still believe that. In those circumstances, Russia would have no interest in putting its missiles in a launch-on-warning posture. Currently the Russian warning system is degraded by age and failures. Because of the breakup of the Soviet Union, many of its early-warning radars are on the territory of other states, and the constellation of warning satellites has some gaps. With the threatened NMD deployment, Russia fears not only a disarming strike but also the likelihood that the relatively few Russian warheads that might survive to be launched would be destroyed by the U.S. NMD system.

China is not a party to the ABM Treaty, but it has benefited from the limitations on missile defense in Russia and the United States. China now has approximately 20 ICBMs, each with a single 3-megaton warhead. These ICBMs are based at fixed locations and have their nuclear warheads stored separately from the missiles, which in turn are unfueled. Since China has no warning system, it is impossible for these missiles to be launched before they are destroyed. Accordingly, China has a program to deploy mobile ICBMs which cannot be destroyed in this way.

According to my arguments thus far, it should be simple for China to defeat the planned NMD system. It could do so by using its bomblets to deliver biological warfare agents (although in violation of their undertaking in the Biological Weapons Convention of 1972), by an antisimulation balloon and decoy balloons, by a large enclosing balloon, or by a cooled shroud around the warhead. Unless Chinese political leaders are capable of more restraint than are the leaders of a democracy, it is highly likely that their military will also use U.S. deployment of an NMD to obtain funds for more missiles and warheads, rather than rely solely on countermeasures.

Both Chinese and Russian authorities hope that the United States would not be so wasteful as to deploy a costly NMD system that will not be effective against a threat of a few warheads or a few tens of warheads. They are not clear, however, as to how the United States will accomplish this task.

It has been argued that even a few hundred interceptors could not seriously interfere with the Russian long-range missile force, but there is more to the possession of a missile force than its use in an all-out response to nuclear attack. For example, in the 1970s and 1980s, Paul

Nitze and others forcefully argued that deterrence by threat of assured destruction was not enough for the United States to restrain the Soviet Union. We needed something called high-quality deterrence, which was variously interpreted as the ability to destroy the Soviet retaliatory force, or the ability to use a few missiles at will to destroy targets anywhere in the Soviet Union. Spending many billions of dollars to achieve high quality deterrence was proposed. It must be assumed that Russia still has the remnants of a similar requirement and that a system with the explicit goal of negating a "light attack" of a few tens of warheads would, if successful, eliminate this prized capability from the Russian force. Even Russian warheads launched in accident, however, will be equipped with effective countermeasures and will not be destroyed by the proposed NMD.

A Better Option? Intercept Missiles in Their Boost Phase

Evidently, these countermeasures that plague the proposed NMD system—intercept in midcourse while warheads and decoys are falling through space—would be ineffective if intercept could take place while the ICBM is still accelerating.[9] Interceptors of a size comparable with those to be used in the NMD system (14 tons) would be deployed either on Russian territory south of Vladivostok and abutting North Korea or on U.S. military cargo ships in the Japan Basin. A vast deployment area of these interceptors would allow them to strike the thrusting ICBM after it had been launched from North Korea and before it could reach full speed to attack Washington, Chicago, San Francisco, Alaska, or Hawaii.

The seeker on the interceptor would not need to be cooled, because its purpose is to detect the intense flame of the rocket rather than the heat radiated by a small warhead in space. The interceptors would be launched on the basis of information from the satellites of the defense support program that have existed for 30 years and have detected every ballistic missile launched in the 1991 Gulf War from their positions at a distance of 40,000 kilometers. The interceptor from a distance of 1,000 kilometers would have 1,600 times as much signal to work with and could use a very simple ground-based radar to aid the interceptor in colliding with its target. The system would be a lot simpler and less expensive than the planned NMD.

Rather than putting a lid over the entire United States and much of the eastern Pacific Ocean as proposed, it seems more reasonable to put a lid over North Korea, a country slightly smaller than Mississippi. Such a system could not be frustrated by deployment of bomblets containing biological weapons or by balloon decoys around nuclear warheads. It would be much less expensive than the proposed NMD system, because it uses hardly any of the components. But whether the challenging task of intercepting an accelerating ICBM stands up to analysis and demonstration remains to be seen.

Missiles that might be developed later and launched from Iraq could be handled from a single site in southeastern Turkey, whereas those from Iran (four times larger than Iraq) could be countered by interceptors based on the Caspian Sea and the Gulf of Oman.

It is not clear that supporters of NMD are really concerned with North Korea. The initial deployment of the NMD system was to consist of 20 interceptors in Alaska or North Dakota, to counter four or five ICBM warheads from North Korea, or later perhaps from Iraq or Iran. In testimony on October 13, 1999, Under Secretary of Defense for Policy Walter Slocombe stated that the president has decided on an architecture to be used for planning and negotiating purposes that would counter "the most immediate threat, that from North Korea. It would be capable of defending all parts of all 50 states against the launch of a few tens of warheads, accompanied by basic penetration aids." This system "would include 100 ground-based interceptors based in Alaska." Such a system feeds suspicions that the real purpose of the NMD system is to counter not North Korea but China, and that suspicion is supported by testimony to the Senate precisely to that effect. The boost-phase interceptors that I propose will be much more capable against North Korean missiles. They would pose no threat to Russian ICBMs, no matter where the interceptor ships might be, and so Russia might be more amenable to modifications to the ABM Treaty, that would not in any way imperil the strategic deterrent.

Conclusion

According to the National Missile Defense Review by the committee chaired by General Larry D. Welch, we are far from ready this year, or in 2001 or in 2002, to make a decision to deploy an NMD. I am persuaded that the Joint Chiefs do not believe that the ICBM threat from emerging missile powers is worth the expenditure of defense dollars, compared with other threats we face—even from those same countries. Additionally, the system as proposed will not be effective against the strategic threat of attack by biological weapon agents in bomblets and can readily be defeated by feasible countermeasures.

If I were president, I would heed advice from both supporters and opponents of the NMD system not to make a deployment decision in 2000 but to leave that decision for the next administration and Congress. I would also direct the Pentagon to work full speed to bring boost-phase intercept along as a prime candidate for meeting a North Korean ICBM threat—if it emerges—and those from Iran and Iraq as well.

Notes

1.   1999 National Security Strategy Report (January 4, 2000).
2.   Strategic aircraft and air defense systems were handled by the Military Aircraft Panel, which I chaired for many of those years.
3.   See <http://www.fas.org/irp/threat/bm-threat.htm>.
4.   The "rocket equation" gives the required initial mass M_i in terms of the mass of the rocket at burnout M_f, the velocity of the exhaust gases E, and the velocity gained by the rocket, V, as $M_o/M_f = e^{V/E}$.
5.   H.R. 4, March 18, 1999.
6.   "The Cochran-Inouye National Missile Defense Act of 1999," S. 257, March 17, 1999.
7.   An extensive technical treatment of countermeasures and their implication for the NMD program is to be found in "Countermeasures: A Technical Evalu-

ation of the Operational Effectiveness of the Proposed U.S. National Missile Defense System" (April 11, 2000) available at <http://www.ucsusa.org> from the Union of Concerned Scientists (UCS) and the Security Studies Program at the Massachusetts Institute of Technology. I am an author of that report, in which a far more extensive analysis of antisimulation balloon decoys may be found.

8. Central Intelligence Agency, National Intelligence Estimate "Foreign Missile Developments and the Ballistic Missile Threat to the United States Through 2015," unclassified version available at <http://www.cia.gov/cia/publications/nie/nie99msl/html> (September 1999).

9. See my proposal for such a system, "Cooperative Ballistic Missile Defense" at <http://www.fas.org/rlg> (November 17, 1999).

Hans Binnendijk and George Stewart

Toward Missile Defenses from the Sea

Events during the past 18 months have created new possibilities for the sea basing of national defenses against intercontinental ballistic missiles (ICBMs). Some conceivable designs would enhance U.S. prospects for defeating a rogue state's missile attack on the United States and its allies, but other deployments could undermine the nation's strategic stability with Russia and China. The most efficacious architecture from both a technical and strategic perspective would include a navy boost-phase intercept program and some sea-based radar.

Where Technology and Policy Stand Today

The Clinton administration developed its national missile defense (NMD) strategy in an effort to defend all 50 states as soon as possible against a limited ICBM threat from rogue states. To secure the nation's strategic stability vis-à-vis Russia, the plan emphasized amending but retaining the 1972 Anti-Ballistic Missile (ABM) Treaty. The resulting architecture relied on land-based midcourse interceptors guided by

Hans Binnendijk is the Roosevelt Professor of National Security Policy at the National Defense University and was at the National Security Council as senior director for defense policy and arms control. George Stewart is a research analyst at the Center for Naval Analyses. The authors' views do not necessarily reflect the views of the U.S. government, the National Defense University, or the Center for Naval Analyses.

The Washington Quarterly • 25:3 pp. 193–206.

land- and space-based sensors. The technologies needed for this architecture had not matured by September 2000, however, and President Bill Clinton decided not to deploy the system in 2001. Although the researchers made significant progress toward developing naval-based theater missile defenses during the Clinton administration, the basic NMD architecture had no naval component because that administration sought actual deployments by 2005–2006.

Once in office, the Bush administration was determined to accelerate progress on missile defenses, expand research and development efforts, accept a greater degree of technological risk, and redesign the NMD architecture. They have not, however, proposed any new missile defense architecture. The clear line established in 1997, which delineated theater missile defenses and national missile defenses, became blurred. The strategy opened the door to a greater seaborne contribution to defense against ICBMs, and the navy began to analyze this possibility's new potential. The government developed a broad array of options to exploit the progress that had been made in the navy's theater programs. Then, three events occurred in December 2001 and January 2002 that further shaped the navy's program.

On December 13, 2001, the Bush administration announced that the United States would withdraw from the ABM Treaty in June 2002. Despite this step's diplomatic drawbacks, the United States can now experiment with ship-based missile defenses that the treaty constrained. When the treaty expires in June, the Pentagon will test the ability of the navy's Aegis radar to track both interceptor and target missiles. The decision to withdraw from the ABM Treaty also removes constraints from the development of navy systems designed to be effective against shorter-range ballistic missiles. As a result, tests of future sea-based systems will begin to move from the virtual world of high-speed computers to the test range.

The day after it announced its intention to withdraw from the ABM Treaty, the administration terminated the Navy Area Missile Defense Program, the navy's program for terminal defense against short-range ballistic missiles, because of cost overruns. Up to that point, some administration officials had envisioned using Navy Area as an emergency boost-phase interceptor against North Korean missiles. This program had been scheduled to begin testing this year, with operational deployment to begin by 2004. One likely consequence of the decision to terminate the program will be the delay of any operational (as opposed to an experimental or test-bed) sea-based missile defense system by some two to five years.

Then, the navy successfully flight-tested the first fully functional SM-3 (Standard Missile) interceptor on January 25 and scored a direct hit, using hit-to-kill technology against a Scud-type test missile. The SM-3 is the missile associated with the core of the navy's Midcourse (formerly Navy Theater-Wide) system. The Midcourse system is the only navy missile defense program that enjoys any significant funding, with seven SM-3 test firings now scheduled, although there is no funding for procurement or any official plan for transitioning what is currently an effort at risk reduction and proof of principle into a procurement program. No one is certain when the project's leaders will meld the technologies tested as part of the navy's Midcourse program into an operational system—an optimistic guess is about five years from now; pessimistic guesses are ten years.

These three events encouraged additional testing of naval missile defense systems while significantly delaying development of the foundations of that system. Developers are reengineering the navy program, taking much of the steam out of efforts to focus it on ICBM defenses.

Defending the Nation against ICBMs

One should place the U.S. Navy's contribution to missile defenses in the context of threats from emerging rogue states and the need to maintain strategic stability with former adversaries. During the past several years, national intelligence estimates have indicated a growing missile threat from North Korea, Iran, and Iraq that will continue to increase throughout this decade. At the same time, relations with former adversaries have improved, and the recent Nuclear Posture Review suggests that the United States is no longer sizing its offensive nuclear forces based primarily on the need to strike specific Russian targets. In this context, a reasonable architecture to defend against ICBMs would

- be oriented primarily against missiles launched from rogue states;
- try to intercept a missile as early as possible in flight before counter-measures are dispersed and to allow time for secondary attempts, if necessary; and
- contain a "thin" layer of ground-based interceptors designed to attack a missile during its midcourse, should the missile leak through the first line of defenses.[1]

These principles call for emphasis on boost-phase missile defense systems. Unless the boost-phase missile defense system is space based, its operating area will necessarily be within about 1,000 kilometers of the ICBM launch site. This range greatly limits the effect that a terrestrial boost-phase missile defense system could have on Russia's or China's strategic deterrents. Deploying boost-phase interceptors in space are not recommended because such deployments could intercept Russian and Chinese missiles and would therefore prove destabilizing. Similarly, deploying ground-based boost-phase interceptors would require stationing them in Russia to deal with the North Korean threat.

Boost-phase missile defense systems also have the advantage of attacking an ICBM during the most vulnerable portion of its trajectory. During the boost phase, an ICBM is a large object with a bright booster plume. Because of the large stresses of launch, even the slightest amount of damage to the ICBM can result in total destruction of the entire system. Boost-phase missile defense systems also attack the ICBM before the offense can disperse countermeasures or multiple warheads. Another strong advantage of focusing on boost-phase defenses is the U.S. ability to defend its allies while defending itself.

The technical and operational challenges of the boost-phase defense require launch of the missile interceptors within a very short time line—less than three to five minutes after the missile's launch. (Some advanced ICBM flight concepts, such as "fast burn" and "depressed tra-jectories," can reduce this time still further, but rogue states' first-gen-eration ICBMs are unlikely to have this capability.)

Because development of most missile defenses to date has concentrated on midcourse or terminal defense, the technical challenges of building a system capable of detecting, identifying, tracking, and engaging a ballistic missile during its boost phase have not yet been fully addressed. Even if the system were fully operable, a barrage attack could result in a few missiles leaking through any boost-phase defenses. Augmenting the boost-phase missile defense systems with a "thin" layer of perhaps 100 midcourse inter-ceptors that could engage leakers from the boost-phase layer is therefore prudent. Provided that the interceptors can handle the problem of midcourse countermeasures, midcourse defense systems are also advanta-geous in that they allow a single missile interceptor base to defend large ar-eas. For example, under the Clinton administration's NMD program, a single site in Alaska could defend the United States against an ICBM launched from much of the Northern Hemisphere. Such a midcourse in-surance policy should not affect Russia's deterrent posture.

Although the United States need not have many sites from which missile interceptors are fired for a midcourse defense, the system would require a large network of sensors (radars, infrared, visible, and so forth) to detect, identify, and track all the components of the ICBM.

This proposed architecture would be both highly effective against a rogue state and relatively cost effective. During the next few decades, rogue states are unlikely to possess more than about 20 ICBMs. Assum-ing all are launched at the same time, a robust boost-phase system should successfully engage considerably more than 60 percent of those missiles. In this stressful scenario, the remaining eight missiles, contain-ing a total of eight warheads, and additional decoys would face 100 U.S. midcourse interceptors. The United States could afford to launch four midcourse interceptors against each real warhead and up to 17 de-coys as a further insurance policy. The cost of this system would be no more than the two phases of the system that Clinton proposed, which included as many as 250 midcourse interceptors.

Pros and Cons of Sea Basing

Given the events of the past 18 months, the U.S. Navy and the new Missile Defense Agency are now considering systems for a sea-based ICBM defense that are not unique to ships; at an appropriate site, officials could deploy all these missiles equally well on land. Thus, asking why the United States should deploy the ICBM defense systems at sea is reasonable. The primary advantages offered by sea basing include:

- *Flexibility offered by making part of the ICBM defense architecture mobile.* The radars and missile interceptors required for defense against ICBMs are large and heavy. Placing them onboard a ship is a very cost-effective way to make them mobile. Mobility offers two advantages: it makes the defensive missile system less vulnerable to a preemptive strike, and it would allow the United States to change the architecture quickly in response to changes in the world situation. Officials could withdraw ships if they were no longer needed or move them if new threats appear.
- *Unambiguous control over ICBM defense sites in international waters.* Oceans cover more than two-thirds of the world's surface. Navy ships can operate year-round in any ocean—with the notable exception of the ice-covered Arctic Ocean—without the approval of foreign governments. Thus, sea basing may allow the appropriate placement of ICBM defense elements outside the United States without a host nation's permission, which the host nation could revoke under different circumstances if their and U.S. interests diverge.

Officials must balance the advantages of sea basing, significant though they may be, with potential disadvantages, including:

- *Operation of a single ICBM defense site continuously requires multiple ships.* No matter how efficiently the U.S. Navy operates, ICBM defense–capable ships will eventually need to return to port for maintenance and rest for their crews. Consequently, the United States will need to purchase multiple copies of each ICBM defense system if it desires a continuous presence on one station. In addition to cost and efficiency, the potential ability to put all the ships to sea at the same time may create political concerns.

- *Officials must integrate missile defenses deployed on navy ships with other combat systems.* Current navy ships are complex platforms capable of performing multiple missions. Technicians must resolve shipboard integration problems of each new combat system added to the ship, as well as the technical issues inherent in the system itself. This integration requires significant resources, particularly when the system is as complex as the Aegis weapons system, which has figured prominently in many proposals for hosting missile defense capabilities on navy ships. Officials can resolve integration issues, but they must factor these issues into the costs and the time required to put a missile defense system to sea.

- *Missile defenses deployed on navy ships create the potential for conflicts between defending against ICBMs and other navy missions.* In practice, several considerations may rule out simultaneous usage of ships for their traditional missions and defense against ICBMs. Some ICBM defense areas overlap neatly with expected navy crisis-operating areas, but others do not. For example, the Clinton administration's original architecture relied on radars in the United Kingdom and Greenland. If a host nation's concerns prompted the United States to place these radars on navy ships instead, the radars would not be very useful for other missions during a crisis in the Middle East. In addition, executing many of the navy's traditional missions requires putting the ship in harm's way. If a ship is participating in defending the United States against ICBMs, limiting that ship's exposure to risks not associated with ICBM defense might be preferable.

Policymakers must make an important decision regarding hosting missile defense systems at sea: will existing navy ships or new special-purpose ships host the missile defense systems? For example, interceptor missiles could be deployed on special ships akin to the canceled arsenal ship, and radars could be deployed on special radar ships, similar to the Cobra Judy radar on the USNS *Observation Island.*

Hosting the systems on existing combatant ships such as an Aegis cruiser offers the advantage of enabling the ship to participate in its own defense. Solid policy reasons also call for keeping major weapons systems such as missile interceptors on military platforms. As pointed out above, however, adding missile defense to the list of existing missions incurs overhead both in the form of integration of the missile defense system with other combat systems and a potential opportunity cost of diverting the ship from its original mission designations. Hosting sea-based systems on special-purpose navy ships avoids the integration and potential opportunity costs but does not eliminate other costs. The United States must still procure additional platforms and provide for their defense. Nevertheless, this solution might be preferable for some applications.

Potential Contributions to Boost-Phase Defense

Although the radar currently in place on Aegis combatants has enough power and resolution to detect and track ICBMs during the boost phase, the navy has optimized the system's performance and displays to defend against targets such as cruise missiles and missiles launched from airplanes. The required modifications for ICBM defense are not trivial, but they are achievable. What is totally missing at present is a suitable boost-phase missile interceptor.

Some U.S. Navy officials proposed using SM-1 missiles to engage boosting ICBMs in the upper atmosphere; that proposal, however, was fraught with a great deal of technical risk and required the ship to be within 50 kilometers of the launch site, making the ship itself vulnerable. A more practical approach may be developing a missile interceptor intended to engage the boosting ICBM later in its boost phase above the atmosphere, allowing ships to be as much as 1,000 kilometers from the launch site.

Developers could use the SM-3 test missiles being produced for the navy's midcourse risk-reduction effort as a starting point for suitable interceptor missiles.[2] Successful boost-phase intercept missiles, however, would have to be faster than the test missiles. Fortunately, the launching system on navy combatants has enough growth potential to support a variety of solutions.

One can only speculate about the length of time required to develop a suitable missile and to integrate it with the Aegis weapons system. Prior to the cancellation of the Navy Area program, optimistic estimates by some navy officials were as low as six years to produce boost-phase missile interceptors for ship tests. Because all work on shipboard integration of missile defense systems is currently suspended, this time line has probably increased.

Using the modified SM-3 or wide-diameter missiles (fast-accelerating interceptors with high terminal speeds), the ship could be as far as 1,000 kilometers from the launch point. U.S. Navy ships thus equipped in international waters could engage missiles launched from all of North Korea or Iraq. The effectiveness of sea-based boost-phase missile interceptors against ICBMs launched from Iran would depend on the part of the country from which the ICBMs were launched. In some cases, U.S. forces would need ground-based or airborne supplements.

A sea-based boost-phase capability has clear political advantages and some disadvantages. Its main advantage is the ability to provide a potential defense against ICBMs launched from North Korea and most parts of the Middle East. At the same time, sea basing would present no threat to Russia's and China's land-based ICBM deterrents because those launch points are far inland.

As for disadvantages, a sea-based boost-phase system would potentially threaten Russia's submarine-launched deterrent, assuming a capability existed to estimate the general location of the submarine. Second, any boost-phase defenses would require the establishment of a "no-launch zone" or other special procedures over the rogue state and a willingness *in extremis* to delegate the engagement decision to the local U.S. commander. Both requirements may be difficult to sustain politically. Finally, any boost-phase concept would require launching the interceptors in the direction of the country launching the ICBMs as well as toward third parties that may not be involved. For example, launches against North Korean missiles with boost-phase missile interceptors would entail launches on azimuths toward both North Korea and China. When defending against Iraqi and Iranian missile launches, the boost-phase missile interceptors would fly over several countries on an azimuth toward Russia. Additionally, debris from the engagement (damaged warheads, spent interceptor boosters, and so forth) could have an impact on uninvolved countries.

If the United States accepts these political disadvantages, the operational advantages of a sea-based boost-phase interceptor are significant. With the potential exception of Iran, these interceptors are most effective against the countries in need of dissuasion and deterrence, and they are less effective against former adversaries that need reassurance. If the United States requires continuous protection, the mission would require the deployment of several missile-defense ships, but that investment is relatively small compared with the potential cost of a missile strike against the United States. Considering the short time frame involved in such an attack, however, developing an additional layer that would help achieve the goal of designing a robust defense against ICBMs launched by rogue states seems prudent.

Midcourse Defense

Any midcourse ICBM defense system depends critically on sensor support. Therefore, the possibility of basing high-power, fine-resolution radars at sea in order to provide sensor support must precede a discussion of the possibility of sea-basing midcourse missile interceptors. These two issues are treated separately, but putting both on the same ship would be quite possible.

SEA-BASED RADARS

Although the ABM Treaty has prohibited formal testing, the current S-band radar (SPY-1) used by the Aegis weapons system can track large objects, such as boosters, at distances well above the atmosphere. Testing is required to determine the extent of the current SPY-1 radar's contribution to a midcourse defense system, but any solution to the countermeasure problem will likely require the development of radars with even higher power and finer resolution.

Navy officials have stated that using the existing SPY-1 radar coupled with software modifications to track objects in space is one near-term possibility. Depending on the target, the radar's maximum detection and tracking range would be 500–1,000 kilometers. This capability would support midcourse engagements of early-generation ICBM systems developed by rogue states with few or no countermeasures. The same navy officials estimate that it will take about nine years to increase the power and resolution of the systems to detect objects, to provide discrimination clues, and to track all the individual elements of a cluster as far away as 3,000 kilometers. The effort will also involve developing new-technology X-band and S-band radars.

Using the current X-band technology developed for the NMD program, adapting it for use at sea, and placing it onboard a ship is another possibility. The maximum detection and tracking range of these radars is 2,000–4,000 kilometers. Whereas the navy could retrofit these radars onto existing navy combatants, their weight, power, and cooling needs would require removal of many combat systems currently in place. As a result, some proponents of this idea suggest that the sensor ship should be a noncombatant and should use a commercial hull. The minimum time required for the integration, design, and conversion of an existing hull is approximately five years.

Sea-based radars contribute uniquely to midcourse intercepts. The earth's curvature limits the detection and tracking ranges of any radar. Officials will find presumably appropriate land-based sites for radars to track incoming missiles as they approach the United States. Sea basing can place a radar that is totally under U.S. control much closer to the launch site than is possible from sovereign U.S. territory. Indeed, if support from a host nation is not forthcoming, sea basing might be the only option for placing high-power radars closer to the launch site. Two factors make this radar placement very desirable:

- Sea basing would help develop sufficient information to engage the ICBM in early midcourse—an important consideration in a battle that will be over, for better or for worse, in 15–30 minutes.
- Observing deployment of the payload would provide additional information of possibly great value in identifying the warhead(s) amid the cluster of debris and deliberate countermeasures.

Naval deployment of radars to detect ICBMs might be useful for two other reasons. First, both Great Britain and Denmark have been reluctant to accept the Clinton administration's suggestion to deploy X-band radars at Fylingdales and Thule, respectively. Even though ground-based radars are more reliable, naval deployments provide an alternative. Second, if the Space-Based Infrared Systems (SBIRS)-High and -Low now in development continue to face technological and funding problems, demand for naval radar deployments could be greater.

Sea-based radars should not undermine strategic stability. They would not enable similar early detection and tracking of ICBMs launched from the interior of Russia and China, reducing the political risks. Verification for future arms control regimes, however, is one potential political complication. If the United States links existing Aegis radars (or any other radar the navy uses widely) into an ICBM missile-defense network, then all ships with that radar become potential strategic assets and a likely topic of future arms control negotiations with Russia. Russia would probably seek on-site inspections, restrictions on the ships' operating areas, and limits on the number of capable ships, inhibiting the navy's freedom to use these ships in other missions.

Using radars onboard existing naval combatants for a midcourse defense system against ICBMs appears feasible and may have definite advantages. The disadvantage again would be the potential opportunity cost of diverting those ships from the missions for which the navy originally constructed them. This disadvantage is offset somewhat when the ships are employed in forward locations where they might simultaneously participate in other missions that do not put their strategic mission at risk.

SEA-BASED MISSILE INTERCEPTORS

Defense missiles currently procured for testing have a maximum speed of about 3.1 kilometers per second. This speed would adequately defend against intermediate-range ballistic missiles, but designers must increase the interceptor missile's speed for a robust capability against ICBMs. Engineers estimate that they could modify the current launch systems used on navy combatants to accept missiles with larger diameters and capable of speeds of 6.5 kilometers per second or more. That type of interceptor missile could defend an area the size of a continent or larger and could handle ICBMs with advanced capabilities. Generally, developing these newer, faster missile interceptors with improved kill vehicles will take 6–15 years.

A priority for the U.S. Navy and for the regional commanders in chief is developing missile defense systems effective against longer-range theater missiles under development in some rogue states. Given appropriate sensor support, such missiles would also possess at least a rudimentary capability against ICBMs. In fact, at times these missiles could perform both missions simultaneously. For example, with proper sensor support, a ship with fast midcourse missile interceptors in the North Sea could defend large parts of Europe and the U.S. eastern seaboard against missiles launched from the Middle East. This feature is beneficial because it enhances the utility of these weapons systems, but damaging because it blurs the boundary between strategic and nonstrategic uses regarding strategic stability.

Notwithstanding the large areas that a single missile-interceptor facility can defend, launching midcourse-system missile interceptors from multiple sites has several advantages:

- Suppression of the sea-based midcourse missile-interceptor system is more difficult.
- These interceptors offer greater flexibility regarding the location of target engagement—an important consideration when dealing with nuclear warheads designed to detonate when successfully engaged.[3]
- Midcourse interceptors allow for a "shoot-look-shoot" firing doctrine: the defense fires one interceptor missile, evaluates the results,

and fires a second (or more) interceptor missile only if the first interceptor misses. The shoot-look-shoot concept preserves missile inventory and greatly simplifies battle management by minimizing the number of interceptor missiles in flight at any given time—an important consideration when one envisions defending against small raids of more than one ICBM.

The ability to build a land-based capability on U.S. territory to permit more than one engagement in the latter part of the midcourse suggests that decisionmakers should choose operating areas for ships with midcourse ICBM interceptors based either on the ability to engage the ICBM early in the midcourse or the extension of the defensive area to cover allies or U.S. forces deployed forward in portions of the world far from the United States. Nevertheless, even with these general guidelines, determining definitive operating areas for navy ships in support of midcourse missile defense against ICBMs is difficult.

Maintaining Strategic Stability

Without the ABM Treaty, which will effectively end in June, the United States must maintain strategic stability with Russia and China in other ways requiring even more vigilance, now without the treaty's negotiated guidelines. For the Bush administration to conclude a new strategic framework with Russia successfully, the United States must accept some constraints on missile defenses. Would those constraints allow for the eventual deployment of a limited number of naval ships with radars and interceptors capable of defeating an ICBM?

The United States could negotiate such a new framework without abandoning sea-based missile defenses. If the sea-based interceptors are limited to the boost phase, they would not have adequate range to intercept ICBMs launched from Russia. Line-of-sight radars based on ships deployed near North Korea and the Persian Gulf would also have very limited capabilities against Russian ICBMs. Russia might seek to limit the number of ships deployed with ICBM defense capabilities, their stationing area, or the range of sea-based radars. Moscow might also seek assurances that the United States will not use sea-based systems against Russia's submarine-launched missiles.

The most difficult strategic stability problem to resolve is the possibility that Russia might assume that all Aegis radars and all interceptors have at least some NMD capabilities if some naval systems with theater missile defense capabilities are networked into the NMD system. Thus, during negotiations for a new strategic framework, the task will be to convince the Russians that this capability is limited and does not undermine Russian deterrence. One possibility would be creation of a boost-phase interceptor that requires a modified launch system visible from outside of the ship for inspection and verification purposes and then a limit on the number of those systems deployed on Aegis ships.

The problem vis-à-vis China is more difficult because the Chinese have only a few dozen land-based single-warhead missiles capable of striking the United States. Sea-based boost-phase interceptors should not present a threat to Chinese ICBMs launched from the country's interior. On the other hand, China could view sea-based X-band radars linked to even a limited number of midcourse interceptors as affecting their current deterrence. The Chinese are modernizing their ICBM force anyway, though, and the number of warheads capable of striking the United States could multiply several times during the coming decade, even without U.S. missile defenses. Ideally, China will not pursue options to place multiple warheads on its missiles. The missile defense architecture suggested above provides the best prospect to dissuade the Chinese from this path while still providing credible protection against rogue states.

The Sea-Based Advantage

Using missile interceptors based at sea to defend the United States against ICBMs offers several advantages, the most important of which are flexibility and control. The system involves costs as well, however, including operational limitations for other missions and competition for resources to build new ships.

The most cost-effective option for a potential seaborne deployment is the use of upgraded Aegis radars and modified SM-3 missiles for boost-phase intercepts onboard existing combat ships stationed near Korea and the eastern Mediterranean. In addition to providing a layer of boost-phase defense, ships at these locations would provide radar coverage early in the flight of an ICBM—a valuable asset to the midcourse defense layer. These locations overlap with current navy forward-operating areas, which would help mitigate the opportunity cost to existing missions that the new mission entails.

Estimates on the availability of this capability are difficult. Assuming the United States decides to pursue this approach in the near future, the end of the decade is a reasonable deadline expectation. Land-based systems for the midcourse defense layer could mature earlier. Then, deployed ships could initially provide radar support, and the boost-phase capability could be added as it becomes available.

This option involves several costs that officials must manage. The United States must maintain strategic stability with the Russians and Chinese and convince them that such deployments would not undermine their deterrents—a difficult task but not impossible. The U.S. Navy would need to accept that Aegis ships deployed with this capability would have missile defense as their principal mission and that all other missions would be secondary. Finally, the president would have to delegate the authority to shoot down a missile in boost phase to the commander of the ship or to some other commander who could act in seconds. That situation might cause potential diplomatic problems, but in practice other missile defense concepts would probably also entail delegation of similar authority to personnel at the operational level.

An alternative, which might benefit arms control and operations, would be the construction of separate ships designed solely for intercept and radar missions. The missile defense ships would then be separate from the Aegis fleet, and the other side could verify any limitations more easily. The cost constraints associated with new construction, however, might slow the navy's existing shipbuilding program.

Sea basing of midcourse missile interceptors or terminal defense systems against ICBMs is a much less attractive alternative. Better land-based alternatives for midcourse intercepts, which would be less destabilizing and would not mix theater and national missile defenses, are available. Defense of a large enough area to be anything other than the last-ditch defense of very important strategic facilities is simply impossible for terminal defense systems of the continental United States. Those defense facilities, however, generally do not move; therefore, paying a premium for making the defense system mobile does not seem sensible.

In summary, deployment of a small number of sea-based radars and boost-phase interceptors is sensible for dealing with a limited threat from a rogue state. The United States must manage the difficulties, not the least of which is persuading Russia and China that such deployments do not undermine strategic stability. If U.S. military officials properly design the architecture, however, overcoming that problem should not be an impossible task.

Notes

1. See Hans Binnendijk, "How to Build an International Consensus for Missile Defense," *International Herald Tribune*, March 7, 2001.

2. The SM-3 was designed to intercept a shorter-range missile during the midcourse of its flight and is therefore often called a "midcourse interceptor," but the missile could be used against an ICBM during its boost phase.

3. Commonly called salvage-fusing, the premature nuclear detonation temporarily blinds sensors attempting to detect targets in the vicinity of the explosion and creates a potentially damaging pulse of electromagnetic energy that can damage nearby systems in space and on the ground below.

Kevin McLaughlin

Would Space-Based Defenses Improve Security?

One could almost hear the gears shifting in the United States and around the world as President George W. Bush announced on December 13, 2001, that the United States would withdraw from the 1972 Anti-Ballistic Missile (ABM) Treaty on June 13, 2002. Although the formal announcement was not greatly surprising, it served notice that the United States was replacing its rhetoric regarding the deployment of missile defenses with action. The precise implications of withdrawal are still somewhat undefined, but the administration has indicated it plans to pursue an operational national missile defense system aggressively. Undoubtedly, historians will link Bush's legacy inextricably to the successes and failures in the ongoing global war on terrorism. Significant changes in the decades-long debate about national missile defense, however, will also define the first U.S. presidency of the twenty-first century. Accordingly, Bush and Secretary of Defense Donald Rumsfeld have indicated they will pursue a prominent role for space-based components in the U.S. missile defense program.

Lt. Col. Kevin McLaughlin is a National Defense Fellow at CSIS. He commanded the squadron that operates the U.S. Global Positioning System satellites and served as a staff member on the Rumsfeld Space Commission. The author's views do not necessarily represent the official position of the Department of Defense or the U.S. government.

Copyright © 2002 by The Center for Strategic and International Studies and the Massachusetts Institute of Technology
The Washington Quarterly • 25:3 pp. 177–191.

Given this near certainty, asking whether a move to use space in support of missile defenses will improve U.S. security and, if so, how is appropriate. A full understanding of the answers to these questions requires recognition of the ways space systems can contribute to the missile defense mission, as well as the strategic and operational benefits that space-based missile defense components could provide. This understanding addresses only one dimension, however, of whether such a move improves U.S. security. Determining the effects of deploying space-based missile defenses on today's geopolitical framework is also important. How will such a move affect strategic stability, and how will the international community view these actions? Finally, has technology progressed to a stage that will make space-based missile defenses possible?

Ballistic Missiles Explained

The ballistic missile defense (BMD) mission is highly complex and requires the integrated use of air-, land-, sea-, and space-based systems. From the advent of the German V-2 ballistic missile in World War II to the latest intercontinental ballistic missiles (ICBMs), planners have tried to determine how they might defend their nations against the ballistic missile threat. When the October 4, 1957, launch of Sputnik I brought the world into the space age, analysts began to examine the possibilities of using space to support BMD requirements. During the past four decades, military officials have explored many space-based missile defense concepts but have deployed very few.

Although ICBMs are highly complex weapons, their basic operational philosophy is simple. A powerful, multistage rocket boosts a nuclear payload into a ballistic trajectory calculated to deliver the payload to a specific target location. All ICBMs have three well-defined phases of their mission—the boost phase, the midcourse phase, and the terminal phase.

- *Boost Phase.* The missile's rocket engines accelerate the payload to speeds of more than 15,000 miles per hour in this portion of the ICBM's mission. On a typical ICBM, the boost phase consists of the sequential firing of several separate stages that lasts for four to five minutes. The ICBM must attain extremely high speeds to allow the payload to reach targets on the other side of the world—targets that can be more than 6,000 miles from the launch site. The payload of the ICBM consists of three primary elements—nuclear warheads, decoys, and a postboost vehicle. The postboost vehicle is a small satellite that automatically functions like a high-tech taxicab for its deadly cargo of warheads and decoys, maneuvering to different points in space and dropping off each warhead and decoy at the exact speed and location required for the warhead to fall along the necessary trajectory to hit its target. Some modern ICBMs can carry as many as 10 independently targetable warheads. The boost phase is completed when the last booster stage stops firing and the booster separates from the payload.

- *Midcourse Phase.* Once the boost phase is completed, the warheads, decoys, and postboost vehicle begin the longest portion of the so-called midcourse mission, which can last up to 20 minutes. During this phase, the postboost vehicle pirouettes through the darkness of space at speeds of more than four miles per second, dropping each warhead and decoy at their preplanned time, location, and velocity. If the postboost vehicle performs properly, the decoys will confuse BMD systems into believing that they are warheads while the real warheads will hit their intended targets.

- *Terminal Phase.* Finally, the terminal phase of the mission begins, during which the warheads reenter the earth's atmosphere and detonate in the vicinity of their target. The earth's atmosphere slows each warhead a great deal during the 30-second terminal phase; despite slowing, however, the warheads are still traveling at speeds in excess of one-half mile per second.

Functions of Space-Based Systems

Current U.S. BMD strategies aim to engage ballistic missiles in all phases described above. Developing a range of capabilities to intercept a missile in the boost phase, the midcourse phase, and the terminal phase of flight increases the chances that the BMD system will destroy the missile and its payload. Layering the defense throughout each phase will require sophisticated technology, however, much of which might be based in space.

Missile Warning. Space already plays a key role in fulfilling the missile-warning mission, which focuses on detecting and reporting an ICBM launch. Its primary purpose is providing the earliest possible warning and characterization of a nuclear attack on the United States, allowing the president and senior military commanders sufficient time to make appropriate decisions about the response. The United States requires this mission even without an operational missile defense system. Leaders can use the same warning needed to launch a nuclear counterstrike, however, to cue a missile defense system. Defense Support Program (DSP) satellites have performed the missile-warning mission for more than three decades. DSP satellites, orbiting 22,500 miles above the earth, use infrared detectors to see the hot missile plumes from the ICBM's booster motors and can quickly determine the location of the launch, the type of missile, and the direction in which it is headed. Unfortunately, the aging DSP satellites can detect and characterize the missiles only during the four-to-five-minute boost phase.

During the next decade, a much more sophisticated satellite system called the Space-Based Infrared System (SBIRS) will replace the aging DSP satellites. This system will have two responsibilities critical to the BMD mission: assuming responsibility over the missile-warning mission and tracking objects during the midcourse phase, which is a brand new mission focused solely on BMD.

Midcourse Tracking. SBIRS will be able to track objects during the midcourse phase, thereby eliminating a potential blind spot for any U.S. BMD systems. In this role, SBIRS will be able to observe, track, characterize, and report on postboost vehicle maneuvers, nuclear warhead deployments, and the use of various types of decoys from launches to anywhere in the world. This last capability is vital because SBIRS's sophisticated sensors will be able to discriminate rapidly between real warheads and decoys as well as provide targeting data to interceptors based on the earth, in the air, or in space. The operational advantages of such a capability are obvious. Any midcourse or terminal-phase interceptor system must receive the necessary targeting information quickly to maximize opportunities to intercept the numerous warheads associated with the launch of even a few ICBMs. Ideally, SBIRS will ensure that intercept opportunities are not wasted on any decoys flying alongside the actual warheads. Without this capability, BMD interceptors will not react quickly or accurately enough to destroy incoming warheads effectively.

Communications. Any modern BMD system will have a very sophisticated battle management/command, control, and communications capability. For the United States, this activity will ensure that all elements of the system are properly integrated and interoperable with external systems, including those of U.S. allies. The backbone of this capability will be the system-wide communication links that allow all components to exchange data and enable transmission of command and control orders to weapons and sensors. Operating as part of a larger communications architecture, the critical connectivity required for this mission will necessitate communications satellites and dedicated communication channels.

Boost-Phase Intercept. The ability to destroy ICBMs during their boost phase is the most difficult and controversial of all BMD missions envisioned for space systems. Boost-Phase Intercept (BPI) has tremendous operational advantages over midcourse or terminal interceptors, perhaps the most significant advantage being the ability to destroy the ICBM at its most vulnerable point and before it has deployed its deadly mix of warheads and decoys. In addition, destruction of the ICBM over the launching state's territory confines any associated hazardous debris within a relatively small area.

Many space-based BPI concepts exist on paper, but no system has ever been operationally tested or deployed. Officials have explored various technologies during the years, include particle beams, lasers, and kinetic-energy weapons. The Bush administration's Missile Defense BPI program for fiscal year 2003 will focus on research and development for two space concepts—a chemically fueled space laser and a space-based kinetic-energy interceptor. An effective space-laser BPI system would destroy ICBM boosters with a laser beam, traveling at a velocity of 186,000 miles per second. This feature is attractive when the target is accelerating to speeds of four miles per second, because the system has more time to respond. Space-based kinetic-energy interceptors accomplish their mission by physically colliding with the warhead, which many have described as "hitting a bullet with a bullet." This system type must detect and confirm the threat missile within a few seconds of launch or the interceptor will not catch a fast-moving ICBM that has a head start.

Launcher Attack Operations. Officials could conduct another potential missile defense mission—launcher attack operations—from space, even though the Department of Defense does not technically define this mission as a missile defense program. Launcher attack operations would preemptively attack launch silos or mobile ICBM transporter erector launchers (TELs) before ICBM launch. This mission, especially when employed against mobile missiles, might require the combined efforts of two space capabilities. The first would be a global space-based radar system that could detect and track mobile missiles as they departed their home bases for their operational deployment areas. This system would close a gap in current U.S. capability: the inability to track mobile missiles continuously. The second space capability needed to support this concept would be a space-to-earth weapon capable of destroying an ICBM silo or a TEL.

New Geopolitical Constructs for Space Contributions

In discussions of how space is or could be used to meet BMD requirements, one must also examine the effect of such moves on strategic stability and the international community. To understand if using space in support of missile defenses can enhance or weaken U.S. national security, one must consider the environment that has shaped the debate on this important but poorly understood topic. Since the dawn of the missile age, analysts dealing with international and security policies have argued about the proper role space should play in programs designed to defend the United States from ballistic missile attack.

From these concepts flowed a calculus that produced a family of interlocking ideas such as nuclear deterrence, mutual assured destruction, and mutual vulnerability that guided the United States through the Cold War. During this era, the ABM Treaty and U.S. policy constrained any serious attempts to utilize space in ways deemed destabilizing. In particular, both the treaty and U.S. policy prohibited using space-based weapons for any purpose—missile defense or otherwise. Other space capabilities that could be directly tied into BMD architectures also caused concern. For example, strategic analysts viewed a missile-warning satellite as a stabilizing factor if it provided enough warning for U.S. decisionmakers to launch retaliatory nuclear strikes and preserved the concept of mutual assured destruction. The missile-warning satellite might also enhance the effectiveness of missile defenses, however, and some analysts viewed that possibility as a destabilizing influence because it would reduce U.S. vulnerability. Within this framework, the national security community carved out mature policy positions on how space and missile defense affected nuclear stability, arms control, force structure, and other important aspects of defense policy.

The dawn of the twenty-first century has turned this issue on its head. Revolutionary advances in the use of space to support nonstrategic and nonmissile defense missions have led to calls for the normalization of space in support of U.S. objectives. Recent high-level studies, such as the one authored by the Commission to Assess U.S. National Security Space Management and Organization, chaired by Rumsfeld, have described space as a vital national interest that the United States must protect and use to support U.S. national interests. International perceptions and reactions are evolving in ways that the United States may not fully recognize or acknowledge, particularly as European and Asian nations move to deploy satellites that will support their security needs. The European Galileo navigation satellite is a key example of a satellite system that will likely revolutionize the manner in which European nations use space to meet national security requirements. The French Ministry of Defense is also interested in developing a space-based system to provide early warning of ballistic missile attacks. These facts suggest that strategic analysts and policymakers should strive to understand these new dynamics fully and resist efforts to use old and outdated methods to solve new problems. Unfortunately, entire bureaucracies and constituencies have evolved on all sides of the debate, and adjusting to the realities of how the world has changed around them is often difficult.

The nation's best thinkers, strategists, and planners must intellectually engage these changes to allow a full and proper debate on the issue. In other words, the time has come for the Cold Warriors and arms controllers to surrender their old guards. Without this transition in the intellectual and academic approach to the problem, characterizing the new environment accurately or developing a new calculus for analyzing current strategic issues, including those associated with integrating space capabilities into U.S. ballistic missile defenses, will not be possible.

EFFECTS OF U.S. DOMINANCE

No examination of this topic is adequate without a short discussion of how new geopolitical realities mandate a new approach. First, the United States occupies a predominant position in the new millennium—economically, technologically, and militarily—relative to all other countries. The U.S. dollar is the benchmark currency in a world that increasingly uses English as the global language. To define this new reality, French foreign minister Hubert Védrine has labeled the United States a "hyperpower."[1] Although his use of the term is not complimentary, the term does reflect the perception and, in many ways, the reality of the current global dominance of the United States.

The level of U.S. dominance gives rise to some predictable and some unanticipated results. Europe, driven primarily by French and German concerns, will strive mightily to forge a common European identity that might be capable of keeping U.S. power in check and will work to maintain a strong role for Europe in global affairs. Russia and China will continue to use their limited resources in broad efforts to reduce the relative imbalance between their national power and that of the United States. Other countries and regions may also act in ways designed to counteract U.S. strength. These possibilities are not new ideas; commentators have extensively written about them. No one has given much thought, however, to how this new reality shapes the potential effect that more extensive use of space may have on strategic stability.

The current geopolitical landscape is a multilateral maze of unequal partners, increasingly proliferated technology (including the technology needed to develop and deliver weapons of mass destruction [WMD]), and a suddenly unsatisfying U.S. stance on deterrence and vulnerability.[2] U.S. and Russian nuclear stockpiles are moving toward their lowest levels in decades, and the risk of a massive Russian nuclear strike on the United States is no longer a primary concern. In this new environment, the nation's deterrent forces do not counter the threats that give rise to its greatest concerns. The strategic vulnerability that perversely formed the basis of U.S. security during the Cold War has become a glaring weakness and perhaps an invitation to those who might harm the United States. In this context, developing and fielding capabilities that reduce U.S. vulnerability and deter the most dangerous threats apparently best enhance U.S. security and strategic stability. Missile defenses are one of the areas that could potentially reduce U.S. vulnerability, and officials should carefully examine the use of space to its fullest extent.

Observers have not yet fully understood or analyzed another possible reality. The current striking disparity between the United States and all other countries in economic, technological, and military endeavors places extreme limits on most countries' abilities to respond meaningfully. Old concerns that U.S. advances in missile defense or space would spawn undesirable arms races may no longer be valid.[3] For example, the United States is the only nation capable of implementing and sustaining decisive military force on a global basis. The war in Afghanistan provided a snapshot of this ability. The nation's development and use of many capabilities—modern airpower; long-range precision weapons; command, control, and communications and intelligence; and highly skilled soldiers, sailors, marines, and airmen—have drastically outpaced all other countries. No other country could carry out the mission that the United States is executing in Afghanistan. Any other country or alliance, such as the proposed 60,000-person European Rapid Reaction Force, performing a similar mission in the near term or in the midterm is equally doubtful. Even more significantly, in the current global war on terrorism, the United States is working to increase the scope of its capabilities to operate simultaneously in several spots around the world.

Primarily, U.S. wealth, global responsibilities, and national security needs drive this reality. The administration's FY 2003 defense budget request of $379 billion is more than six times larger than that of Russia, the second-largest spender, and more than the combined spending of the next 25 nations.[4] This disparity creates its own dynamic with unique qualities, one of which may be the elimination of the incentive for many nations even to try to compete, decreasing the likelihood that U.S. developments will face traditional countermeasures. For example, the B-2 stealth bomber provides the United States with an unchallenged military capability that other nations would have viewed as destabilizing only a few years ago. The airplane can fly anywhere in the world undetected and can attack targets through defenses that officials previously thought were impenetrable. Yet, this revolutionary capability has not given rise to a race to build stealth bombers, nor has it resulted in a huge defensive investment by the Chinese, the Russians, or the Europeans to develop technology to counter it. Other nations have not cried out in indignation—an indication that the United States can use such overwhelming capabilities without threatening the world's strategic stability.

Other than the B-2, any number of U.S. technological advances, such as unmanned combat air vehicles (UCAVs), information dominance capabilities, and the previously mentioned SBIRS system, serve as examples of advanced U.S. warfighting capabilities revolutionizing the nation's military capabilities and further increasing the disparity between the United States and the rest of the world, but that have not seemed to produce arms races or other traditional responses. For these reasons, U.S. development of space-based missile defenses will arguably contribute to U.S. security and possibly in a way neither destabilizing nor likely to spawn an arms race in space.

GROWING USE OF SPACE IN PURSUIT OF U.S. NATIONAL OBJECTIVES

Space capabilities, beyond those contributing to missile defenses, are becoming central to the pursuit of broader U.S. national objectives. In early January 2001, the Rumsfeld Space Commission provided the clearest statements to date of this new reality. The bipartisan commission "unanimously concluded that the security and well-being of the United States, its allies, and friends depend on the nation's ability to operate in space" and that the U.S. national interest lies in taking the following steps:

- promoting the peaceful use of space;
- using the nation's potential achievements in space to support its domestic, economic, diplomatic, and national security objectives; and
- developing and deploying the means to deter and defend against hostile acts directed at U.S. space assets and against uses of space that are hostile to U.S. interests.[5]

The Space Commission recognized space as simply a place where nations conduct business, no different than air, land, or sea. Following this logic, space possesses no qualities that imply special moral or ethical connotations but is simply a physical domain with its own physical properties. Those who operate in space must act in an ethical, moral, and legal manner—no different than the requirement nations have for operating in other domains. Accordingly, the United States should use space to underpin a broader strategy aimed at exercising U.S. economic, military, and technological leadership.

This concept is most evident regarding the use of space to support air, land, and sea operations conducted in the course of traditional military contingencies. Since the Persian Gulf War in 1991, military planners have revolutionized the use of space to support conventional military operations. Recent conflicts in Bosnia, Kosovo, and Afghanistan have matured U.S. concepts to the point where space systems are now woven into the fabric of modern U.S. military operations. The Space Commission summarized:

> Today, information gathered from and transmitted through space is an integral component of American military strategy and operations. Space-based capabilities enable military forces to be warned of missile attacks; to communicate instantaneously; to obtain near real-time information that can be transmitted rapidly from satellite to attack platform; to navigate to a conflict area while avoiding hostile defenses along the way; and to identify and strike targets from air, land, or sea with precise and devastating effect. This permits U.S. leaders to manage even distant crises with fewer forces because those forces can respond quickly and operate effectively over longer ranges. Because of space capabilities, the [United States] is better able to sustain and extend deterrence to its allies and friends in our highly complex international environment. Space is not simply a place from which information is acquired and transmitted or through which objects pass. It is a medium much the same as air, land, or sea. In the coming period, the [United States] will conduct operations to, from, in, and through space in support of its national interests both on earth and in space. As with national capabilities in the air, on land, and at sea, the [United States] must have the capabilities to defend its space assets against hostile acts and to negate the hostile use of space against U.S. interests.[6]

How does this thinking affect the possible use of space to support U.S. missile defense activities? One barrier to using space to support missile defenses has been the belief that the United States should not use space to provide overwhelming U.S. advantage or in any way contribute to a strategic imbalance between the United States and other great powers. Nonetheless, the above paragraphs indicate that the United States quietly crossed this space threshold at the end of the last century in ways that did not pertain to missile defense. The United States now leverages satellites to fight battles in ways that overwhelm adversaries.

Our satellites allow field commanders to see the entire battlefield, communicate globally and instantaneously, attack targets precisely, avoid threats, and warn of aggression in ways that no other nation in the world can match. Arguing that space already affords the United States an overwhelming military advantage is no overstatement.

Defense requirements that do not involve missiles may drive the development of the first weapons to operate from space. U.S. military planners have increasingly stressed requirements for engaging global targets with conventional weapons within a few minutes or a few hours of target identification. This requirement may drive the necessity for power projection through and from space, which U.S. forces could accomplish with almost no delay. Such a capability would arguably provide the United States with a much stronger deterrent and, in a conflict, an extraordinary military advantage. Effective nonnuclear deterrent concepts could also create a safer and more stable strategic environment by potentially reducing reliance on nuclear weapons. Finally, if the United States fields these capabilities in support of nonmissile defense requirements, the absence of a precedent in developing defenses that operate in, from, or through space will no longer constrain missile defense planners and policymakers.

INTERNATIONAL PERCEPTIONS AND REACTIONS

In today's globalized society, the United States must balance its security needs with the implications of U.S. actions on the international community. Despite the changing geopolitical environment, the United States should act only after careful consultation and negotiation with its friends and allies. Earnest consultations do not guarantee agreement, however, and the United States may have to act unilaterally to protect its interests. Such actions may animate other nations to conclude that the United States is too powerful and must be opposed at every level to reduce the level of U.S. dominance in a particular domain. In particular, the idea of using space in support of U.S. missile defense capabilities will quite likely meet with skepticism and disagreement abroad. How can the United States, then, pursue its own interests in a manner that might engender support or at least bring about neutral reactions on the part of others?

First, the United States must try to understand the motivations of those who would be and are concerned about U.S. activities in this area. This exercise is important if U.S. planners and policymakers want to minimize any adverse effects of U.S. pursuits on the international community, including the following actors:

- *Europe.* Characterizing the European position on this issue is difficult because the views differ from country to country. Some European nations fundamentally and philosophically oppose missile defenses and any efforts to militarize the realm of space further. Others fully embrace the concept of leveraging space capabilities in support of national security needs, including those associated with missile defense. Despite these differences, making some general observations about the core group of European countries that typically cooperate on European defense and space policy—France, Germany, Italy, and Great Britain—is possible. Concerns about economic, industrial, and technological competition seem to dominate these nations' views of U.S. military space programs. Current disparities between U.S. and European investment in defense and space capabilities drive a perception, which the French articulate most often, that these disparities are a threat to Europe. Europe will likely resist any effort to field missile defense capabilities in a manner that does not include a strong role for itself and the likelihood of sharing technology with the United States.
- *Russia.* The Russians have a long-standing and mature understanding regarding the use of space in support of their national interests, including military and missile defense missions. Like the United States, the Soviet Union of the Cold War viewed a broad-based space program as a political statement of the superiority of Soviet technical know-how and capability. Their national effort included an advanced military space program with interests in space weapons, antisatellite systems, and missile defense. Since the collapse of the

Soviet Union, the Russian economy has forced the Russian government to reduce the scope of many of its activities, including its national space program, drastically. This cutback has pressured the Russian government to consolidate its space efforts around its most important core capabilities while striving to preserve the perception within the international community that it remains a preeminent space power. Russia resists U.S. plans to deploy a layered missile defense, especially one that heavily leverages space capabilities, because they would highlight glaring weaknesses in the Russian ability to fund and deploy equivalent systems. In addition, such steps would provide ammunition to Russian conservatives who would try and cast U.S. missile defense plans as threats to the effectiveness of the Russian nuclear deterrent force. If successful, such arguments could cause Russia to pursue nuclear modernization programs aggressively and to reject U.S. calls for further cuts in strategic nuclear warheads.

- *China.* China also has deep misgivings about U.S. missile defense plans, but its concerns are different from Europe's and Russia's problems. No country has ever perceived China as a premier economic, military, or technological power. Its limited nuclear deterrent capability is one of its most valued military capabilities, however, especially as a balance to U.S. capabilities and interests in East Asia. China's national potential and ambitions all point toward a desire to challenge the United States as a strategic power in the first half of the twenty-first century. Increases in China's strategic, conventional, and space military investments, as well as a determined effort to enlarge its economy, are evidence of these ambitions. China also recognizes the current U.S. advantages made possible by the integration of space throughout the U.S. economy and national security sector. The Chinese have openly discussed the need in any war with the United States to attack U.S. space capabilities using asymmetric methods, including antisatellite weapons. Within this environment, China objects to U.S. missile defense plans and the use of space to support those plans. Such U.S. efforts throw the viability of the Chinese nuclear force into question and create political pressures for the Chinese to respond in a manner that appears to counterbalance new U.S. capabilities and in ways that other nations might find destabilizing.

U.S. INTERNATIONAL STRATEGY

As the United States refines its missile defense plans, it must work equally hard to craft an effective international strategy that accounts for the international perceptions and concerns discussed above. This strategy, tailored for each nation or region, will establish the best possible conditions for friends and allies to support U.S. actions in this area.

The United States could take the key step of leveraging the global war on terrorism to create the political imperative for protecting itself and its allies against the threat of WMD attacks by extending missile defense concepts to the nation's friends and allies. The United States must make the offer in a manner that all nations involved view as fair and equitable. During a recent trip to Europe, I had an opportunity to speak with various European defense officials, who indicated a strong interest to join the United States on missile defense activities, including those involving space aspects of missile defense. They desire a true partnership, however, as opposed to performing as a sort of U.S. "subcontractor." This position obviously raises difficult technology transfer, industrial base, and proliferation issues, which are worth resolving in order to broaden international involvement and spread the cost burden of expensive missile defense architecture.

In addition, the United States should place cooperation with Russia on missile defense high on the political agenda. Such cooperation could take the form of exchanges of personnel and data, common architectural development, common research and development programs, or even common development programs. A primary goal of these efforts would be providing transparency in U.S. plans and deployments to reduce Russian fears and anxieties that U.S. activities threaten Russian security.

Given the state of current relations between the United States and China, envisioning any U.S. international missile defense strategy that includes a heavy dose of cooperation with China is difficult. Nevertheless, not pursuing a dialogue with the Chinese leadership to clarify U.S. intentions and reduce China's fears that U.S. activities threaten its interests would be a mistake. In this relationship, advances in areas such as human rights discussions, the deepening of economic ties, and cultural exchanges may establish conditions for improved long-term U.S.-Sino relations. Defense cooperation, including space and missile defense, might be possible once the overall relationship matures and improves.

Technological Feasibility

No discussion of this topic is complete without addressing the technical feasibility of the various space concepts in support of missile defense. Obviously, some space systems, such as missile-warning and communications systems, are proven technologies. The SBIRS program and a space-radar system for tracking moving targets are probably within the technological grasp of the United States. Although these programs are approaching state of the art in many areas, most experts agree that their development and deployment will most likely be successful. The technical feasibility of the space laser and the space-based kinetic-energy interceptor is an open question. These spacecraft present difficult technological challenges and perhaps even more difficult problems for battle management and command, control, and communications. The Bush administration evidently recognizes the difficulty associated with space-based BPI concepts and is pursuing technical risk reduction and technology demonstrator programs for both concepts. In summary, most space-based elements for missile defense are within the country's technological grasp, but some will require a few more years of focused research and development before officials can provide any accurate assessment.

Conclusion

The world is changing at an ever-increasing rate. The global war against both terrorism and WMD, the emergence of a consolidated European political entity, instability in the Middle East and in much of the Muslim world, and an uncertain global economy are just a few of the forces transforming the geopolitical landscape. Amid this backdrop, the Bush administration is poised to pursue little by little a missile defense program that will feature a role for space-based components. Even though space systems can clearly help satisfy missile defense mission requirements, fewer people agree that such a move will improve U.S. security. Yet, the radically new geopolitical framework, new threats to U.S. security, new concepts for deterrence, and the important role space can play in satisfying larger U.S. interests underpin my assessment that space systems used in support of the missile defense mission could improve U.S. national security. The United States must balance its security needs with the implications of its actions on the international community and should deploy missile defenses only after careful consultation and negotiation with U.S. friends and allies. Although such consultations do not guarantee agreement, they increase the likelihood that many in the international community will at least understand U.S. efforts and at best support them.

Notes

1. Hubert Védrine, *France in an Age of Globalization* (Washington, D.C.: Brookings Institution Press, 2001).

2. Therese Delpech, "Ballistic Missile Defense and Strategic Stability" (presentation at the forum on The Missile Threat and Plans for Ballistic Missiles Defense: Technology, Strategic Stability, and Impact on Global Security, Rome, Italy, January 2001), pp. 55–56.

3. See Keith B. Payne, "Action-Reaction Metaphysics and Negligence," *The Washington Quarterly* 24, no. 4 (autumn 2001): 109–121.

4. Center for Defense Information, "World Military Expenditures: The U.S. vs. the World," http://www.cdi.org/issues/wme/ (accessed April 10, 2002).

5. Executive summary to the Report of the Commission to Assess U.S. National Security Space Management and Organization, Washington D.C., January 11, 2001, p. 7.

6. Report of the Commission to Assess U.S. National Security Space Management and Organization, Washington D.C., January 11, 2001, ch. 2, p. 13.

James M. Lindsay and Michael E. O'Hanlon

Missile Defense after the ABM Treaty

During his campaign for the presidency, George W. Bush promised to "build effective missile defenses, based on the best available options, at the earliest possible date."[1] As president, Bush took major steps to follow through on this pledge during his first year in office. He increased spending on missile defense substantially; directed the Pentagon to explore a broader array of antimissile technologies; and, most significantly, terminated U.S. participation in the 1972 Anti-Ballistic Missile (ABM) Treaty. Bush accomplished all these tasks at a far lower political cost than anyone expected. The horrific events of September 11 hastened, if not caused, a major shift in Russian policy toward the United States generally and toward missile defense specifically. The attack also quieted, for the time being at least, domestic critics of missile defense.

Although Bush's commitment to proceeding with missile defense development is beyond doubt, his precise plans remain unclear. The administration has not settled on a specific missile defense architecture, and its public statements about future deployments are sketchy at best. This ambiguity is attributable not to a lack of forthrightness but rather to the immaturity of missile defense technology. President Bill Clinton's

James M. Lindsay and Michael E. O'Hanlon are senior fellows at The Brookings Institution and the authors of *Defending America: The Case of Limited National Missile Defense*.

The Washington Quarterly • 25:3 pp. 163–176.

administration had only one long-range missile defense program under development—a midcourse system designed to destroy individual warheads in space—which is far from being deployable. The Bush administration is now scrambling to turn other defensive concepts into systems it can test, an undertaking that will take years to accomplish. In the meantime, the political climate at home and abroad could change, thereby reigniting domestic and international controversies over the wisdom of missile defense.

Bush's Ambiguous Vision for Missile Defense

Bush's discussion of missile defense during the campaign was long on rhetoric but short on details about the kind of defense he would build. This ambiguity persists. The Pentagon no longer distinguishes between so-called theater missile defense (TMD) systems aimed against shorter-range missiles and so-called national missile defense (NMD) systems designed to intercept long-range missiles; the Pentagon instead prefers the generic label "missile defense." The labeling change, however, does not erase the fact that, although TMD systems are relatively uncontroversial because they do not threaten the deterrents of other major nuclear powers, NMD systems are controversial precisely because they can. On the central question of what the long-range missile defense is expected to accomplish, the Bush administration has yet to give a definitive answer.

On May 1, 2001, Bush outlined his vision for missile defense, emphasizing his commitment to protect the country against long-range missile attack but suggesting that his administration was of two minds on the goal of missile defense. Bush implied at times that his goal was a limited missile defense, designed to shoot down the handful of long-range missiles that so-called rogue states might acquire. He said that the most urgent threat facing the United States came not from thousands of Russian nuclear-armed missiles but from "a small number of missiles in the hands of these states ... for whom terror and blackmail are a way of life."[2] Iraq was the only country he named, but he almost certainly had Iran and North Korea in mind as well. He also spoke at length on the need to create a "new strategic framework" with Russia to replace the arms control treaties crafted during the Cold War.

At other times, however, Bush hinted that he wanted defenses capable of doing much more than intercepting a few Iraqi or North Korean missiles. He spoke dismissively of the principles underlying the ABM Treaty, and nothing in his remarks suggested that his proposed new strategic framework would limit the kinds of defenses the United States could build. Given his previously expressed concern about possible accidental or unauthorized Russian missile launches, which could theoretically involve several hundred warheads (the number associated with a single ballistic missile submarine or intercontinental ballistic missile (ICBM) complex), one could interpret Bush's remarks as endorsing robust missile defenses. Even though the distant prospect of the development of technology for building effective large-scale defenses might reassure Russia, China, with its small long-range missile force, could not have been as optimistic.

The administration's subsequent statements and actions have not resolved the ambiguity. Officials have said occasionally that their goals are modest. During a July 2001 trip to Beijing, for example, Secretary of State Colin Powell repeated his frequent refrain that the United States is seeking to build a "limited missile defense that ... would not threaten, [was] not intended to threaten, and I also don't think they would see it actually threatening the strategic deterrents of either Russia or China."[3]

Much of the time, however, the administration seems to favor ambitious long-range missile defenses. Consider exhibit A: the administration's missile defense budget request. The Pentagon requested a $3 billion increase—60 percent—in missile defense efforts for fiscal year 2002, which Congress ultimately provided almost in full. Some of the proposed increase was slated for systems that could defend only against shorter-range missiles, but much of it was requested for defensive capabilities against long-range missile attacks. The components of the request are listed in Table 1.

The Pentagon provided few specifics about potential deployments. By a conservative estimate, however, the budget request suggests that the

Table I. Comparison of Clinton and Bush Administration Missile Defense Budgets (in millions of dollars)

	Fiscal Year 2001	Clinton Plan for FY 2002	Bush Request for FY 2003
Overall System (Design, testing)[a]	$742	$662	$934
Theater Missile Defense Systems			
Patriot Advanced Capability-3 (PAC-3)	442	534	784
Medium Extended Air Defense System (MEADS)	52	74	74
Navy Area Defense[b]	270	297	395
Theater High Altitude Area Defense (THAAD)	531	699	923
Arrow[c]	94	46	66
National Missile Defense Systems[d]			
Clinton Midcourse System	2,029	2,458	3,285
Navy Theater-Wide Defense	456	246	656
Airborne Laser	231	214	410
Space-Based Laser	73	137	165
Sea-Based Boost-Phase Missile	0	0	50?
Space-Based Boost-Phase Missile	0	0	60?
Satellites and Sensors			
SBIRS-Low Sensor	239	308	420
U.S.-Russian Satellites	35[a]	75	75
TOTAL	5,194[a]	5,751	8,298

[a] Budget documents for 2001 use different categories so figures may be slightly inaccurate.

[b] The Navy area program has been terminated, though something similar will probably eventually replace it.

[c] Israel is the primary developer of the Arrow program.

[d] Systems explicitly designed for long-range missile defense or potentially usable for that mission.

Source: July 2001 Pentagon briefing.

Contemporary Nuclear Debates

administration ultimately plans to deploy a fairly large defense. In addition to its plans for dedicated long-range missile defense, including the Clinton midcourse system and other options, the Bush administration plans to give long-range defense capabilities to two TMD programs, the Theater High Altitude Area Defense (THAAD) and Navy Theater-Wide (NTW) systems. Because these programs are intended to have many hundreds of interceptors, the Bush budget implies deploying at least a thousand interceptors capable of long-range defense. Indeed, the budget request probably implies deploying closer to 2,000 interceptors.

Exhibit B is the administration's approach to the ABM Treaty. Throughout the fall of 2001, the nation's newspapers speculated that when Presidents Bush and Vladimir Putin met in Crawford, Texas, in November 2001, they would strike a deal on modifying the ABM Treaty. Washington would get greater freedom to test and deploy missile defense technologies, and Moscow would get limits on the ultimate size and nature of any U.S. defense. The logic behind the proposed deal was straightforward: to maintain Russian cooperation in the war against terrorism, the United States would accept constraints that would prevent it from developing ambitious defenses that would not be ready in any case for years. The pundits were wrong: although both presidents committed themselves to a sharp reduction in their offensive nuclear forces, they could not agree on modifications to the ABM Treaty.

This outcome set the stage for Bush's historic December 13 announcement that he was invoking the six-month withdrawal clause in the ABM Treaty. Thus, as of mid-June 2002, the United States is free to develop, test, and deploy missile defenses in any manner it desires. Immediate need did not drive this decision. No missile defense systems were ready for deployment, and virtually all the research and development that the administration wanted to conduct could have continued for some time within the strictures of the ABM Treaty. Bush's decision to withdraw reflected instead the calculation that the political climate had changed so much at home and abroad that the costs of withdrawal were low. The U.S. public cared far more about stopping terrorism than preserving traditional arms control, and Putin had signaled that he would do nothing more than call the decision a "mistake." With neither the U.S. public nor the Kremlin protesting, domestic and foreign critics were easily ignored.

The 2003 Defense Budget Proposal

In February 2002, Bush released his proposed budget for national security for fiscal year 2003. The budget contained a request for $379 billion to fund the operations of the Department of Defense and another $17 billion in funding for the nuclear weapons programs run by the Department of Energy. Equally important, the budget's five-year plan anticipated that national security spending would rise far more sharply than the administration had projected only a year earlier—reaching $470 billion in fiscal year 2007. The amount would be $100 billion—more than 25 percent—greater than what the Clinton administration's long-term plans had envisioned for that year. After adjusting for the effects of inflation, the figure approaches the peak levels of military spending reached during the Reagan years as well as those of the Vietnam era.

A key question is whether those spending increases will actually occur. If they do, missile defense will be less likely to compete with other defense programs as well as other homeland security programs for funding. Yet, national security spending could also fall well short of what Bush proposes, especially in FY 2004 and beyond, either because the federal budget slips deep into deficit as it did during the 1980s and much of the 1990s or because the absence of new terrorist attacks saps public and congressional support for greater defense spending. Consequently, missile defense could find itself competing against other defense priorities.

In the short term, however, robust spending on missile defense is assured. As Table 2 shows, the Pentagon's FY 2003 budget proposal requested $7.8 billion for overall missile defense, the same level of spending Congress appropriated a year earlier. The Bush administration did propose shifting the spending allocation somewhat among various categories under the missile defense umbrella, such as for shorter-range

Table 2. Missile Defense Budget Request for Fiscal Year 2003, by Program Type (in billions of dollars)

Item	FY 2002 Spending Appropriated	FY 2003 Spending Requested
General missile defense systems	0.8	1.1
Terminal defense	0.1	0.2
Midcourse defense	3.8	3.2
Boost-phase defense	0.6	0.8
Theater High Altitude Area Defense (THAAD)	0.9	1.0
Patriot Advance Capability-3 (PAC-3)	0.9	0.6
Medium Extended Air Defense System (MEADS)	0.1	0.1
Other	0.6	0.9
TOTAL	7.8	7.8

Source: Bush administration budget request for 2003, February 2002.

(or theater) systems and long-range (national) missile defense systems. These shifts were unexceptionable. Most of the FY 2003 funds will be spent on research and development. The Pentagon anticipates that overall missile defense spending will rise to $11 billion by FY 2007. Beyond that point, the budget plans are unclear because the Bush administration has not chosen a missile defense architecture.

What might this spending buy in terms of a defense against long-range missile threats, at least in the short term? Official statements, as well as excerpts leaked from the classified Nuclear Posture Review that the Pentagon undertook at Congress's direction and formally completed in January 2002, suggest that by around 2004 the administration hopes to deploy what it calls "a rudimentary ground-based midcourse system."[4] The system, which would use the technology that the Clinton administration was developing, would consist of a few interceptor missiles based in Alaska. To make rapid deployment feasible, the Bush plan would forgo the dedicated high-resolution X-band radar that the Clinton administration had planned for Shemya Island and instead rely on existing radar systems. This rudimentary deployment would expand in subsequent years and be supplemented by the operation of initial airborne-laser aircraft, which could provide at least "limited operations against ballistic missiles of all ranges"—assuming the aircraft were located nearby when a missile launches. The specifics of this plan, however, are likely to change. Indeed, given the embryonic state of missile defense technology, probably no other outcome is possible.

How much might building the more robust defenses that the administration seems to envision cost? Neither the Pentagon nor the White House has offered an estimate—a reasonable response, given that they have made no final decisions about what the system would look like. In early 2002, however, the Congressional Budget Office (CBO) offered one broad estimate of the long-term costs of a long-range missile defense.[5] Envisioning an architecture consisting of a land-based midcourse system, a sea-based midcourse system, and a space-based system, the CBO guessed that total development and deployment costs could approach $200 billion during the next two decades. Assuming a roughly steady level of overall spending for TMD programs, that estimate would imply an overall spending level for all missile defense efforts of about $15 billion a year, plus operating costs for various systems once they are deployed. Such projections should be treated cautiously; until the administration decides on a long-range missile defense architecture, all talk about cost will be speculative.

Threats and Technology

Bush's success in building effective defenses depends not only on his commitment to the cause but also on whether the public shares his perception of the threat and whether technology enables these systems to be built. Bush's first year in office saw important developments on both scores.

In a narrow sense, the threat of a ballistic missile attack did not change significantly during 2001. In December 2001, the National Intelligence Council released an unclassified version of the National Intelligence Estimate (NIE), summarizing the official views of the U.S. intelligence community on the nature of the ballistic missile threat.[6] The report's conclusions about the threat from long-range ballistic missiles largely tracked the previous NIE, released in September 1999.[7] Both NIEs note that North Korea could probably test a multiple Taepo-dong-2 missile theoretically capable of reaching parts of the United States with a payload of several hundred kilograms within short order if North Korea made the political decision to do so. Similarly, both NIEs indicate that Iran is not likely to test its first ICBM until the last half of the decade, if then.

In a broader sense, however, September 11 dramatically changed the perception of the ballistic missile threat. Some observers initially speculated that support for missile defense would plummet because people would want to concentrate on stopping low-tech methods of attacking the United States. Yet, most of the U.S. public drew a different lesson from September 11, namely, that some of the country's adversaries are prepared to do the unthinkable against the United States, actually using missiles if they get their hands on them. That heightened perception of the threat now helps drive the missile defense debate.

On the technological front, the Pentagon has made modest progress with the existing midcourse system. In July 2001 and again in December, a prototype interceptor successfully destroyed a target warhead some 140 miles above the Pacific Ocean; a similar if slightly more challenging test involving three decoys instead of one succeeded in March 2002. These results were encouraging, but they do not mean that a working system is within reach. Pentagon officials have repeatedly acknowledged that none of the tests conducted so far mimic real-world conditions for a number of reasons: (1) the target warheads have not used realistic decoys; (2) the interceptor missiles have used relatively slow-moving booster rockets that place less stress on the kill vehicle rather than using the faster booster rockets that would be included on an operational system; and (3) the programmers artificially placed the kill vehicles on a trajectory heading straight for the desired intercept points. None of these decisions is improper or deceptive. All tests of new weapons systems are partial and limited at first; one must learn to walk before learning to run, as Pentagon officials like to say. By the same token, however, the fact that the midcourse system is learning to walk does not mean it will soon be ready to run.

Moreover, the Clinton midcourse system is the only program dedicated to shooting down long-range missiles that the Pentagon had under development when Bush came into office. The administration is now exploring an array of other technologies. Indeed, the administration argued, not entirely convincingly, that U.S. withdrawal from the ABM Treaty was necessary so that the Pentagon could test all technological possibilities. Nevertheless, proceeding from initial concepts to operational systems will take years or decades. The Bush administration hopes to shorten the time needed to prepare for deployment by giving long-range capabilities to the THAAD and NTW programs. These systems have yet to meet their initial design goals, however, making their effectiveness in a long-range mode anytime soon debatable. In addition, the airborne-laser program has experienced developmental delays. The Pentagon has now postponed its first test against a missile in flight from 2003 to 2004. Additional delays in the schedule would not be surprising.

Although the technology for shooting down long-range ballistic missiles under real-world conditions remains a hope rather than a reality, the political feasibility of one kind of long-range missile defense—earth-based boost-phase systems—rose considerably in 2001. Boost-phase defenses, which attempt to shoot down missiles while their rocket motors are still burning, have one decided advantage over midcourse systems such as those contained in the Clinton program, which try to destroy individual warheads in space. Boost-phase defenses would intercept missiles before they could deploy countermeasures, thereby greatly simplifying the defense's job. To accomplish this mission, however, earth-based boost-phase systems must be based within several hundred miles of the enemy's missile launch. Although geography makes defenses situated on ships at sea possible against a North Korean missile attack, the geography of Iran makes a system based to its north—in the Caspian Sea, in Turkmenistan, or possibly in Kazakhstan or Uzbekistan—essential. Before September, such a deployment would have been doubtful. Today, however, with greatly improved U.S.-Russian relations and U.S. troops now based in Central Asia, the idea is at least conceivable.

The Politics of Missile Defense

Although changes in threats and technology cloud the future of missile defense, the political climate shifted dramatically in its favor after September 11. Abroad, Putin made the pivotal decision to align Russia closely with the United States, even if doing so meant abiding by U.S. policies that Moscow had previously deemed unacceptable. Putin's restrained reaction to the U.S. withdrawal from the ABM Treaty, in turn, effectively derailed criticism of the decision from China and from major U.S. allies.

Domestically, missile defense appeared to be emerging as a potentially divisive political issue during the summer of 2001. Democratic leaders in the Senate hoped to reprise the Star Wars debates that had proven politically profitable for them during the 1980s. Following the attacks on the World Trade Center and the Pentagon, however, the Democratic majority quickly dropped its effort to cut missile defense spending and limit missile defense tests. Contrary to most predictions of six months earlier, Bush's decision to withdraw from the ABM Treaty caused barely a ripple on Capitol Hill.

Despite these developments, the chances are good that missile defense will resurface as a contentious political issue, especially if the threat of terrorism recedes in political importance. Moscow's acceptance of the U.S. withdrawal from the ABM Treaty does not mean that Russia is indifferent to the Bush administration's missile defense plans. The treaty's demise had obvious symbolic significance but no immediate practical effect. The same cannot be said about actual deployments. Russia will evaluate how the specific technological capabilities of proposed systems affect its national interests. The perspectives of those in power—and the overall state of relations between the two countries at that time—will inevitably shape those evaluations.

The prospect of Russia's negative reaction to U.S. missile defense deployments is evident from the tensions between Moscow and Washington in early 2002 over offensive nuclear forces.[8] Although both sides agreed in late 2001 to reduce their long-range nuclear arsenals substantially—to between 1,700 and 2,200 operational warheads on the U.S. side and down to 1,500 warheads in Russia—they disagreed over whether to make the cuts irreversible. The Bush administration argued that friendly U.S.-Russian relations made binding ceilings unnecessary and that future events might force the United States to return to a larger nuclear force. To make this option possible, the administration said it would keep many of the retired warheads in a reserve force it could reactivate if events warrant. Russia objected to this laissez-faire approach and pushed for a binding agreement that would limit how many weapons each side could possess. The two sides will likely resolve their differences eventually, though perhaps not to either side's total satisfaction. The relevant lesson for the missile defense debate is that the details of the nuclear balance continue to matter, at least to some in Russia.

China may be an even more likely source of international opposition. In many respects, U.S. missile defense deployments are more important to Beijing than to Moscow. China, with less than two dozen long-range missiles, is far more vulnerable to a U.S. missile defense than Russia is. China is also more prone to conflict with the United States based on strategic realities. This possibility presents a potential problem for Washington because Beijing has the wherewithal to make the United States pay a substantial strategic price for building missile defenses that China finds threatening. Beijing can expand its plans to upgrade its own nuclear missile force, frustrate U.S. efforts to stem nuclear and ballistic missile proliferation, and obstruct U.S. policy in other areas. The Bush administration's proposal to open a dialogue with China on strategic stability may lessen the chances of a rift, but Beijing will clearly be watching not just what Washington says but also what it does.

The domestic missile defense debate is also likely to revive as Bush's extremely high public approval ratings erode and critics decide that they can question his defense proposals without being labeled unpatriotic. Yet, the debate probably will not be fought on the same terrain that dominated discussion before September 11, when the debate was primarily theological in nature: Is missile defense good or bad? Should we keep or jettison the ABM Treaty? Are we undermining three decades of arms control? The terrorist attacks and the passing of the ABM Treaty pushed those theological issues into the background, though not entirely off the agenda. In the forefront now are more prosaic questions about the cost and technological feasibility of the system.

This change in the terms of the debate does not necessarily favor proponents of missile defense, and the shift could actually complicate their cause. In U.S. politics, holding coalitions together on abstract principles rather than on specific decisions is usually easier. Should the cost of missile defense be high, or should a deteriorating budgetary picture intensify the competition for federal dollars, weak supporters of missile defense could easily switch sides, as happened during the Reagan defense buildup in the mid-1980s. Moderate northern and midwestern Republicans abandoned that cause when it threatened other programs important to their constituents.

Technological feasibility may be an even bigger stumbling block. Political support typically fades for weapons systems that cannot demonstrate their workability, and missile defense programs have experienced their share, if not more, of developmental snafus. For instance, development of the interceptor rocket that is supposedly part of the existing midcourse system is far behind schedule. That problem has forced the Pentagon to substitute booster rockets that are far slower and do not accurately mimic the stresses and strains that the actual interceptor will place on the kill vehicle during its tests. Secretary of Defense Donald Rumsfeld's decision to exempt missile defense programs from many standard oversight requirements, including oversight by the Pentagon's own test evaluation office, may also fuel doubts about the state of the technology. Ostensibly intended to expedite the development of the missile defense system, the decision will likely raise questions about whether the Pentagon is adequately testing these systems.

A Look Ahead

Three principles that should guide U.S. policy on missile defense in future years stand out:

- Missile defense has a potentially important role to play in U.S. defense and foreign policy. September 11 provided the world with a warning that the unthinkable can happen. Ballistic missile technology may not be spreading rapidly, but it is spreading, and the threat it poses to the United States and its allies will likely grow during the next decade. Having protection against this threat, especially in the context of the war on terrorism, would be useful. If a terrorist group found refuge on the territory of a state possessing long-range ballistic missiles and warheads outfitted with weapons of mass destruction (WMD), the United States and its allies would face grave difficulties trying to pursue the group or overthrow the regime of the country that harbored it. In other words, without a reliable missile defense system, the United States could not use the strategy that worked so successfully against the Taliban in Operation Enduring Freedom.
- Officials must soberly assess the potential capabilities of missile defense technology. Debates about missile defense have frequently oscillated between two poles—arguing either that it cannot work or that only a lack of will stands in the way of success. The reality is more complicated. Missile defense is truly "rocket science." The Pentagon has made progress in the last decade, but destroying ballistic missiles in flight is extraordinarily difficult, especially because the attacker will always look for ways to counter any defense. Consequently, in assessing whether to proceed with deployments, honesty about what proposed systems can and cannot do is crucial. Building systems that do not work, or forgoing ones that do, does not serve U.S. interests.
- The potential benefits of missile defense must be weighed against the

costs. The direct budgetary costs of missile defense are important, but so too are the indirect costs. Competing national priorities—within the realms of defense and homeland security as well as nondefense items—argue for restraining the size of missile defense programs that could become major budget busters. Decisionmakers must also take foreign policy interests into account. Proceeding with deployments that threaten Russia or, even more likely, China, could weaken U.S. security. Out of spite or out of a desire to complicate U.S. strategic planning and thereby preserve the viability of their own deterrents, these countries could accelerate the transfer of missile technology to countries hostile to the United States. Moscow and Beijing have behaved badly in this regard in the past, but they could behave far worse in the future. They could also become less willing to work with Washington to improve the security and safety of their existing WMD or to cooperate in the struggle against terrorism. The chances of nuclear theft, accidents, and other catastrophes would then be higher than they should be.

Rather than walk away from the ABM Treaty and leave nothing in its place, the United States might therefore consider accepting some limitations on its future long-range missile defense capabilities. Even if not codified in a treaty, such limitations could be useful. A politically binding framework, or even a unilateral statement accepting constraints, could help preserve the benefits of cooperation by the great powers on security issues while permitting development and deployment of missile defenses. We suggest that, for the next 15 years or so, the United States pledge to limit any long-range missile defenses for itself and its allies within the original numerical bounds of the ABM Treaty—meaning 200 interceptor missiles. (Airborne lasers might be counted as the equivalent of perhaps five interceptors.) Abiding by such a limit means not giving long-range missile defense capabilities to TMD systems such as THAAD and NTW.

We also suggest that, for the time being, the United States forgo testing and deployment of missile defense weapons in space. These constraints need not be permanent, but they could help avoid any derailment of the ongoing improvement in the U.S.-Russian partnership while also avoiding excessive disruption in U.S.-Sino relations.

Missile defense, against long-range and short-range threats, continues to make sense for the United States as well as for its allies. Too much missile defense or too little diplomatic care to go along with the defense systems, however, can be harmful to U.S. security. The year 2001 may have ended the old debate about the ABM Treaty, but it hardly changed the list of issues that complicate the pursuit of missile defense.

Notes

1. George W. Bush, "New Leadership on Security," Washington, D.C., May 23, 2000, www.brook.edu/dybdocroot/fp/projects/nmd/bush1.htm (accessed April 2, 2002) .

2. George W. Bush, "Remarks to Students and Faculty at National Defense University," Washington, D.C., May 1, 2001, www.whitehouse.gov/news/releases/2001/05/20010501-10.html (accessed April 2, 2002).

3. U.S. Department of State, Office of International Information Programs, "Secretary Powell Press Conference in Beijing," July 28, 2001, usinfo.state.gov/topical/pol/arms/stories/01072802.htm (accessed April 2, 2002).

4. Excerpts from the Nuclear Posture Review are available at www.globalsecurity.org/wmd/library/policy/dod/npr.htm (accessed April 2, 2002).

5. Congressional Budget Office, "Estimated Costs and Technical Characteristics of Selected National Missile Defense Systems," January 2002, www.cbo.gov/showdoc.cfm?index=3281&sequence=0 (accessed April 2, 2002).

6. National Intelligence Council, "Foreign Missile Developments and the Ballistic Missile Threat through 2015," December 2001, www.cia.gov/nic/pubs/index.htm (accessed April 2, 2002).

7. National Intelligence Council, "Foreign Missile Developments and the Ballistic Missile Threat to the United States through 2015," September 1999, www.brook.edu/dybdocroot/press/companion/defendingamerica/appendix_d.htm (accessed April 2, 2002). Exact comparisons are impossible because the reports discuss their results in different formats.

8. See Ivo H. Daalder and James M. Lindsay, "A New Agenda for Nuclear Weapons," Brookings Policy Brief, no. 94 (February 2002), www.brook.edu/dybdocroot/comm/policybriefs/pb94.htm (accessed April 2, 2002).

Part II

Global Perceptions of Missile Defense

François Heisbourg

Brussels's Burden

Well into the year 2000, a strategic analyst can only be struck by the lack of public debate in Europe on the United States' projected NMD. Part of this is attributable to ignorance: European politicians tend to know as little about U.S. NMD as most U.S. politicians do about the new defense policy of the European Union (EU). Until NMD becomes a political reality, Europeans not specialized in defense matters are not going to focus on it. Those Europeans who do follow strategic affairs do not, as a rule, like NMD, much in the same way that the congressional armed services committees and the U.S. secretaries of state and defense are not exactly enthusiastic about the new European Defense Policy (EDP).

There is another similarity between NMD and EDP. In both cases, these policies are graduating from concepts into the real world. The Europeans most directly involved know, as Ivo Daalder and others put it, that NMD deployment is not a question of whether but of how,[1] in the same way that the relevant U.S. policymakers now assume that EDP will happen.

The EDP is now firmly established as part of the transatlantic dialogue. The EDP includes the creation of defense institutions within the EU, including *inter alia* a military committee, and the creation of a Eu-

François Heisbourg is a professor at the Institut d'Etudes Politiques, Paris.

Copyright © 2000 by The Center for Strategic and International Studies and the Massachusetts Institute of Technology
The Washington Quarterly • 23:3 pp. 127–133.

ropean rapid reaction force of 60,000 soldiers by the year 2003. A move toward establishing a European defense identity raises U.S. fears of duplication with, and discrimination within, the North Atlantic Treaty Organization (NATO). NMD, on the other hand, has been the subject of relatively little debate and could erupt on the political scene in a brutal and uncontrollable manner, poisoning U.S.-European relations. As a French saying goes, one should beware of sleeping waters. Although the degree of virulence of European reactions will depend on the exact circumstances of the NMD decision, the backlash will be stronger because there has not been much of a debate, with limited exceptions such as U.S. secretary of defense William Cohen's hard-sell of NMD at this year's Wehrkunde.[2] The discussion should be nurtured, on both official and nonofficial tracks, before the actual decision is made.

How Europe's Interests Will Be Affected by NMD

The assumption here is that NMD will be what the current U.S. administration says it will be (a limited system capable of dealing with a small number of ballistic missiles) and, furthermore, that it will actually do what it is supposed to. That may be an excessive leap of faith as to what the technology can accomplish. But, if the tests preceding the deployment decision prove satisfactory, this is a sensible way to focus the transatlantic debate. Europeans are well advised to assume that the decision on NMD will be made by the United States, irrespective of what the Europeans might think or say about its technical feasibility. European analysts understand that this scheme is not a remake of Star Wars, which elicited vehement European opposition on doctrinal and political grounds, but which was often and rightly dismissed as a technological fantasy that eventually collapsed under its own weight.

Four main areas of European interest would be affected by NMD. First, there would be the opportunity cost of the scheme. The funds involved would be considerable, with a $28 billion figure on a 20 year period mentioned by the General Accounting Office. The part devoted to the total procurement, $10 billion for NMD, would represent the equivalent of 11 percent of this year's U.S. procurement spending at fiscal year 2000 levels.[3]

In the absence of NMD, these are resources that would presumably have been available for defense items upon which there is a degree of transatlantic agreement. Improving U.S. force projection capabilities, or sustaining the U.S. force presence in Europe and Asia. Nevertheless, even if the project encountered the usual cost overruns, the amounts are not such that this will be more than a second-order issue, an unwelcome distraction as it were. In the unlikely event that the United States convinced Europe to allocate a fraction of its already tight defense spending on a European variant of NMD, however, Europe would experience high opportunity costs.

No doubt, U.S. lobbying could enlist the support of this or that European defense contractor, who could in turn put pressure on its national government. The only thing that would be more unwelcome than a U.S. attempt to draw European resources into NMD, however, would be a successful U.S. attempt to do so. We have enough on our plate with the current collective shift by the EU to force projection, a belated but welcome development. Weakening this priority in the name of NMD would not be helpful.

The strategic impact of NMD is a second realm of interest. At one level of analysis, the United States is right to dismiss some European fears. NMD is not going to negate the credibility of NATO deterrence, even if Russia built a copycat NMD capability with U.S. help. The French and British nuclear forces were prepared during the Cold War to cope with the Soviet antiballistic missile (ABM) system around Moscow. At the time, this system used nuclear-tipped, antiballistic missiles, with a much bigger "kick" than all-conventional NMD. At worst, Paris and London would be compelled to use available warhead potential. For instance, each of Britain's four nuclear submarines currently carries 48 warheads on 16 Trident II missiles, an average of 3 warheads per missile; this average could be readily built up to 8 warheads per missile. Additionally, NMD will not prevent the United States from extending its nuclear guarantee to its European NATO partners. Similarly, the United States is right to point out, in the case of Asia, that it is easier to defend Seoul against North Korea if NMD provides assurance that putative Taep'odong 2s cannot hit U.S. territory.

At another level, however, there is a legitimate European-U.S. divergence concerning the broad impact of NMD on deterrence as a means of war prevention. What Washington is telling the world through NMD is that the United States, which already commands 35 percent of the world's military expenditures, considers itself secure only if it now gets a missile shield in addition to the world's most powerful conventional and nuclear forces. And this is not in the face of a monstrous military challenge but against a famine-ridden, Asian backwater with a yearly GDP representing one month's worth of WalMart's sales. Since no one country in Europe is a continental-scale superpower, it cannot afford such a level of absolute security. Europe is, in effect, reduced to a second- or third-class rank not only from the standpoint of its status vis-à-vis the United States—most of us understand that the United States is in a class of its own in terms of power—but also in terms of the quality of our security which would appear to be second rate. This is not as dire as it sounds, if only because the Europeans, as shall be seen, do not always or entirely share the U.S. threat assessment which underlies the NMD project. Nor do they generally believe that NMD is an appropriate means to deal with that threat. But Europeans (as other non-Americans) will feel resentment toward this confirmation of U.S. hyperpower which, coming on top of other causes, will complicate the transatlantic relationship.

In theory, this contradiction could be eased by U.S. efforts to transfer NMD technology to the Europeans, thus "equalizing" the degree of security on both sides of the Atlantic. But such a policy would fuel the European fear that an NMD "transfer" to Europe would interfere with other defense priorities, notably force projection. More generally, the offer, however generous, would still rub salt into the wound by pointing out that all and sundry U.S. strategic decisions, however ill advised, call the tune. In sum, in a "damned if you do (offer NMD technology), damned if you don't" situation, the "do" would not be as bad as the "don't."

The third highly specific, and potentially deeply divisive, impact of NMD on Europe is related to the role played by European-based elements of the future U.S. NMD system. These are located at the Fylingdale's facility in Yorkshire, England, and at the Thule base on the Danish island of Greenland. Powerful, U.S.-managed, over-the-horizon missile warning and tracking radars are based there, completing similar ballistic missile early warning installations based in Clear, Alaska.

It is as yet unclear what the exact degree of integration of Fylingdale's and Thule would be in the NMD system. Publicly available details are lacking about the amount of work entailed at these locations to eventually include them in an NMD. If it were to become a highly contentious item in transatlantic relations, then Britain and Denmark would find themselves caught between their bilateral relationship with the United States and their other, national or European, allegiances.

Finally, we have the distant, but potentially powerful, impact of NMD on Europe's relations with China. NMD is seen by Beijing as a direct threat to China's comparatively limited nuclear forces, with only a clutch of inter-continental ballistic missiles (ICBMs) capable of reaching the United States.[4] On this issue, Chinese statements have been harsh, sometimes to the point of shrillness. Therein lies an apparent opportunity for Europe, insofar as China may offer economic and political advantages to Europeans as a way of "punishing" the United States. "It was not by chance," to use a Soviet-era phrase, that France made a bid last November to get the United Nations (UN) General Assembly to condemn U.S. moves in the ABM arena.[5] Just a few weeks before, Chinese president Jiang Zemin visited Paris on a high profile, extremely friendly state visit. The transatlantic relationship would suffer if the Europeans succumbed to Chinese blandishments and were seen by the United States as working in tandem with Beijing.

Meanwhile, the Europeans cannot but note that Washington will waste precious goodwill in its relations with Beijing and Moscow, with whom the West's relations are difficult (and important) enough without complicating them further with NMD. The diplomatic opportunity costs of NMD will be tremendous, hampering the pursuit of other, more worthwhile objectives such as democratization and human rights in China and Russia.

"It's the Treaty, Stupid!"

If Moscow accedes to U.S. requests for Anti-Ballistic Missile (ABM) Treaty modifications, the European reactions will be disgruntled but relatively quiet. Unhappiness would be compounded by the revival of the Cold War feeling that Washington and Moscow settle matters above their allies' heads. Provided the modification, and the corresponding quid pro quos in the Strategic Arms Reduction Talks (START) process, were of a limited nature,[6] the Europeans would live with the consequences.

The alternative scenario, in which the United States breaks out of the ABM Treaty without an agreement with Russia, would cause a furor which will make foreign reactions to the U.S. Senate's rejection of the Comprehensive Test Ban Treaty seem tame in comparison. U.S. unilateralism, along with the dismantling of the last vestiges of cooperative nuclear arms control, would be universally condemned. No doubt the United States would try to limit the political damage by emphasizing the reasonable nature of the requested modifications. The fact would remain that a treaty is a treaty is a treaty. Even if the ABM Treaty contains an exit clause which the United States could invoke, the international and transatlantic impact of the United States pulling out of the treaty would be immense, barring an act of absolute foolishness by North Korea which would provide a credible basis for such a U.S. withdrawal. A harsh reaction, in which Europe would be seen as teaming up with Russia and China, could in turn elicit a U.S. backlash, with the United States turning against European defense initiatives. EDP could thus become a hostage of NMD.

We also have the issue of future U.S. developments in the ABM field, beyond NMD. To what extent will an NMD decision by one U.S. administration be a prelude to moves by a different administration down the "Star Wars" road? The Europeans understand that there can be no absolute answer here; but again, a cooperative agreement with the Russians on the ABM Treaty would be of the essence to assuage fears about this "slippery slope." That, of course, assumes that the Senate would ratify the treaty changes, a prospect in which the Europeans have little reason to place confidence if the vote were taken under the outgoing administration.

One Man's Rogue Is Another Man's Partner

Last but not least, U.S.-European differences vis-à-vis NMD rest on different threat perceptions. One of the differences is purely that of location: North Korea is relatively close to Alaska and rather far away from Europe. Even if the Europeans shared U.S. analyses about North Korea's intentions and capabilities,[7] they would not feel as directly threatened. As for the other so-called "rogue states," the Europeans tend to have a more laid-back attitude than the United States. Khatami's semi-democratic Iran certainly doesn't strike most European analysts as being more of a rogue state than Mao's China or Stalin's USSR, and certainly not a threat implying a drastic departure from a combination of deterrence and engagement. Iraq is seen as being in a box, in terms of acquiring a long-range missile capability, and Libya no longer causes sleepless nights. The point here is not to decide whether the United States or Europe is right on the threat assessment. Simply, there is not much of a chicken-little syndrome in Europe today. Every loud-mouthed dictator is not considered a wildly irrational rogue elephant, unamenable to classic mixes of deterrence, military pressure, and diplomacy. Indeed, the one thing dictators share is an appetite for power and, for that reason, they tend to be prudent when it comes to putting their power base under a direct, existential threat. Saddam Hussein did not use his biological and chemical weapons during the Persian Gulf War. He had, conversely, used them during the Iran-Iraq war, against a foe that could not retaliate with weapons of mass destruction.

Contemporary Nuclear Debates

Policy Paths

In order to defuse the alliance-splitting potential of NMD, several policy paths are available. The first, insofar that NMD is going to happen anyway, is that the United States should do the utmost to secure a cooperative agreement with Russia. The corollary of this path is Europe should not attempt to deter Russia from agreeing to a limited modification of the ABM Treaty along the lines mentioned above. Europe should make such a view clear in Moscow as in Washington. In terms of public diplomacy, this so far has not been the case.

The second recommendation is that the United States should not attempt to foist NMD upon Europe. The line to tread here is a relatively fine one. On one hand, the United States should deal with NMD as a national defense decision, not calling for alliance endorsement or, *a fortiori*, alliance participation. On the other hand, the United States could display to Europe the same sort of openness it has, or is contemplating, with Russia in terms of sharing of early warning data and other missile related information.

On the European side, there should be a symmetrical readiness to live with a U.S. NMD decision without mounting diplomatic offensives in the UN or elsewhere—as long as the decision is conducted in a cooperative mode with Russia and strictly limited to the current definition of NMD.

In the same way that Europe does not appreciate the United States grousing about EDP, the United States is entitled to follow its own policies, however unreasonable they may appear to many, provided that they are kept within these bounds.

Notes

1. Ivo Daalder et al., "Deploying NMD: Not Whether, But How," *Survival* 42, no. 1 (spring 2000).
2. "Speech of Secretary of Defense William S. Cohen," Thirty-Sixth Munich Conference on Security Policy, February 5, 2000.

3. This is out of $87.4 billion (including RDT&E). Nineteen percent, if one in-cludes the acquisition of $53 billion.

4. Fifteen to twenty, according to "The Military Balance 1999-2000," IISS, Lon-don, 1999.

5. The bid was moderately successful, the corresponding resolution (A/RES/54/54F) having been carried by only 80 UN members out of 188, with the major-ity abstaining or not taking part in the vote.

6. Along the lines described by Sam Nunn, Brent Scowcroft, Arnold Kantor in "A Deal with Russia on Arms Control," *Boston Globe*, September 13, 1999.

7. There is clearly room for difference here. The Ikonos satellite imagery of the North Korea launch facilities displayed on the Federation of American Scien-tists website at <www.fas.org> is difficult to square with official assessments. See "Foreign Missile Developments and the Ballistic Missile Threat to the United States Through 2015," National Intelligence Council, September 1999.

Yoichi Funabashi

Tokyo's Temperance

The current debate on U.S. NMD has, without a doubt, placed Japan in a deep quandary as it struggles to articulate its position while valuing its alliance with the United States. For Japan, NMD can no longer be ignored on the grounds that it is merely an "internal American debate," characterized simply as a clash of "Democrats versus Republicans." Nor can it be neglected based on the argument that it is only a Russian-U.S. bilateral issue. If the United States proceeds with its own NMD deployment while disregarding the international implications of such an action, there is a danger that Japan could also face a backlash from Russia and, especially, China. The NMD issue needs to be addressed in the context of its ramifications for Japan's long-term security interests. Furthermore, Japan must accept the hard reality that the current U.S. NMD debate warrants a serious domestic Japanese discussion of its implications for the U.S.-Japan alliance management process, as the United States could pursue an NMD policy that would be adverse to Japanese interests. Under a worst-case scenario, Japan's own missile defense program could be compromised as a result of the currently planned U.S. NMD system.

Yoichi Funabashi is columnist and chief diplomatic correspondent of *Asahi Shimbun*. He also directs Project Alliance Tomorrow, a security studies project, at the Tokyo Foundation.

Copyright © 2000 by The Center for Strategic and International Studies and the Massachusetts Institute of Technology
The Washington Quarterly • 23:3 pp. 135–144.

Three Security Shocks for Japan

To fully understand Japanese NMD perspectives, one must consider three "security shocks" that Japan experienced in the latter part of the 1990s. These shocks have had a psychological impact on the Japanese, which is sure to tangibly influence the direction of the Japanese debate on the U.S. NMD strategy.

The first of these shocks was the Chinese missile tests over the Taiwan Strait in 1995 and 1996. China executed unarmed launches of its DF-15 missile during military exercises near Taiwan. This incident led Japan to doubt China's commitment to a no-first-use policy, while acutely heightening Japan's perception of China's missile threat. To make matters worse, a recent intelligence report revealed that the total number of coastal-deployed M-9s and shorter-range M-11s has been increased to 150-200 missiles and will reach 600 by 2005, should the current deployment trend continue.[1] The incident has manifestly affected the Japanese security psyche, as it prompted Japan to join the West in criticizing China for its missile diplomacy and added to Japan's motivation to formulate new Japan-U.S. defense guidelines.

The second shock was the North Korean test launch of the Taep'odong 1, which provided direct impetus for both the U.S. NMD and Japan's theater missile defense (TMD) initiatives. Besides the fact that the missile was lobbed over Japanese territory, the decisive factor behind the joint U.S.-Japanese signing of the 1999 TMD Memorandum of Understanding was the rude awakening that North Korea's program, which now included a multi-stage missile, progressed farther than either the United States or Japan had imagined.

The third shock was a chain of events that rocked the foundations of the global nonproliferation regime: nuclear testing by India and then Pakistan in 1998, and the U.S. Senate's decision not to ratify the Comprehensive Test Ban Treaty (CTBT) in the fall of 1999. As the only country to have suffered a nuclear attack, nonnuclearization and nuclear disarmament are very powerful themes for the Japanese, which explains Japan's desire to play a larger diplomatic role in the global nonproliferation regime such as the Nuclear Non-Proliferation Treaty (NPT) or CTBT. These recent events were thus a blow to Japan, and international confidence in the existing nonproliferation regime eroded as a result. Japan was particularly shocked by the U.S. Congress's rejection of CTBT ratification, giving credence to Japanese suspicions that the United States is no longer willing to sustain its commitment to allied cooperation on nuclear nonproliferation and that it is only interested in its own security.

Five Key Japanese Interests

The discussion on U.S. NMD thus far in Japan has neither been adequately broad nor candid, and views expressed on NMD have been minimal, with only a few individuals venturing to address the issue. Missile defense is a highly divisive issue in Japan, even on governmental and bureaucratic levels. While most Japanese affiliated with, or close to, the government are pro-TMD, there is a clear lack of consensus among them on the U.S. NMD. Views vary even within the Ministry of Foreign Affairs. Foreign ministry officials affiliated with arms control and disarmament agendas are likely to express perspectives and positions that differ significantly from those iterated by their counterparts working in the security policy field, for instance. On the one hand, there are those who express a high level of concern that the U.S. NMD could undermine the current Russo-U.S. strategic equilibrium, while, on the other, there are those who contend that that balance will not be greatly affected even by an abrogation of the Anti-Ballistic Missile (ABM) Treaty. The Japan Defense Agency is similarly divided, reflecting the diverse concerns and interests of its various divisions and service branches.

In the Diet as well, missile defense has only been discussed briefly and then only in terms of the defense budget, implications for a regional arms race, and its legal limitations. Government responses to questions on TMD have also been provided at only a cursory level. The Diet has not, as one foreign ministry official pointed out, yet attempted to engage in any extensive discussion that addresses deterrence and security simultaneously, which explains its historic lack of a "decoupling" debate.

At present, there are roughly five key areas of interest when NMD is discussed within a Japanese context: (1) Its effect on extended deterrence and fear of a "Fortress America"; (2) differing perceptions of North Korea; (3) the connection with TMD; (4) Russian and Chinese reactions; and (5) the aim of long-term missile defense architecture. Let's look at each of these points in more detail.

EFFECT ON EXTENDED DETERRENCE AND FEAR OF A FORTRESS AMERICA

How will NMD affect U.S. extended deterrence? This question, as critical as it is, has been inadequately addressed by the Japanese security community. While there are those who argue fervently that NMD would strengthen the credibility of the U.S. nuclear umbrella, there are others who express concern that it could bring about a decoupling in Asia.

An example of the former opinion can be seen in a piece carried in a recent edition of the *Sankei Shimbun*, which was printed in response to the Defense Department's Annual Report 2000. It positively appraised the U.S. effort to develop an NMD system to counter "uncertain" threats and argued that Japan should also look in the same direction.[2] Some military experts are also beginning to contend that U.S. allies, including Japan, should closely follow the U.S. debate on NMD and support its position in the international arena. They state emphatically that NMD is certain to strengthen the credibility of the U.S. extended deterrent, which is good reason for its allies to give the issue close attention.[3]

Such explicit views on NMD are, however, few and far between, with a discussion on NMD being close to nonexistent in Japan. It is highly likely, though, that this discussion will be innervated and expanded as a decision to deploy NMD draws nearer. Without a doubt, the debate will be shaped by the psychological impact of these shocks touched upon earlier.

The current missile defense debate also gives rise to a critical question concerning U.S. and Japanese differences over "who will protect whom from whom?" To date, no agreement sufficient to close this perception gap has been reached in the U.S.-Japan relationship. For example, the crux of the U.S. missile defense discussion is focused on how to protect Americans and U.S. troops from ballistic missile threats. There is, however, very little talk about the ramifications of U.S. NMD on the U.S.-Japan alliance, particularly with regard to U.S. extended deterrence over Japan.

It is true that Under Secretary for Defense Walter Slocombe recently described the U.S. missile defense as a system that "further complement[s] deterrence by enhancing the United States' ability to fulfill its global security commitments" to its allies by rendering useless any ballistic missiles equipped with weapons of mass destruction (WMD), thereby "reinforcing" America's commitment to its allies.[4] Yet, this statement by itself falls far short of an explanation of the linkage between missile defenses and U.S. extended deterrence. Many Japanese are simply unconvinced. Some worry that U.S. NMD plans are the foundation for a Fortress America, a unilateralist defense posture that may lead to complacency and, ultimately, disregard for its allies' security interests.

Poised behind a magnificent shield erected to protect itself and only itself, how will the United States respond on the eve of a missile attack on one of its allies—say, Japan? Will the United States actually execute its nuclear retaliation option to protect a foreign country? Will a unilaterally defensive fortress end up threatening the very roots of the U.S.-Japan alliance? The dialogue until now has permitted an ambiguous answer to questions concerning U.S. "extended deterrence" policy; the current NMD debate, however, highlights a need to clarify the nature of the U.S. nuclear umbrella.

Beyond technological and financial aspects, there are other issues posed by the deployment of missile defense systems. For example, one of the selling points of missile defense for Japan is its ability to help integrate Japan into the U.S. command system, thereby increasing U.S.-Japan military interoperability and bilateral intelligence information sharing. Nevertheless, Japan, at this point, feels uncertain about these prospects, not being firmly convinced that such a rosy scenario will come to fruition. This presents a new dilemma for U.S. allies in an RMA (revolution in military affairs) era—many are unsure whether U.S. RMA initiatives will have a unifying or a dismantling effect on the system of post-Cold War alliances.

DIFFERING PERCEPTIONS OF NORTH KOREA

As noted earlier, Japanese debate over the U.S. NMD deployment is far from being advanced, let alone settled. True, it was the same Taep'odong shock that prompted Japan to opt for TMD while causing the United States to rush toward NMD in defense of its mainland. This has, in fact, been a reason for some Japanese to rejoice, believing that the United States and Japan now share—for the first time in many years after the end of the Cold War—a common, concrete security threat. Others, however, question America's rush to NMD, believing that the current U.S. NMD debate reflects an exaggerated level of U.S. apprehension over the prospect of its vulnerability to North Korean missiles. They fear that the Japanese may perceive a more acute North Korean missile threat than the United States recognizes. Although these people exhibit, to a certain extent, an understanding of the U.S. drive to deploy NMD deployment in response to North Korea, they question the U.S. justification for prioritizing NMD over TMD.

CONNECTION WITH TMD

As many Japanese experts point out, the relationship between NMD and TMD has yet to be adequately articulated. This has been the source of confusion in recent discussions on the two missile defense systems.

For example, due partially to the U.S. decision to dramatically increase funding for NMD, there is a growing concern in Japan over the complementarity between TMD and NMD and attendant role sharing between Japan and the United States. As research moves ahead, plans for TMD and NMD, previously discussed separately, are becoming increasingly intertwined, or so it would appear. Could this lead to a cut-throat battle over who gets the bigger piece of the pie? Some worry that Japan's TMD could be compromised as a result of the priority being given by the United States to NMD development, and that this, in turn, could result in Japan having to bear a greater financial burden for missile defense. Some Japanese express concern that missile defense is being used as a pretext by the U.S. military establishment to acquire larger budget allocations than would otherwise be granted, and argue that this is leading to a chronic lack of U.S. interdepartmental policy coordination over TMD.

Whether the United States and Japan signed the TMD agreement without first conducting a sufficient policy dialogue on relevant issues, such as the notion that TMD is part of a Japanese hedging strategy, is something that has been discussed only within an extremely small circle of security professionals—the so-called security "high priests." Discussions on TMD have been minimal within the Diet, which explains the lack of solid support from the public. The foundation of support for Japan's TMD option, fragile to begin with, has thus eroded further.

RUSSIAN AND CHINESE REACTIONS

While Japan is attracted by the potential unifying effect of U.S. missile defense systems, it realizes that closer collusion with the United States could complicate its relations with Russia and, even more so, with China. The following incident illustrates the extent of this dilemma. As the United Nations (UN) First Committee (Disarmament and International Security) began discussing arms control in October 1999, China, Russia, and Belarus jointly introduced a resolution related to U.S. missile defense, one that demanded strict compliance with the 1972 ABM Treaty. Faced with voting on this UN resolution that registered strong Chinese and Russian opposition to U.S. missile defense plans, Japan chose not to side with its ally but to abstain.

Underscoring Japan's quandary is the need to address the NMD issue both in the context of its own foreign and defense policies and simultaneously heeding Russian and Chinese concerns over NMD and their implications for Russo- and Sino-Japanese relations.

If the United States fails to reach an agreement with Russia over amendments to the ABM Treaty and decides to unilaterally deploy a massive NMD system, both Russo- and Sino-U.S. relations will surely deteriorate. This will give Russia and China a free hand to move toward an uncontrolled arms race. Subsequently, it would give India an excuse to do the same with, inevitably, Pakistan following suit.

Such a spillover effect would most certainly not be in Japan's security interests. If the problem can be contained among the three powers, it will probably not pose a problem for Japan. Chances are, however, that a unilateral move by the United States would trigger a deteriorating of both Russo- and Sino-Japanese relations as well. To put it mildly, this would not be in Japan's diplomatic or security interests. The worst scenario for Japan would be a massive backlash against its own missile defense system, caused by a U.S. decision on NMD deployment that disregards the security interests of other players, both allied and nonallied.

The question of how to address China in the overall context of the missile defense debate is a particularly contentious one in Japan, as the Japanese perception of China is markedly divided (although the threat perceived over Chinese missiles has become generally more acute since 1996). Some Japanese are becoming uneasy about the direction in which China's regional security strategy is headed and are worried that the Sino-Japanese perception gap on regional security may have become too wide to rectify.[5] Others note the lack of legally binding treaties that could act to cap Chinese military expansion. Still others see China as being saddled with too many domestic problems to be able to move forward aggressively with a military modernization agenda.

A danger lies in such differences and fluctuations in Japanese perceptions of China, as they may exert an overly strong influence on Japan's view of NMD. For example, some Japanese, especially those close to Japan's defense establishment, view China as the "next Soviet Union" and accordingly support the idea of using the U.S. NMD to contain it, much like the Strategic Defense Initiative was advocated to corner the USSR in the 1980s.

AIMS OF LONG-TERM MISSILE DEFENSE ARCHITECTURE

As noted earlier, what worries China most in this missile defense scenario is the Taiwan factor. They fear that sooner or later Taiwan will also be integrated into a U.S.-led command and control system, which will enable a de facto military alliance between the United States and Taiwan. Additionally, many Chinese are concerned about the prospects of Japan being included in such a U.S.-led RMA architecture, as they worry that a shared control over TMD could mean a fundamental change in the nature of the U.S.-Japan alliance and, consequently, an alteration in Japan's military posture. Such sentiment is reflected in certain Chinese statements that it would be best for China if TMD would be under the sole control of the United States rather than a shared control.[6]

The Chinese preoccupation over a "seamless" international system should not be taken lightly as it is actually a crucial question for Japan as well. This leads to the question, "What will be the ultimate purpose of the U.S. NMD?" Is it the U.S. intention to expand the defense system into a global command and control system, in which each TMD will function as a regional terminal? If so, what will this mean for Japan's own defense and foreign policy and its alliance with the United States? Will such a "globally-seamless" command and control system be compatible with Japan's recent moves toward acquiring its own intelligence satellites? At present, such discussions have yet to take place, either in Japan or in the United States—as the United States, in particular, is busily going about constructing a Fortress America exclusively for the benefit of Americans.

Although U.S. NMD is a long-term goal, it is not prudent to put off or neglect these questions. The United States ought to be willing to treat the NMD issue in truly comprehensive terms, a component of which should be to address the questions of the system's ramifications on Japan and other allies.

In addition, some in the United States oppose the development of a ground-based NMD system, opting instead for a boost-phase NMD (involving land-based, naval, or airborne boost-phase interceptors) that could hit a theater ballistic missile during its booster phase from hundreds of kilometers away.[7] If the technological and legal challenges[8] could be overcome and such a system was developed, it could potentially be deployed in U.S. bases on Japanese soil in order to counter the North Korean missile threat, posing a serious problem for Japan both constitutionally and politically. Nonetheless, discussions on such issues are nonexistent in Japan, underscoring the lack of frank discussion among Japanese and U.S. security leaders. The psychological and political inertia resulting from the long-standing taboo to openly discuss the U.S. nuclear presence in Japan has unfortunately been passed along to the current missile defense debate. Hence, no Japanese in their right mind dares to address the issue directly, for it touches upon one of the most sensitive spots of the U.S.-Japan alliance: the chronic lack of real security policy consultation.

These five concerns, elaborated above, illustrate an obvious lack of policy coordination on missile defense between the United States and Japan, and a clear need for the two parties to begin a comprehensive discussion on the NMD issue. Both parties need to come to grips with the serious ramifications for the U.S.-Japan alliance if the NMD issue is not addressed on a comprehensive basis, transcending the current framework of an internal American debate and a bilateral U.S.-Russia dialogue.

Conclusion

Given recent international events, it would behoove Japan to pay closer attention to the ongoing debate over U.S. NMD, particularly given its potential to affect Japan's security, defense, and foreign policies. As the juxtaposing of NMD and TMD becomes increasingly opaque, Japan has ample reason to involve itself in this discussion from as holistic a perspective as possible.

Similarly, there is a clear need for the United States to hammer out a balanced policy that resolves conflicting foreign policy and defense objectives pertaining to NMD deployment. Most reactions to date from U.S. allies as well as from Russia and China have been against NMD deployment, especially if it means withdrawal from the ABM Treaty. While some of these reactions could be dismissed as rhetorical, it would be a serious mistake for the United States to proceed without regard for the serious security concerns of other states.

This is not to denote that the United States should refrain from deploying NMD altogether. The U.S. NMD option as an "insurance" against emerging ballistic missile threats, particularly those posed by the rogue states, is legitimate in light of its national security concerns—as has been the logic behind Japan's rationale to opt for its own missile defense (refered to by Japanese defense officials as "Japan's NMD"). Considering that Japan too has moved forward with its own missile defense research largely as a response to regional missile proliferation and that no effective global or regional missile control regimes exist as of yet, the U.S. move toward NMD is not entirely inconceivable. The question is not whether the United States should opt for NMD but how the United States can defend itself from emerging ballistic missile threats without disregarding security concerns of others, allied and nonallied alike.

The U.S. NMD debate has become far too politicized, particularly in light of the fact that no realistic technological assessment has yet been made of the system. The current debate lacks a holistic approach to include such factors as nonproliferation, arms control, disarmament, alliances, and multilateral negotiating frameworks as well as the Russia-U.S. strategic equilibrium. Without this systematic approach, some Japanese are beginning to question the credibility of the U.S. commitment to TMD. If the current NMD discussion is allowed to proceed unchecked, it may unnecessarily complicate America's strategic calculations and its relations with other powers, not just Russia and China, but even its ally—Japan.

Notes

1. "U.S. Missile Defence: Strategy, Technology and Politics," IISS Strategic Comments 5, no. 3 (April 1999).

2. "The U.S. Defense Report: Japan Headed in the Same Direction" (in Japanese), *Sankei Shimbun*, February. 10, 2000.

3. Interviews with Japan Defense Agency officials, March, 2000.

4. Remarks by Under Secretary of Defense Walter B. Slocombe to the CSIS Statesmen's Forum, November 5, 1999.

5. Hideshi Takesada, "If Even TMD Cannot Be Introduced, Japan Will Remain 'Naked' When Faced with Coming Asian Crises (in Japanese)," *Sapio*, January 13, 1999, 37.

6. Interviews in China, November 1999; see also Thomas Christensen, "China, the U.S.-Japan Alliance, and the Security Dilemma in East Asia," *International Security* 23, no. 4 (spring 1999): 75.

7. For further detailed discussions on boost-phase interception systems, see Dean Wilkening, "Amending the ABM Treaty," *Survival* 42, no. 1 (spring 2000); Theodore Postol, "Hitting Them Where It Works," *Foreign Policy* (winter 1999-2000): 132-133.

8. For example, on the technological side, an ABL-equipped Boeing 747 aircraft would have to be in the proximity of the launch sites to be able to knock out enemy ballistic missiles on launch, which means that it would be ineffective for missiles deployed deep in the interior. On the legal side, all three boost-phase interception systems would violate the ABM Treaty.

Brahma Chellaney

New Delhi's Dilemma

The U.S. debate on NMD is taking place at a time of deteriorating relations among the three major world powers whose policies and actions have the greatest impact on Indian security. The Sino-U.S. and U.S.-Russian relationships have soured due to several disputes and conflicting interests. The issue of missile defense will further aggravate tensions between these powers which, in turn, will affect India's strategic options and interests.

With international politics and security in flux, U.S. NMD has introduced a disruptive new element. Although unipolarity has become stronger in the past decade, emerging rivalries in the world point to a new cold war in the offing, a reality likely to become clearer following a U.S. decision in favor of NMD.

Today, the global strategic environment is more competitive than ever. The revolution in military affairs (RMA) is producing new destructive capacities. In the past century, weapons of mass destruction (WMD) and missiles came to occupy a central military role. That is likely to remain the case in the foreseeable future. The growing attraction of missiles—which are much cheaper and easier to operate and maintain than manned bomber aircraft—flows from the fact that the attacking nation does not have to bring its forces in harm's way. As the

Brahma Chellaney has served as an advisor to India's National Security Council. He is a professor of security studies at the Center for Policy Research in New Delhi.

Copyright © 2000 by The Center for Strategic and International Studies and the Massachusetts Institute of Technology
The Washington Quarterly • 23:3 pp. 145–153.

disarmament process has stalled, missile defenses have been justified and encouraged. In the distant future, NMD could make the strategic environment even more competitive as missile-defense research yields technologies for offensive space-based weapons.

Policy Implications for India

Antiballistic missile (ABM) systems are theoretically of great interest to New Delhi. Few countries in the world confront the multitude of missile threats that India does. These threats stretch all around—from China in the north to the missile-armed foreign naval fleets in the Indian Ocean to Pakistan and Iran in the west. Further afield is Saudi Arabia, with its traditionally close military ties to Pakistan and its China-supplied, intermediate-range ballistic missiles (IRBMs) that can reach India. Two of India's neighbors, Pakistan and Iran, startled the world by testing IRBMs in a space of three months in 1998.

Through China's new generation of solid-fueled, multiple-warhead missiles, however, India's largest neighbor is conducting the biggest expansion of missile capabilities anywhere in the world. The first of these new missiles, the Dongfeng (DF) 31, last tested in July 1999, can reach every corner of India but little of U.S. territory. This multiple-warhead, truck-mobile missile,[1] and China's other planned solid-fuel intercontinental ballistic missile (ICBM), the DF-41, are "most destabilizing" weapon systems as they are precisely the kind of multiple-warhead, land-based missiles that START II seeks to eliminate.[2]

The growing proliferation and use of missiles carries serious implications for Indian security. First, missiles have come to symbolize power and coercion in international relations. They are useful not only to achieve military objectives but also to realize aims through political intimidation and coercion. Second, there is, unlike in the case of nuclear weapons, no international legal structure to control them and no taboo related to their use. Although nuclear weapons have not been employed for nearly 55 years, missiles are being used with increasing frequency. China used ballistic missile "tests" in 1996 as a means to intimidate and blackmail Taiwan. Its M-9 maneuvers against Taiwan were the first instance in history when ballistic missiles were employed for political warfare and blackmail in peacetime. In a span of less than eight months during 1998 and 1999, the United States fired with impunity cruise missiles at targets in Sudan, Afghanistan, Iraq, and Yugoslavia. The low-flying, slower cruise missiles, unlike the much-faster ballistic missiles, strike with a high degree of accuracy.

Third, the 1999 U.S.-led North Atlantic Treaty Organization (NATO) air war against Yugoslavia, more than the 1991 Persian Gulf War, provided a vivid reminder of the high costs of being defenseless against a foe firing missiles and other high-tech, remotely fired conventional weapons. The RMA process is only increasing the costs of defenselessness. Had India not embarked on building a nuclear deterrent, it would have remained vulnerable to vindictive strikes by an adversary. As John Mearsheimer has said, "Nuclear weapons are an excellent deterrent against aggression, and India lives in a dangerous neighborhood."[3]

Fourth, only nations without the capability to hit back are falling victim to missile strikes. In fact, these states are becoming guinea pigs for the testing of new missile systems. Iraq was turned into a testing ground for upgraded Tomahawks in 1996. The tests showed that not all the target-locating defects from the Gulf War had been purged. Two years later, another improved Tomahawk variant was field tested on Sudanese and Afghan targets. During the strikes on the hideouts of Afghanistan-based fugitive Osama bin Laden, however, a few stray Tomahawks landed on Pakistani territory, underlining the need for a still-better Tomahawk version.

So far, India has looked at only one way to deter missile terror and blackmail—a reliable missile-deterrent capability to ensure a proportional response. Without the capacity to effectively strike back with missiles, India will remain vulnerable to the type of blackmail China mounted against Taiwan or the kind of missile warfare waged by NATO against Yugoslavia. Since the best and only reliable method to defend against a missile strike is to deter an attack from occurring in the first place, India has concentrated on building operational missile forces to ward off the growing range and intensity of threats. The lack of a missile-deterrent force had been the main deficiency in Indian defenses.

Before India succeeds in erecting a credible missile-deterrent force, it faces new issues relating to missile defenses. India will be directly affected by the larger Asian consequences of a U.S. deployment of theater missile defense (TMD) against short-range ballistic missiles and national missile defense (NMD), a system that will employ space-based sensors to track incoming ICBMs and have interceptor missiles and radars based on land.

India will be affected by NMD in three different ways.[4] First, it will trigger a new arms race in Asia, at the center of which would be China and Russia. Yet, India will be most affected by the response of China, with which it shares its longest border. China is likely to retort by sharply accelerating its already ambitious nuclear and missile modernization programs. The buildup will have a direct bearing on India's security. No other country is placed in as adverse a nuclear environment as India, with its two nuclear neighbors, China and Pakistan, engaged in close strategic collaboration. U.S. missile defenses can only make that environment more adverse to Indian security.

A major motivation for India's 1998 nuclear tests was the growing military asymmetry with China, compounded by Beijing's continuing covert nuclear and missile assistance to Pakistan. Right after the first round of tests, Indian prime minister Atal Bihari Vajpayee spelled out those concerns in a letter to heads of government of the G-8 states: "We have an overt nuclear-weapons state on our borders, a state which committed armed aggression against India in 1962. To add to the distrust, that country has materially helped another neighbor of ours to become a covert nuclear-weapons state." China bared its animosity toward India by responding menacingly to the tests, warning New Delhi of "serious consequences" and demanding global action to "stop" it from developing nuclear weapons. Official Chinese newspapers started attacking India with a vehemence reminiscent of the period leading to the 1962 Chinese invasion across the Himalayas.

India has no real ally in a world in which most states of consequence are in economic and military alliances. Not only does India have to fend for itself, it faces a growing imbalance of power in Asia inimical to its long-term interests. At the center of this imbalance is an increasingly powerful and assertive China, whose rapid rise has been accentuated by the decline of Russia and Japan. China, with its pursuit of naked power politics, has done everything possible to keep India contained, employing Pakistan as a surrogate and gaining a strategic foothold in Burma.

Any plan that can possibly limit China's growing power and arrogance should aid Indian interests. NMD threatens to weaken China's "minimal" nuclear deterrent, despite Defense Secretary William Cohen's contention that it is aimed at the alleged rogue nations. So India, with its growing friendship with the United States, should not in principle be opposed to NMD. To see the Chinese rattled by U.S. missile defenses is surely an agreeable sight for India. The problem, however, is that Beijing's Leninist rulers, thriving on a burgeoning trade surplus with Washington, will use NMD as a justification for going on a frenzied nuclear and missile buildup.

Second, India's existing modest deterrent capabilities will be gravely undermined as China builds up its nuclear and missile armories. The Sino-Indian asymmetry will increase to the extent that New Delhi will be compelled to respond by diverting more of its scarce resources to new nuclear and missile development projects. An Indian ICBM program in that situation will become inevitable.

ICBMs are already an idiom of big-power status. To a country like India that aspires to be a permanent member of the United Nations Security Council, their attraction is strong. In a situation where China begins a major program to expand its ICBM arsenal,[5] India will have every incentive to acquire similar assets that play a primary role in power-projection strategies. In addition to intercontinental missile-strike capability, power-projection assets also include a hardy naval force of indigenously-built submarines, instruments of precision strike in the form of cruise missiles, and space-based information systems. Missile defenses will put India on that path.

India's current focus is on building a minimal but credible nuclear deterrent based on survivable, second-strike assets. India's no-first-use policy (or retaliation-only nuclear posture) places it in a sitting-duck position, making second-strike assets essential. While supporting a nuclear-powered submarine program, India so far has not funded ICBM development, although it has demonstrated its latent capability through construction of civilian space launch vehicles.

India wishes to ensure that China's ongoing nuclear and missile modernization, as well as its reported theft of U.S. nuclear secrets, does not undercut its nuclear-deterrence posture. India also would like to ensure that Pakistan does not continue to match India in nuclear and missile technologies through the assistance Pakistan covertly receives from China. It is obvious that China is the root of the proliferation problem India faces. That problem will be greatly exacerbated when China responds to U.S. missile defenses, making strategic stability in larger southern Asia harder to achieve.

Third, China, once it begins to build more modern NMD-resistant systems, will have commercial motivations to recover some of the costs of its new buildup by transferring to Pakistan its older technologies. Beijing has repeatedly broken its assurances with impunity to halt clandestine strategic transfers to Islamabad. As a Central Intelligence Agency (CIA) annual report states, "China has provided extensive support to Pakistan's WMD capabilities."[6] Beijing has found ingenious ways to proliferate, according to a Pentagon intelligence report, "on a consistent basis without technically breaking agreements with the [United States]."[7] One way is to help set up production facilities in Pakistan. Another is to employ North Korea as a conduit for transfers, as evidenced by Pakistan's Ghauri IRBM.[8]

The reported Chinese theft of advanced U.S. nuclear and missile blueprints has already set the stage for increased transfers of older technologies to Pakistan by Beijing. But as China builds newer systems to outwit missile defenses, commercial and strategic reasons are likely to further goad it to sell no-longer-needed technologies to Pakistan. Faced with the growing capabilities of its two hand-in-glove neighbors, India will be left with no option but to step up its indigenous efforts in the nuclear and missile fields.

Larger Ramifications

In addition to the more specific implications for its national security, India also has to be concerned about the likely larger ramifications of an early U.S. decision to go ahead with NMD deployment. The change of the original 3+3 to a 3+5 NMD plan—three years of research and development up to 2000 to be followed by the prospective deployment of a land-based system over a five-year (instead of three-year) period— has not diminished international concerns. Indeed those concerns have been heightened in anticipation of a Clinton decision this summer to go ahead with deployment.

One cannot fault U.S. policymakers for looking at ways to meet future missile challenges. A prudent policy should always look ahead and anticipate threats. U.S. policymakers and lawmakers, however, have to carefully weigh the strategic benefits and costs of erecting ambitious missile defenses against hypothetical threats. Compounding matters is the manner in which the issue of national missile defenses has become entangled in U.S. national politics.

The political demand in the United States for ICBM defenses has to be traced back to the Clinton administration's initial "cry wolf" approach. The Clinton team spent its first years in office conjuring up all sorts of missile threats. The "rogue-states doctrine" came in handy to shield defense spending from deep cuts and fashion a military strategy aimed at concurrently waging and winning two major regional conflicts. That doctrine also has spawned the controversial counter-proliferation initiative, based on America's "duty" to deny other nations, through military means if necessary, the right to develop weapons it has in its own arsenal. Having whipped up national passions on supposed missile threats, the Clinton administration then began pouring cold water over the threat scenarios it had itself advanced. A National Intelligence Estimate suggested that tangible missile threats were still 15 years away. Then as Republican criticism mounted, the Clinton team has taken pains to deny it is downplaying threats by saying "the threat is here today."[9]

The irony is that after having first shifted from strategic to theater defenses, the Clinton administration is now reemphasizing defenses against long-range missiles. NMD has overtaken the earlier top priority, TMD, with the major research and development effort today focused on a strategic option originally conceived as a hedge against a future ICBM threat.

NMD's potential benefits could help strengthen and expand U.S.-led security arrangements. If NMD is seen to work, the United States could extend a "missile umbrella" to its allies the way it presently holds out a nuclear umbrella. As the U.S. Ballistic Missile Defense Organization has stated, such a globally expansive missile defense system would help safeguard unipolarity, providing the impetus to other nations to enhance their military arrangements with the United States and come under its missile-defense umbrella.[10]

India, as a potential strategic partner of the United States, could avail itself of such benefits and reduce its burden of developing appropriate countermeasures against a burgeoning Chinese missile might. While nations as far afield as Japan, Taiwan, and Israel express interest in defenses against a potential missile attack, India (with its multitude of missile threats from different directions) has more reason to seek cooperation in that field with the United States. In a world marked by rapid change, it is conceivable to think of a future India with its own nuclear force but under a U.S. strategic missile-defense umbrella.

The psychological benefits of missile defenses also should not be underrated. Although the 1991 Gulf War showed that defending against even unsophisticated short-range missiles is problematic, with the Patriots causing most of the civilian damage in attempts to intercept incoming Scuds, it also demonstrated the same Patriots' morale-boosting role. NMD will yield valuable psychological benefits against any major power that attempts to flex its nuclear muscles and impose its writ on any continent. The contention that NMD will have a destabilizing effect in Asia has to be seen against the already existing power disequilbrium in Asia.

The drawbacks of NMD, however, are equally compelling. Despite spending tens of billions of dollars, the United States is still encountering serious technical difficulties in developing a reliable protective system, even against theater ballistic missiles. Even if an NMD system were successfully developed and deployed, it could be frustrated by an adversary in different ways: by firing a barrage of missiles rather than one or two at a time, by concealing a nuclear warhead inside a mylar balloon and releasing dozens of decoy balloons, or by cooling the warhead's nose cone with liquid nitrogen to foil heat sensors. Defenses against medium- and long-range missiles, because of their faster speed, are technologically more challenging.

NMD will compel states already armed with a range of different missiles to build even more sophisticated missiles that can foil defenses of any kind. NMD reminds India that it faces the challenge of not only deterring regional missile threats but also catching up with fast-changing technologies. The emerging missile defenses mean that India will have to arm its ballistic missiles with decoys and other countermeasures, as Russia is doing with its new Topol-M and China is planning to do. With its fast-growing capabilities, China would seek to defeat any NMD system by saturating or fooling its defenses, as would Russia, which lacks the money to develop its own NMD. While China and Russia will go ahead with their countermeasures, India may be forced to seek U.S. help.

While U.S. research on futuristic space-based X-ray lasers continues, a covey of ground-based hit-to-kill interceptors, supported by a Space-Based Infrared System, will form the NMD system, whose deployment could demolish the central pillar of strategic stability —the 1972 Anti-Ballistic Missile Treaty. NMD also raises the prospects of developing space-based weapons. Space-based platforms and other weapons such as antisatellite lasers could undermine strategic stability and global peace, even though they would ensure continued U.S. military preeminence.

NMD's biggest casualty, however, will be international arms control. China is already holding up the agenda of the Geneva-based Conference on Disarmament, including negotiations on a fissile-material cut-off treaty, by linking everything to U.S. missile defense plans. Under President Vladamir Putin, Russia will be more assertive, although it will be more willing than Beijing to work out some honorable compromise with Washington on NMD. The bare fact, however, is that NMD will allow Washington to both deliver a nuclear punch and shield itself from counterattack. In the aftermath of a U.S. deployment decision, therefore, the already-stalled process of arms control and disarmament is likely to disintegrate.

On balance, India can take an unruffled, nonjudgmental view of any U.S. decision to go ahead with NMD deployment. After all, it is the sovereign right of every nation to defend its security by appropriate means. Nevertheless, the likely response of those states whose security will be directly affected, particularly China, will significantly affect India's interests. This is what India has to worry about. U.S. missile defenses will not threaten India's security. In fact, India could potentially seek to derive, in partnership with Washington, some benefits from such defenses. In due course, the action-reaction cycle triggered by missile defenses could drive India closer to the United States.

Notes

1. The DF-31 likely benefited from stolen U.S. secrets. James Risen and Jeff Gerth, "China Missile is Said to Use US Secrets," *International Herald Tribune*, May 15-16, 1999, 1.

2. Therese Delpech, "Nuclear Weapons and the 'New World Order': Early Warning for Asia?" *Survival* 40, no. 4 (winter 1998-99): 63.

3. John J. Mearsheimer, "India Needs the Bomb," *New York Times*, March 24, 2000.

4. Nearly all of these implications will also arise from a U.S. TMD deployment in Asia.

5. China has only about two dozen ICBMs at present, with most of its nuclear arsenal made up of short- and intermediate-range weapons of direct conse-

quence to neighbors such as India.

6. "China Aiding Pakistan's Nuclear Program: CIA," Associated Press, July 23, 1998.

7. Bill Gertz, "China Still Shipping Arms Despite Pledges," *Washington Times*, April 15, 1999.

8. Joseph S. Bermudez Jr., "DPRK-Pakistan Ghauri Missile Cooperation," Federation of American Scientists (FAS), p. 4.

9. "Defense Secretary Cohen on National Missile Defense Program," March 24, 2000, *Wireless File*, U.S. Government, Washington D.C., March 27, 2000.

10. *Space-Based Laser Programme,* <www.fas.org/spp/starwars/program/sbl.htm>.

Efraim Karsh

Israel's Imperative

From the Israeli perspective, the U.S. deployment of an NMD contains several strategic and technological benefits and a number of secondary drawbacks. Having just begun the deployment of its own national anti-ballistic-missile (ABM) defense system, the Arrow II, Israel cannot but welcome the NMD. To be sure, there is a fundamental difference between the two defensive systems. The U.S. NMD is designed to meet a limited tactical threat: for instance, an attack on a small number of U.S. cities by "rogue states" such as Iraq and Iran. Nonetheless, the strategic threat to the national security of the United States continues to be posed not by the rogue states, but by the great nuclear powers, notably Russia and China, and requires a wholly different range of military, technological, and political measures. By contrast, given Israel's minute size (approximately the size of New Jersey), the nonconventional threat posed by these very rogue states is of the highest strategic order, indeed, a matter of national existence. Given the concentration of Israel's social, industrial, technological, and economic heartland in the tiny triangle of

Efraim Karsh is a professor and the head of the Mediterranean Studies Program at King's College, University of London, as well as the founding editor of the scholarly journal *Israel Affairs*. He is the author and editor of some twenty books, including most recently *Empires of the Sand: The Struggle for Mastery in the Middle East 1789-1923* (Harvard University Press, 1999).

The Washington Quarterly • 23:3 pp. 155–161.

some 30 kilometers long by 10 kilometers wide which comprises metropolitan Tel Aviv, the Jewish state is fatally vulnerable to a nonconventional, and particularly a nuclear, strike.

It is precisely these narrowest of security margins that makes the potential benefits of the NMD so appealing to Israel, regardless of the fundamentally different circumstances for the two countries. To start, there are the technological spinoffs, to be gained through acquisition or cooperation, that could help improve Israel's Arrow II defense system (e.g., upgrading of early warning satellite systems, computer software to deal with the most modern missiles, and so on). The Arrow II is the only operational ABM national defense system with a capacity to destroy warheads in the stratosphere. It has effectively been a joint U.S.-Israeli program, with the United States footing a substantial part of the $1.2 billion bill to date and Israel doing the lion's share of the research, thus serving as a backdoor platform for the testing of new technologies, weapons systems, and strategic concepts that could benefit the U.S. research and development program in general and the NMD program in particular. Once the U.S. NMD is launched, this symbiosis would be reversed, and Israel would become the beneficiary of a far more encompassing development effort than before.

Mutual gains would not be limited to the technological sphere. The political and strategic implications for the United States of the ups and downs of the Arrow II program have not been lost on NMD supporters or critics. Once the NMD is up and running, Israeli policymakers can be expected to exploit its operational success as a means to curb domestic skepticism regarding the Arrow's value and to curb opposition in the United States to further appropriations for Israel's strategic defense.

The importance to Israel of such technological and political benefits cannot be overstated, given the horrendous destruction that could be inflicted on the Jewish state by the strike of a single nuclear missile and the attendant operational requirements of its ABM defense system. Hence, it is of critical importance to Tel Aviv that all internationally available technological, doctrinal, and political resources be pulled together to readily give Israel a measure of added security.

Indeed, a major concern among many analysts over the past few years has been that the spread of nuclear, chemical, and biological weapons in the Middle East has not been accompanied by either practical steps or rigorous conceptual theories to prevent, or at least limit, the use of these terminally destructive weapons. Concern has been further compounded by the speed at which proliferation has taken place. This has meant that concepts of deterrence and strategies of restraint have failed to become firmly embedded in national decision making, injecting an added level of insecurity into the process. The extremist qualities of the policy aims of various regional protagonists mean that scenarios could well arise in which weapons of mass destruction are used in desperate situations.

This is what makes the NMD's strategic rationale so important for Israel, and indeed for the international community at large. Until the Iraqi occupation of Kuwait in August 1990, the Western powers had been largely oblivious to the concept of "rogue states" or their increasing nonconventional threat to international security. The few warnings in this regard were cavalierly swept under the carpet as European (and, to a lesser extent, U.S.) companies lined up to sell Saddam Hussein the latest and deadliest technological know-how and materiel.

This fecklessness, seen all too clearly in the Bush administration's opposition to the Senate's attempts to enforce sanctions against Iraq just days before Iraq's invasion of Kuwait, is not difficult to understand. Support for Third World dictatorships has been more of a norm rather than the exception as Western countries have often subordinated their high ideals to pragmatic (if not purely venal) considerations of financial gain and political influence. The West is once again confronted with a familiar scenario: totalitarian regimes armed to their teeth with the most deadly and sophisticated weapons systems and harbouring far-reaching hegemonic designs on their neighbors. Now, however, it lacks a stable framework to structure its relations with these regimes. This combination of factors gives the rogue state a new and far more dangerous meaning than the old-fashioned style of Third World dictatorship, so instrumental in the realpolitik of the Cold War.

Some of these rogue states are well on their way to obtaining nuclear weapons, on top of their formidable chemical and biological weapons arsenals. Furthermore, their strategic rationale underpinning this nonconventional proliferation is diametrically opposed to that of the existing nuclear powers (or for that matter, Israel). The latter views nuclear weapons in purely deterrent terms, as a means of last resort; for the rogue states, by contrast, they are a perfectly usable instrument in both international hostilities and domestic strife. This is not due to these states' inherent irrationality—to the contrary! They have often acted in a perfectly rational way, albeit devoid of any moral inhibitions. Saddam Hussein's use of chemical weapons, as in the indiscriminate gassing of civilians in Kurdistan, was carefully calculated and took place where there was absolutely no risk of retaliation. It is precisely the ruthless rationality of these rogue states which makes their possession of nuclear weapons and ballistic capabilities all the more dangerous. In a political system where absolute leaders supersede state institutions and the notion of national interest is highly personalized; where power is concentrated in the hands of a tiny minority (e.g., the Alawites in Syria or the Sunnis in Iraq); where no orderly mechanisms for political participation or peaceful transfer of power exist; and where the goal of regime survivability supersedes everything else, physical force is the most eloquent mode of political discourse—from civil strife, to interstate wars, to domestic repression. Should such rulers and/or regimes deem themselves to be in mortal danger, they would have no scruples about resorting to nonconventional means, including nuclear weapons, against their own population, let alone external enemies.

The more widespread the international recognition of these stark facts, the deeper the potential sympathy for Israel's strategic predicament; indeed, achieving such recognition should be a major goal of Israeli policy. A key potential benefit that may accrue to Israel from such an effort is the possible relaxation of pressures for nuclear disarmament. For quite some time, Israel's nuclear program has been singled out as the foremost catalyst of regional proliferation, a point eagerly canvassed by the Arab states. Yet the historical record shows no linkage between Israel's nuclear program and similar regional endeavors. Iran's nuclear quest, for instance, was in fact the offspring of Shah Muhammad Reza Pahlavi's imperial aspirations, and the Islamic Republic continued it after his demise as an integral part of its hegemonic worldview. Iraq's mid-1970s decision to embark on the same route came in direct response not to Israel but to the Iranian threat, and represented Saddam Hussein's stark determination to hold power whatever the cost.

Now that the potential nuclear threat by Iraq and Iran has been recognized by the United States and other Western powers (as demonstrated *inter alia* by Britain's expressed interest in benefiting from the program[1]), the United States has little moral or strategic ground to pressure Israel into surrendering its nuclear program. For one thing, the threat to Israel by these two states is infinitely more direct and lethal than that they pose to the United States. After all, unlike Israel, the United States has never been threatened with national extinction by either Iran or Iraq; and, unlike Israel, the threat to the United States by these rogue states is tactical rather than existential.

The only conceivable drawback of the NMD from Israel's point of view revolves around the possible retreat of a more self-assured United States into isolationism, expressed among other ways in a decreasing readiness for international engagements such as support of local allies in distress or obstruction of rogue states' nuclearization.

The NMD is not likely to have a discernible effect on U.S. antiproliferation policies in the Middle East, for the simple reason that that battle has virtually been lost. Despite longstanding U.S.-Soviet unanimity on the need to control the spread of nuclear arms, these powers have been unable to impose the Nuclear Non-Proliferation Treaty (NPT)—the global nonproliferation regime agreed upon in 1969—on their Middle Eastern allies. The Middle Eastern states that joined the NPT, notably Iraq and Iran, have unscrupulously violated the treaty. The disintegration of the Soviet Union, far from stopping the Middle Eastern nonconventional arms race dead in its track, seems to have brought the region closer than ever to a nuclear threshold, not least due to the seepage of nuclear know-how and expertise, and possibly fissible materials as well, following the breakdown of central control over its nuclear arsenal.

Moreover, the unfortunate limits of verification and coercion have been vividly illustrated by the failure of the international community to dismantle Iraq's nonconventional arsenal following the 1991 Gulf War. Here was a longtime member of the NPT, which had consistently sought to develop nuclear weapons in flagrant violation of the treaty and under the very nose of the international organization that was supposed to prevent this from happening, confronted with an unprecedented international coalition made possible by a unique convergence of regional and international conditions. These conditions ranged from the brutal nature of the Iraqi regime, manifested in domestic repression and external aggression, to the astonishing occupation and elimination of Kuwait as a sovereign state, to the strategic and economic importance of the Middle East and the Persian Gulf, to the momentous events in Eastern Europe and the Soviet Union and the consequent diminution of great power rivalry in the Third World. And yet, even this exceptional global cooperation, forged during the Gulf conflict of 1990-1991 and maintained—with great awkwardness and diminishing efficiency—in the wake of the war, has encountered formidable obstacles with disappointing results. Is it realistic to assume that a new international effort, operating under far less favorable circumstances, would be able to identify and monitor similar nuclear violations by members of the NPT, such as Iran?

Conclusion

The economic and political *cordon sanitaire* around Iraq has been decisively loosened to the point of total breakdown, even as the policy of "dual containment" has been effectively drained of real substance by international reluctance to participate in sanctions against Iran. This all occurs just as the attainment of nuclear weapons by these two states is in the offing. There should be no relenting in the effort to prevent this eventuality, or at least to slow it down—but it should now be apparent to all that its chances of success are meager. What is important now is to think through the strategic consequences and requirements of nuclearization. Given the regional mass proliferation of long-range ballistic missiles, such a development would not only endanger Middle Eastern stability, but could also pose a real threat to Europe (including Russia) or even the United States.

Such dim prospects can hardly be expected to encourage the Israelis. Given Israel's two-pronged vulnerability—featuring prominently on the rogue states' "hit list" and of being an ideal nuclear target due to its minuscule size—Israel has long accompanied the development of its own ABM system with efforts to induce the U.S. administration to pressure Russia to contain the seepage of nonconventional technology and expertise to Iran. "The Americans have effectively given up the effort to obstruct the nuclear and missile capabilities of such states as Iran, Iraq, and North Korea," an unnamed senior Israeli official has recently complained. "This is best evidenced by the administration's plan to deploy a national missile defense against Third World countries."[2] This stark assessment is bound to be confirmed in Israeli perceptions by such acts as Secretary of State Madeleine Albright's recent extension of an olive branch to Iran, regardless of the latter's continued quest for nuclear weapons.

These frustrations notwithstanding, Israel is keenly aware of the formidable constraints attending U.S. pressure on Russia, not least the desire to avoid alienating the former superpower at this critical juncture of power transition in the post-Yeltsin area. Nor has Israel been oblivious of the voices in Washington advocating a U.S.-Iranian rapprochement, some hypothetical advantages of which could conceivably benefit Israel as well. Given the extraordinary threat to its national existence from the Middle East's imminent nuclearization, Israel cannot but welcome NMD. It could follow the British, opting for participation in the development process, or it could seek to acquire the complete product.

There is no guarantee that nondeployment will lead to a greater U.S. effort to forestall rogue states' nuclear and missile programs or that such an effort would meet with practical success. On the other hand, NMD can potentially enhance the Arrow system through technological and scientific cooperation and support, greater financial assistance, and a more understanding approach in Washington to Israel's strategic needs, in particular the preservation of its nuclear deterrent posture— a complex, multifaceted combination of political and military efforts.

It should be clear that the NMD is not a solution in and of itself. It should not be conceived as an autarkic system but rather as a part of an integrated defensive package comprising the traditional components of nuclear deterrence and preemption. Israel's Arrow II system cannot be expected to stop a nuclear missile attack on its own. An ABM defense system should be viewed as the nation's final, not primary, line of defense—a means of last resort when all other measures have failed. Hence, were Israel to surrender its nuclear program it would totally eviscerate its deterrent posture vis-à-vis Iran and Iraq. There would be nothing to prevent them from hurling their nuclear missiles with impunity at Israel, since it would not require more than one nuclear strike against metropolitan Tel Aviv to extinguish the Jewish state.

By contrast, the foremost line of defense should be a proactive foreign policy, whose aim is precisely to forestall the need to retreat, under duress, to a final protective line. From this point of view, the NMD, if anything, would expand the United States's room to maneuver rather than narrow it. Had Saddam Hussein been in possession of nuclear weapons at the time of his Kuwaiti misadventure, an effective NMD could have only strengthened our resolve to confront him or, better yet, dissuaded him from attacking in the first place. One can only hope that, in some similar crisis in the future, we do not have to learn this the hard way—again.

Notes

1. *Times* (London), January 31, 2000.
2. *Ha'aretz*, March 17, 2000.

Scott Snyder

Pyongyang's Pressure

North Korea (DPRK) has been an inadvertent catalyst and the primary ostensible threat cited by Clinton administration officials as motivating the accelerated U.S. drive for an NMD program.[1] Despite limited progress in addressing nuclear issues through the U.S.-DPRK Geneva Agreed Framework of 1994, deep mistrust between the United States and North Korea has driven repeated cycles of tension followed by protracted negotiation. In the United States, the primary concerns continue to be about North Korean nuclear and missile development programs. North Korea's leadership expresses concern about the continued U.S.-led drive (along with increasingly sophisticated South Korean forces) for military modernization, including U.S. development of sophisticated missile defense systems, as an attempt to "dominate the world."[2]

North Korea's missile development and export efforts, when seen from Pyongyang's perspective, have been a primary source of hard-won foreign currency through exports to Iran, Syria, Iraq, and Libya. For North Korea, unconventional weapons development is also a relatively inexpen-

Scott Snyder is the Asia Foundation's recently appointed representative in Korea and author of a newly published book entitled *Negotiating on the Edge: North Korean Negotiating Behavior* (U.S. Institute of Peace Press, 1999). The views expressed here are his personal views and may not represent those of the Asia Foundation.

Copyright © 2000 by The Center for Strategic and International Studies and the Massachusetts Institute of Technology
The Washington Quarterly • 23:3 pp. 163–170.

sive means of maintaining deterrence by enhancing weapons of mass destruction (WMD) delivery capabilities against perceived enemies including the United States, Japan, and South Korea. The overt North Korean response to U.S. NMD development efforts has come primarily in the form of vitriolic media attacks against U.S. characterizations of North Korea's own missile development efforts as the primary driver for pursuing NMD. The North Korean media has also responded strongly to Japanese cooperative involvement in the development of theater missile defense (TMD).[3] The emergence of NMD as a major issue in the U.S.-North Korea relationship has complicated an apparent North Korean willingness to hold negotiations over missile exports and development, although both sides have yet to put forward realistic proposals necessary to give serious momentum to such a negotiation.

North Korean public reactions to U.S. NMD efforts predictably presume that NMD really is all about Pyongyang. This is not surprising, given the self-aggrandizing nature of the regime's propaganda and the fact that North Korea is indeed consistently named as the primary threat justifying the pace of NMD development efforts. North Korea's own unorthodox invitation to a missile negotiation with the United States in June 1998, the catalytic political impact of North Korea's August 1998 rocket launch on the U.S. political debate over NMD, and subsequent North Korean public comments through the spring of 2000, suggest that both sides have been talking past each other all along.

North Korea's Missile Gambit

North Korean missile development and export of the Hwasong (300- to 500-kilometer range) and No Dong (range of up to 1,300 kilometers) missiles, adapted from Scud technology, were most active during the Iran-Iraq War of the 1980s. Yet it was North Korea's nuclear program, rather than its missile exports, which received paramount attention in the United States until the signing of the Geneva Agreed Framework.[4] That agreement froze known North Korean plutonium reprocessing activities and suspended construction of two large graphite-moderated reactors in return for U.S.-led provision of two proliferation-resistant 1,000 megawatt light-water reactors through the Korean Peninsula Energy Development Organization. The Agreed Framework also indicated that the United States and North Korea would address other issues, including concerns about North Korean missiles, as part of a process of improving the bilateral relationship over time. Several sporadic unsuccessful rounds of missile negotiations with North Korea were led by then-Deputy Assistant Secretary of State for Political-Military Affairs Robert Einhorn in 1996 and 1997 without significant progress beyond a restatement of opening negotiating positions.

Two reports released during the summer of 1998 set the stage for a negative action-reaction cycle between North Korean missile development and U.S. NMD efforts. First, in an aggressively worded June commentary entitled "Nobody Can Slander the DPRK's Missile Policy," the North Korean government both foreshadowed its own progress in developing the multi-stage Taep'odong rocket and indirectly offered a renewed negotiation over missiles with the United States. The commentary criticized U.S. assertions that North Korea, as a "leading missile power," should freeze the development and export of its missiles as a precondition for lifting of the U.S. economic embargo against the North. Upholding North Korean missile development efforts as a matter of sovereignty and self-defense against the "military threat from outside," the commentary ties negotiations over missile development to the signing of a U.S.-DPRK peace agreement and the removal of the "U.S. military threat." Second, the commentary states that DPRK "missile export is aimed at obtaining the foreign money we need at present," and demanded lifting economic sanctions as the price for a North Korean pledge to discontinue missile exports. The commentary essentially laid out an opening negotiating position (however unrealistic from a U.S. government perspective) over the price it would demand to give up its missile exports as well as missile development, and invited the United States to respond at the negotiating table.[5]

The Report of a Commission to Assess the Ballistic Missile Threat to the United States (the Rumsfeld Report), issued in July 1998, underscored the expansion of the ballistic missile threat and of the capacities to utilize ballistic missiles to deliver nuclear or biological weapons against the United States. In particular, it highlighted the fact that missile development by newer entrants to the field are harder to track because they are not following the old Soviet or Chinese path in developing ballistic missiles. There are a wider availability of relevant technologies and applications on the international market, and enhanced capabilities to conceal ballistic missile development programs from the view of the international community. North Korea (along with Iran) was accused of leading efforts to pursue ballistic missile capabilities, in particular by developng the long-range (up to 6,000 kilometers) Taep'odong 2 ballistic missile. The fact that North Korea subsequently launched a three-stage Taep'odong 1 missile (with a range of 2,500 to 4,000 kilometers) less than two months after the release of the report served as a major catalyst for the NMD effort. In addition, the launching fixed North Korea as the leading potential proliferant of ballistic missile technologies.[6]

North Korean Strategic Counterresponses

Thus far, there has been no public evidence of a strategic North Korean counterresponse to NMD other than to continue Pyongyang's own indigenous missile development efforts to reach the continental United States. Statements by U.S. intelligence officials suggest that North Korean efforts to develop longer-range Taep'odong missile capabilities have continued to receive top priority within North Korea's rather limited resource base. Yet, Pyongyang did provide an oral pledge in Berlin in September 1999 not to conduct additional missile tests concurrent with U.S.-DPRK negotiations over the North's missile program.[7] North Korea is deemed unlikely under current circumstances to give up a program that has so effectively garnered international attention disproportionate to North Korea's relative size and aggregate power. It is unlikely that development or deployment of the U.S. NMD will deter North Korean missile development efforts, which are useful to Pyongyang both for tactical negotiation objectives and the broader strategic purpose of maintaining deterrence.

The U.S. public debate over whether NMD is viable and leakproof against rogue military threats has provided North Korea with the guidebook for how to effectively respond to NMD. Richard Garwin, chairman of the Arms Control Advisory Committee of the U.S. Arms Control and Disarmament Agency, said in recent testimony before the U.S. Congress, "It [NMD] would have strictly zero capability against the much more realistic and important threat from North Korea, Iran, or Iraq—short-range cruise or ballistic missiles fired from merchant ships near U.S. shores, a nuclear weapon detonated in a harbor, or biological warfare agent disseminated in the U.S. from a ship in harbor."[8]

Presumably, a strategic counterresponse to NMD might include the expansion and reorientation of past North Korean special forces operations primarily directed against South Korea to focus on penetrating U.S. bases in the Asian theater and the continental United States.[9] This type of North Korean operation on a global scale has not been attempted for more than a decade. The prospect of a response that would jeopardize North Korea's increasing dependence on external resources from South Korea and the United States would constitute an extraordinarily risky and desperate (but not unimaginable) counterresponse, given North Korea's own post-Cold War isolation and economic weakness.

Response to the Taep'odong Test: How to Achieve Effective Deterrence?

North Korea's 1998 Taep'odong launch reshaped the Northeast Asian regional security agenda and complicated U.S.-DPRK nuclear negotiations designed to allay doubts about North Korea's adherence to its pledge not to develop nuclear weapons that had been raised by the discovery of a suspicious site at Keumchang'ri. These latter tensions were subsequently resolved by the initiation of a review of policy toward North Korea led by former Secretary of Defense William Perry and specifically by North Korea's willingness to allow inspections of the site in question in return for several hundred thousand tons of U.S. food assistance.

Pyongyang's Taep'odong test launch demonstrated that the ballistic missile threat to the continental United States was potentially real but not immediate. U.S. intelligence about North Korea's program had succeeded in predicting the launch but had underestimated the level of technical capability North Korea would display. At the same time, the launch provided a benchmark for the intense political and technical debate in the United States over the timelines necessary for adequate testing and deployment.

North Korea's own assertions that the Taep'odong 1 launch was designed not to test a missile but rather to put a satellite in orbit (a claim later confirmed by the U.S. government) accomplished two things. It preserved a fig leaf of ambiguity regarding North Korea's intentions. And, as a failed satellite launch, it demonstrated that much work would be required before North Korea could effectively master the technical aspects of flight control and atmospheric reentry necessary to effectively target the continental United States using intercontinental ballistic missile (ICBM) technology (an effort that would require development and production of the Taep'odong 2, rather than the Taep'odong 1, which cannot reach the continental United States from North Korea). In testimony to Parliament, a senior Canadian defense official has succinctly suggested that currently the most dangerous threat from North Korean ICBMs is "that when they aim at Colorado Springs they may hit Toronto."[10] Yet, the mixed record of U.S. intelligence regarding the pace of North Korean missile development is not reassuring.

In combination with deterrence, regional diplomatic activity has been more active in recent months in response to the specific challenge posed by North Korean missile development efforts. Perhaps most notable has been the trilateral (United States, South Korea, and Japan) coordination process initiated as part of the Perry Review. The review has made North Korea's pledge not to pursue further missile tests an essential prerequisite for enhanced engagement (along with North Korea's continued adherence to the Geneva Agreed Framework). One result has been that the North Koreans made an oral pledge to the United States in September 1999 in Berlin to forgo additional missile tests for the duration of U.S.-DPRK negotiations over the missile issue. In return, the United Stated pledged to lift economic sanctions against North Korea.

The Berlin statement marks a starting point for further missile negotiations analogous to the limited understanding over nuclear issues that resulted from the initial U.S.-DPRK meeting held in May 1993, at which North Korea suspended its withdrawal from the Nuclear Non-Proliferation Treaty (NPT) for the duration of nuclear negotiations. Of course, the road to a nuclear agreement that followed nearly led to U.S.-DPRK confrontation in June 1994 and even now has come under criticism for failing to prevent alleged North Korean nuclear conversion. The Berlin pledges come close to restoring the status quo ante in U.S.-DPRK relations that had existed in the immediate aftermath of the Geneva Agreed Framework. At that time, a much larger sanctions-lifting effort by the United States had been implied by the Agreed Framework but was not forthcoming as a result of political concerns on the part of the Clinton administration in the aftermath of the 1994 Republican takeover of Congress. The Berlin statement has put a temporary brake on a possible second Taep'odong launch, leaving open the door to additional negotiations.

Will NMD Hit the Wrong Target?

Following North Korea's Berlin pledge, several rounds of meetings have been held to arrange for a higher-level exchange of officials and to follow through on North Korean pledges to continue regular U.S.-DPRK negotiations on nuclear and missile issues. Those talks have made little progress through three rounds held from November 1999 to March 2000 toward setting dates for a high-level visit or resuming U.S.-DPRK nuclear and missile negotiations. Meanwhile, the North Korean media has been unusually sensitive to high-level U.S. administration characterizations of North Korea as a threat and as a rationale for NMD.

North Korean officials have reacted negatively to the perceived double-standard of continued U.S. NMD testing while they have pledged a moratorium on North Korea's missile tests. Following the January NMD test, the spokesman for the North Korean Ministry of Foreign Affairs stated,

> The DPRK and the U.S. are now negotiating a solution to the issues of common concern including the missile issue. ... However, the U.S. conducted the test of a missile interceptor this time. It is one more grave challenge to the magnanimity and good faith shown by the DPRK in its efforts to settle the outstanding issues through negotiations. The U.S. behavior has compelled the DPRK to take our moratorium into serious consideration.[11]

The North Koreans have mistakenly assumed that NMD is indeed targeted at Pyongyang rather than a response to ballistic missile proliferation more broadly. One result is that Pyongyang's leadership has failed to understand that U.S. NMD efforts may have been catalyzed by a North Korean threat but are not driven solely by North Korean missile development activities. According to Under Secretary of Defense Walter Slocombe, "Even if the North Korean threat were to disappear entirely, we would still be concerned about threats from other parts of the world."[12] Nonetheless, the action-reaction dynamic that has developed between NMD and North Korea's own missile development efforts suggests the risk that premature collision is more likely than accommodation.

One unintentional casualty of the political atmosphere surrounding the NMD development effort may indeed be the time necessary to see if North Korean and other missile development efforts can be constrained through negotiations. Such a strategy assumes, of course, that the United States itself would be willing to put an offer on the table. The offer would have to be sufficient to give North Korea something to lose, rather than simply demanding that the cash-strapped country voluntarily give up one of its primary foreign currency-earning exports as part of its duties as a global good citizen (a category for which North Korea consistently fails to qualify). At the same time, North Korea's demand of upwards of $1 billion to end exports totaling no more than $100 million annually is an equally outrageous starting position. Any potential bargain requires provisions that verify that North Korea's missile development capacity has been frozen.

Conclusion

North Korea's own hedging strategy against a decisive post-Cold War shift in the balance of power on the Korean peninsula has led to its pursuit of WMD development to compensate for the inability to keep pace with U.S. and South Korean weapons modernization—insurance against invasion from Pyongyang's precarious perspective. Yet such programs have perpetuated U.S. distrust and have ironically even become the catalyst for a U.S. global counterstrategy against the rising threat of ballistic missiles. This counterstrategy now takes the form of a global project that with a $12.7 billion budget (although some estimates suggest that the budget may nearly double to over $20 billion) is larger than the DPRK's total annual reported budget of $9 billion to $10 billion. North Korea's awkward, blustering efforts to extract economic concessions as a tangible assurance that the United States will support its regime survival have been widely misunderstood, resented, and rejected as extortion in Washington. Yet critics of Pyongyang's strategy also can not imagine a state such as North Korea voluntarily giving up what is probably perceived as the "ace" that can assure survival and economic gain of an otherwise failed system. It should not be surprising that in such a context, and absent a greater basis for cooperation to overcome half a century of mistrust, North Korean missile development efforts and NMD might be the sparks that put the United States and North Korea back on a course toward rhetorical collision if not military confrontation.

Notes

1. See Walter Slocombe, "National Missile Defense," speech given at Center for Strategic and International Studies, November 5, 1999.
2. Associated Press, "North Korea Denounces U.S. Missile Defense System," February 22, 2000. See also William S. Cohen, "Rogue States Cannot Hope to Blackmail America or Her Allies," *Times* (London), March 1, 2000.
3. For one example, see BBC World Wide Monitoring, "North Korea Blasts Japanese-US Research into Theater Missile Defense," February 7, 2000 (based on KCNA Web site reports, February 6, 2000).

4. For a comprehensive review of recent developments in North Korean missile development efforts, see Joseph S. Bermudez, Jr., "A History of Ballistic Missile Development in the DPRK," Occasional Paper no. 2, Monitoring Proliferation Threats Project of the Center for Nonproliferation Studies, Monterey Institute of International Studies, November 1999.

5. Korea Central News Agency, "Nobody Can Slander DPRK's (Democratic People's Republic of Korea) Missile Policy: KCNA commentary," June 16, 1998 (quoted in English from BBC Summary of World Broadcasts).

6. "Executive Summary of the Report of the Commission to Assess the Ballistic Missile Threat to the United States," July 15, 1998, available on the Internet at http://www.fas.org/irp/threat/bm-threat.html.

7. See Cohen, "Rogue States Cannot Hope to Blackmail America or Her Allies."

8. Brad Glosserman, "Missile Defense Opens a Pandora's Silo," *Japan Times*, January 23, 2000.

9. See Joseph S. Bermudez Jr., *North Korean Special Forces* (Annapolis, Md.: Naval Institute Press, 1998).

10. Edward Alden, "U.S. Missiles Make Canada Defensive over Arms Control: Plans to Deploy Ballistic Missiles in Alaska Are Compromising Ottawa's Principles," *Financial Times*, March 1, 2000, 4.

11. Korea Central News Agency, "North Korea 'Compelled' to Reconsider Moratorium by U.S. Missile Test," January 22, 2000.

12. See Slocombe, "National Missile Defense."

Anoushiravan Ehteshami

Tehran's Tocsin

America's prospective development and implementation of a national missile defense system will provide countries targeted by the system intriguing diplomatic and military opportunities. This is especially true for Iran, one country that would be "targeted." Throughout Iran, a tocsin has sounded in response to the perceived threat of NMD.

Should Iran, regarded as one of the countries intent on developing a long-range missile and nonconventional capability, worry about this new U.S. initiative? If so, how might Iran react to the U.S. defense shield, if at all? At first glance, one may be forgiven for assuming that the two countries are already so far apart politically and geographically that such a deployment will not affect their rather strained bilateral relations. But Iran watchers will testify that Tehran actually does note, quite carefully and more systematically than most people care to know, what the United States does and what it says it is going to do in its foreign and strategic policies. The NMD then is likely to be of interest to Iran.

In the short term, Iran's response is likely to be heavy on rhetoric and light on concrete action. Although the rhetorical exchange between the two sides is unlikely to affect the slow pace of progress in bi-

Anoushiravan Ehteshami is a reader in International Relations and director of the Centre for Middle Eastern and Islamic Studies, University of Durham, UK.

Copyright © 2000 by The Center for Strategic and International Studies and the Massachusetts Institute of Technology
The Washington Quarterly • 23:3 pp. 171–176.

lateral relations, Tehran will probably use the NMD as a perfect opportunity to enhance its political-military relations with China, Russia, and North Korea. Short of political posturing, however, Tehran has no concrete military alternatives to explore as countermeasures.

Before embarking on an analysis of possible Iranian responses to the U.S. NMD deployment, it is appropriate to consider the basis of Iran's outlook toward the United States. It is true that the Islamic elite as a whole has little love for the U.S. way of life. Their responses thus far to U.S. actions, however, have been based less on ideological grounds and more on pragmatic and realistic calculations about the balance of power between the two at any one time. Iran has based much of its strategy toward the United States in political terms, not unlike other actors in the international system. Iran's pragmatic calculations toward the United States are driven by a widely shared perception.

Iran holds an almost paranoid and conspiratorial view of the United State's role and actions in the Middle East and sees almost every U.S. initiative as a direct or indirect assault on Iran's regional interests. Since the Cold War, the United States has been in strategic competition with Iran and is the main challenger in the Middle East and the Transcaspian region north of Iran. The view that the United States is Iran's main regional rival is shared by both the political elite and large sections of the military establishment.

For an oil-rich country like Iran, sitting in the middle of the two strategically important oil zones of the Persian Gulf and the Caspian Basin, America's words and deeds, particularly in the defense and security realms, matter a great deal to those who will inform Tehran's strategic thinking.

NMD and Iran's Foreign and Defense Policy

Iran can explore several responses through its foreign policy. It can intensify its extremely slick charm offensive, by making noises of compromise on the status of the three islands in dispute with the United Arab Emirates, and effectively remove itself as a threat from the calculations of its Gulf Arab neighbors. In this way, Iran would politically remove one of the key rationales for the continuing U.S. military presence in the Persian Gulf and force the United States to rethink its Gulf Arab allies. Removing U.S. military forces from the region, of course, will be seen by the more forward-looking groups in Tehran as a way of reducing U.S. attention on Iran and as a way of minimizing the dangers of NMD emboldening the Pentagon to plan direct action against Tehran. Yet, these actions are unlikely.

NMD development will undoubtedly be seen by target countries as the United States' gaining first-strike capability. In response, they will search for effective deterrence measures. Iran is no exception, though it is almost impossible to say whether the NMD will generate a military response from Iran. What then, might Iran's deterrence mechanism be?

Again, we can speculate that the best deterrence in Iran's case will have to incorporate measures that aim to buildup its conventional military capabilities and force structures in order to allow it to present a greater potential challenge to U.S. forces in the Persian Gulf and the wider Middle East. Such weapon systems as long-range bombers, missile systems, and sea mines will be the basic requirements of this type of planning. The strategy would be built around the idea that the United States must be made to think twice about a confrontation with Iran.

Next on the list will probably be whether Iran should renege on its international obligations and actively develop its nonconventional weapons capabilities. In an atmosphere where Iran's membership in nonproliferation regimes is openly debated in Tehran, a nonconventional weapons capability combined with a credible delivery system will be seen as providing a well-structured deterrent—even countermeasure—against possible attack by U.S. forces. Thus, the NMD may actually encourage this line of reasoning amongst the Iranian security establishment and strengthen the hand of those who do want to give Iran a credible weapon of mass destruction profile at any price.

Whether Iran would have the resources to further modernize its armed forces, as well as a nonconventional weapons capability, is a different matter altogether. For one thing, Iran will probably have to turn to traditional arms suppliers (Russia, China, and North Korea)—hungry for hard currency—for the required advanced equipment and training. Whether these suppliers can fill Iran's increasingly sophisticated military and military-related needs is an open question. Also, can Iran itself afford the services of its suppliers? For one thing, Iran's economy cannot as of yet generate the sorts of surpluses that would allow a massive military program—even with the beneficial impact of high oil prices since early 1999. For another, Tehran's offer of oil-for-weapons is probably an insufficient incentive for the three suppliers to absorb the wrath of the United States over significant military trading with Iran.

Although it is unlikely that Iran will pursue alternative (conventional or nonconventional) military systems in response to NMD, it is not impossible. In foreign policy terms, however, Tehran is likely to capitalize on the NMD issue to strengthen its already close relations with the other targeted nations, each of which ironically regards itself as the real target of the NMD initiative. Iran would thus take a step closer toward its dream of creating close strategic partnerships with the two continental powers of Asia—Russia and China—and the strategically placed North Korea. NMD also enables Iran to tie itself more closely to an Asian balance of power game, in which the United States is viewed by all four parties as an intrusive military power. Such strategic alliances, if made to work, can pose serious challenges to Washington's Asia-Pacific interests.

What are Iran's medium-term countermeasures to the NMD? Assuming that Iran actually felt threatened by the NMD, it is conceivable that Iran could try and make life for the United States and its citizens in the region less pleasant. It could raise the premium on the U.S. presence by (directly or indirectly) threatening its vital interests in the Middle East and putting undue pressure on its allies in the Persian Gulf and the Levant, as well as try to stretch U.S. resources in Central Asia and the Caucasus. The least that Tehran may have to do is to encourage its Islamist allies in the Arab and Muslim worlds to be more proactive in their challenges to the status quo, which they managed with great effect in the 1980s.

In military terms, Iran could consider other factors. For instance, the United States is spending substantial sums (some $60 billion per year) on defending its interests and allies in the Persian Gulf—a matter that the U.S. Congress is not too happy about. In the context of a response to the NMD, Iran might be tempted to raise the premium on U.S. military commitments in the area and hope to find a tradeoff between the longer-term impact of the NMD on its own national security and the protection of U.S. regional interests.

Focusing more closely on the implications of the NMD, Tehran will probably regard the U.S. missile defense shield largely in Middle East regional terms. One direct consequence of this perception is likely to be how Iran will regard the NMD as aiding U.S. military allies in the Middle East. This is likely to form a significant part of Iran's strategic calculations about the NMD. Its impact on the resources and abilities of one U.S. ally in particular, Israel, is likely to be scrutinized. Iran already confronts Israel in other ways as it is seen as the protector of U.S. interests in the region. In the conspiratorial world of Middle East politics, it is believed Israel and the United States, already known to be close military partners and cosponsors of the Arrow antimissile defense project, are developing an elaborate defense pact. With this pact, the United States would commit to Israel's defense in case of attack. Israel's regional rivals can be forgiven for calculating that the NMD's virtues for the United States will also directly benefit Israel. In the Iranian view, where a steady flow of U.S. military know-how to Israel is assumed, there is a direct relationship between NMD and Israel's missile defense shield. In this sense, a totally unintended level of tensions could creep into Middle Eastern regional dynamics and adversely affect different aspects of U.S. regional strategy, whether the United States engages or contains independent regional actors.

In purely military terms, the mere perception that Israel stands to gain from the NMD could intensify the regional arms race and encourage countries like Iran to seek regional partners (like Syria) to form a military front against Israel. Paradoxically, it would be this sort of response, spawned from the United States' own defense strategies, which would encourage the United States to discuss the provision of a security umbrella for Israel.

Relations with the United States

What about the NMD and Iranian-U.S. relations? Let us be clear: We are starting from an already low base and the NMD will only become the latest on a long list of items for discussion between Tehran and Washington. Its impact, therefore, on the glacial process of dialogue between the two countries is likely to be minimal. But hard-liners in Iran will draw lessons from the NMD and the fact that Iran is often named in U.S. circles as a threat. Such hard-liners could argue that while on the one hand the United States is talking of dialogue and the need to turn the page, its defense establishment is actively planning against the Islamic Republic. Even if untrue, the political impact of such an argument cannot be underestimated, particularly if it is used against the very moderate forces that the United States is courting. Whether the NMD issue is of sufficient importance to affect the domestic balance of power within Iran is hard to say, but one gets the sense that public initiatives such as NMD will not blow the internal debate off course.

But where should the NMD agenda sit in the current Iranian-U.S. bilateral relations? In an atmosphere where the United States seems actively to be courting Tehran, and the U.S. president openly speaks—in what can only be termed his 'Valentine's Day' message to Tehran—of his desire for a partnership, we can afford to be more positive. When President Bill Clinton states that in his view, "one of the best things that [the United States] can do for the long-term peace and health of the Middle East and, indeed, much of the rest of the world, is to have a constructive partnership with Iran," he is really saying that his administration is not only interested in better relations, but in the context of broader dialogue, is actively trying to address some of Iran's security concerns as well.[1]

On the eve of Iran's sixth Majlis elections, when State Department Spokesman James Rubin praised the Iranian electoral process, and his government's interest in the mechanics of the Islamic political system,[2] he was merely reinforcing the message that Washington wants to do business with Tehran and support the reformer democrats to emerge as the administration's negotiating partners. In this interesting situation, and with Iran's reformers having scored a resounding victory in the country's elections, can the United States afford to miss this historic window of opportunity by embarking on a military strategy likely to alienate the forces it must talk to in Iran? Are the two parties able to rise above such distractions and push ahead with establishing a forum for bilateral talks? They may be able to, but only if progress in the relationship advances further.

Notes

1. See <www.CNN.com>, February 14, 2000.
2. Associated Foreign Press, February 16, 2000.

Michael McDevitt

Beijing's Bind

Preserving the Anti-Ballistic Missile (ABM) Treaty intact, unmodified, is the centerpiece of China's diplomatic attempt to forestall NMD deployment. Assuming the United States will, at a minimum, begin to deploy an NMD system optimized to deal with North Korean and other "rogue" state ballistic missiles, even this limited system, known as C-1, includes elements in its architecture[1] that are not currently permitted by the 1972 ABM Treaty, which, among other things, prohibits a nation-wide defense against ballistic missiles.[2] Intended or not, the system would have an impact on China's small intercontinental ballistic missile (ICBM) force, which numbers approximately 20.[3]

Should the Russians not agree to modify the ABM Treaty, the United States will be faced with three alternatives. The first two, either dropping the idea of NMD altogether or developing a new architecture that is ABM Treaty-compliant, seem highly unlikely since neither option would provide protection for the entire United States. The third option would be to withdraw from the ABM Treaty altogether, after giving the required six months' notice. This last alternative, which today seems to be the most likely should modification attempts prove unsuccessful, would be a disaster from Beijing's perspective because it would leave the United States free to select any mix of land and space-based NMD

Michael McDevitt is a retired rear admiral in the U.S. Navy and a senior fellow at the Center for Naval Analysis Corporation.

Copyright © 2000 by The Center for Strategic and International Studies and the Massachusetts Institute of Technology
The Washington Quarterly • 23:3 pp. 177–186.

options unconstrained by international agreement. This means that Beijing, by objecting to changes in the ABM Treaty, is pursuing an anti-NMD policy course of action that has a high probability of making Beijing's strategic circumstances worse.[4]

Background

Until mid-1999, China policy did not clearly distinguish between theater missile defense (TMD) and NMD in its interactions with the United States. This is not because individuals in China did not understand the difference. In fact, both technical and conceptual specialists in China understood what NMD was all about and understood the implications of this latest U.S. attempt to develop a defense against ICBMs. For decades there has been a group of scientists and technologists within China who closely followed the on-again, off-again U.S. missile defense debates—especially Reagan-era Strategic Defense Initiative developments.[5]

China has also appreciated the impact that a successful missile defense could have on its strategic deterrent missile force. But, as a general proposition, this technical and strategic awareness was not translated into an overt policy position until late 1996. At that time, the beginning of an anti-NMD policy line began to publicly emerge. Even then, Beijing's focus was more on TMD and how U.S. theater systems might affect China's ICBM force. Chinese policy did not clearly differentiate between TMD and NMD until the later half of 1999.

Earlier that summer, the United States adopted an official NMD policy when, on July 22, 1999, President Bill Clinton signed legislation that stated U.S. policy was to deploy an NMD system as soon it was technologically possible. The purpose of such a system was to protect all U.S. territory against limited missile attacks from rogue nations. Although not specifically stated, the system would also presumably have the ability to defend against accidental or unauthorized launches from rogues as well as Russia and China.[6] This was followed on October 2, 1999, by a successful NMD test, when an NMD interceptor hit a test warhead that was travelling at ICBM range and speed.

In Beijing, the legislation and subsequent successful test seemed to have had a galvanizing effect. A policy line specifically oriented toward NMD emerged. Before examining Beijing's reaction more closely, a look at China's strategic nuclear circumstances is necessary in order to understand the context in which its policy was formulated.

Vulnerability of China's Strategic Deterrent

Since October 16, 1964, the day China exploded its first atomic bomb, China's declared strategic doctrine has been retaliatory in nature. The official statement made that day continues to guide China's nuclear strategy: "The Chinese government hereby solemnly declares that China will never at anytime, or under any circumstances, be the first to use nuclear weapons."

This "no-first-use" doctrine means that China has adopted a strategy that overtly acknowledges that China will "accept" the first nuclear blow. Its nuclear forces would only be used to retaliate once China was attacked. For such a strategy to be credible, at least vis-à-vis the two nuclear superpowers, its retaliatory nuclear force had to be able to survive an overwhelming first strike from either the Soviet Union or the United States. Because China did not have the means to retaliate against the continental United States until its first ICBM, the DF-5, entered service in 1981, its no-first-use strategy against the United States was really not credible.

It is only over the last twenty years that China's minimum deterrent against the continental United States had the possibility of being credible. ICBM survival still seems problematic, though. As Paul Godwin has written about both the DF-5 ICBM and the shorter range DF-4 intermediate range ballistic missile,

> neither of these weapons is maintained at high levels of readiness. Their warheads are stored separately from the rocket launchers, and the rockets themselves are not kept fueled. The process of loading the liquid fuel tanks and installing the warhead can take 2 to 4 hours.[7]

Furthermore, these silo-based weapons are obviously geographically fixed—and hence can be located from space. Because the Chinese do not have space-based missile launch detection systems necessary to warn them of a U.S. missile launch, China could not institute a launch-on-warning posture even if the ICBMs were fueled and otherwise ready during a crisis.

During the 1980s, any Chinese concerns were undoubtedly mitigated by the relatively close anti-Soviet political relationship between Beijing and Washington. The potential for a Soviet first strike must have seemed much more plausible at the time. Against the Soviets, Beijing had more numerous short-range ballistic missiles, its intermediate-range bomber force, and, from mid-decade on, its single ballistic missile submarine available. This intermediate range "triad" made the likelihood of some retaliatory capability surviving a Soviet first strike much more credible.

During the 1990s, Beijing has seen this calculus flip to its disadvantage. The close Beijing-Moscow "Strategic Partnership" makes the prospect of a Russian first strike remote, while the potential for conflict between Beijing and Washington over Taiwan, dormant since the 1950s, has reemerged during this decade. From China's point of view, the prospect of a U.S. first strike is not nearly as far fetched as it was 10 years ago. Instead of the several hundred weapons that could reach Russia, and thus almost guarantee some ability to retaliate, Beijing today has just about 20 DF-5A ICBMs (8,100-nautical-mile range) capable of reaching the United States.[8]

China's sensitivity to the vulnerability of its retaliatory capability was almost certainly enhanced as the People's Liberation Army carefully analyzed the lessons of the Persian Gulf War. The combination of real-time, space-based surveillance; space-based navigation systems; and very accurate conventional weapons made the possibility of a preemptive strike by conventional weapons another concern. In 1992–1993, preemption with conventional weapons as well as other "revolutionary" possibilities were openly debated in U.S military journals, conferences, and seminars.[9]

As the decade ended, the reality facing Beijing was that its declaratory nuclear doctrine, based on an assured ability to retaliate against the United States, was more rhetorical than real.

Why Does It Matter to Beijing?

Given this assessment, it is fair to pose the rhetorical question, "If Beijing's retaliatory capability against the United States is a strategic fiction anyway, how does an NMD system make China's strategic situation any worse?" Why is Beijing investing political capital in an active anti-NMD policy?

The answer has several aspects. First, from Beijing's perspective there is always the possibility that a few, even one or two, Chinese ICBMs could survive preemption. Even a minimally-sized NMD would be able to deal with these surviving ICBMs. There is some possibility that not all of China's long-range missiles are silo based. Some may be hidden in caves. NMD would have the potential to capture these "concealed" weapons.

Second, and more importantly, there is the concern that a U.S. NMD system would undercut China's ongoing strategic modernization—a program specifically aimed at ensuring a retaliatory force by eliminating China's vulnerability to a preemptive U.S. first strike. Beijing's efforts have largely focused on its ICBM force and, at this time, do not appear to intend to compliment its intermediate-range triad with an intercontinental triad.[10]

Beijing's strategic modernization improves ICBM survivability in five ways:[11]

- *Mobility*: To make it difficult to target China's ICBM force, a move from cave and silo basing to road-mobile ICBMs is underway. This capitalizes on the vastness of China. Two new road mobile ICBMs, the DF-31 (4,300 nautical miles) and DF-41 (6,500 nautical miles), will greatly improve survivability as they are introduced over the next decade.
- *Solid fuel*: China's current ICBM force is liquid fuel propelled. Liquid fuels are highly volatile, and therefore very dangerous to use—par-

ticularly under stress. They are also very corrosive. The new DF-31 and 41 will have solid fuel, which is much safer and eliminates the need to fuel just prior to launch.

- *Command and control*: According to the Pentagon in 1997, China is working to improve its command and control.[12] Improvements make it more likely an order to retaliate would be successfully transmitted and received.
- *Accuracy*: In the same 1997 report, the Pentagon states that China is using the Global Positioning System (GPS) to make significant improvements in accuracy. China has also reached agreements to share in the Russian space-based Global Navigation Satellite System.
- *Greater numbers*: There is no conclusive evidence to indicate how large China's ICBM force might become. More missiles do improve China's retaliatory survivability. The number of missiles currently in China's intermediate range strategic force (about 110 missiles and a similar number of bombers) might provide a clue to how many intercontinental systems Beijing would consider necessary to insure its ability to retaliate.[13]

A U.S. NMD system may be deployed at about the same time China begins to field these survivability steps, raising the specter of mitigating them and returning China to today's vulnerable posture. This relates directly to the third reason China opposes U.S. NMD—the issue of "nuclear blackmail."

Nuclear blackmail is a serious issue from Beijing's perspective. It dates back to the 1950s when the Eisenhower administration threatened to employ nuclear weapons to end the Korean War and then again during the Taiwan Strait Crisis of 1958. In 1964 when China detonated its first atomic bomb, its public rationale for developing this weapon was to "oppose the U.S. imperialist policy of nuclear blackmail and threats. ... China is developing nuclear weapons for defense and for protecting the Chinese people from U.S. threats to launch a nuclear war."[14]

These arguments may appear self-serving to the United States, particularly since these incidents occurred more than 40 years ago, but they are encountered frequently enough from Chinese interlocutors that they cannot be easily dismissed. Even if one judges this argument as specious, one ought not overlook the Chinese penchant for attributing to others the approaches and techniques they themselves might employ. The persistent Chinese belief that the U.S. bombing of their embassy in Belgrade was a deliberate attempt to "teach China a lesson" is a recent example of this phenomenon.

The nuclear blackmail issue is also at the heart of Chinese concerns about a U.S.-dominated unipolar world. Beijing's desired multipolar world with China as one of the poles cannot be realized if the "Chinese pole" can be intimidated by nuclear weapons.[15]

The issue of nuclear blackmail leads to the fourth and final major reason why Beijing opposes NMD—Taiwan. The Chinese combine the blackmail argument and Taiwan in the following way: A U.S. NMD would return China to a position of nuclear vulnerability without a retaliatory recourse. Then any attempt by Beijing to use force against Taiwan would permit the the United States to intervene and threaten to escalate the crisis with impunity. In other words, a replay of the 1958 Taiwan crisis.

Implied in this argument is that as long as China's nuclear retaliatory capability is credible, it possesses a wider range of military options against both Taiwan and the United States than it might otherwise consider if the United States can trump China's nuclear response. It also implies that Beijing's "no-first-use" doctrine may not apply in a Taiwan crisis. That certainly is the impression resulting from the now-notorious statement made in 1995 to a former U.S. official by a senior Chinese official to the effect that the United States would not risk Los Angeles on behalf of Taiwan.[16]

China's Policy Response

Translating these concerns into a sensible policy approach cannot have been easy for Beijing. They could hardly persuade the United States not to field NMD because, if the United States did so, it would constrain China's military options against Taiwan.

Nor could Beijing argue that its current retaliatory capability is a "paper tiger" and that it would not be credible until the DF-31s and DF-41s are fielded in numbers. Not only would this undercut its own attempts to use the threat of nuclear weapons to intimidate the United States during a Taiwan crisis, it could easily embolden those in Beijing who press for an increase in defense spending—particularly those who want to accelerate the strategic modernization program even further.

From Beijing's perspective, the best outcome would be to perpetuate the status quo (i.e., either an ABM Treaty-compliant U.S. missile defense system or none at all). During a recent visit to Washington by a high-level Chinese security official, it was clear that the inviolability of the ABM Treaty was the centerpiece of Beijing's anti-NMD policy. According to this official, the importance of the ABM Treaty was that it guaranteed a second strike, or retaliatory capability, for both the United States and Russia.

In turn, this curbed the nuclear arms race and preserved strategic stability. To tinker now with the ABM Treaty would undo these "great achievements." I hasten to add this is not a unique Chinese perspective, as many experts in the United States and Europe share these views. China's approach should not be considered quixotic.

China has been very active, pressing this policy line globally. They and the Russians are attempting to organize an "international united front" against NMD, all the while hoping that Moscow will not agree to modify the ABM Treaty to permit at least a C-1 NMD system. Beijing has had some success in fueling European concerns—especially France and Germany—about a U.S. NMD deployment and, as a result, U.S. diplomatic efforts are increasingly focused on greater consultation with U.S. friends and allies.

China has also augmented the main line of its argument about the centrality of an unmodified ABM Treaty by appealing to broader world public opinion. The most successful manifestation of this effort took place on November 5, 1999, in the United Nations General Assembly. A draft resolution cosponsored by China, Russia, and Belarus condemned missile defense as destabilizing, arguing such defenses would provoke a nuclear arms race. The First Committee of the General Assembly adopted this draft resolution by a vote of 54 to 4 with 73 abstentions.

The arms race argument is a persistent theme in Beijing's commentary on NMD. This in itself is interesting since no "rogue-oriented" NMD system currently under serious consideration would have a major impact on Russia's ability to hold the entire United States at nuclear risk.[17] It is not entirely clear who, beside Beijing, would become involved in such a race. The arms race line seems to be Beijing's way of publicly putting the United States on notice that it will attempt to outbuild any U.S. NMD system.

The North Korean Pivot

Should Washington decide to go ahead with an NMD system, the initial, and perhaps only, site will be optimized to deal with the North Korean threat. The proposed C-1 system (100 interceptors in Alaska, an X-Band radar on Shemeya Island in the Aleutians, improved early warning radars, command and control at NORAD, and existing Defense Support System satellites) is perfectly located to capture North Korean launches toward the United States. The Alaska site also has a capability against Chinese ICBMs launched from eastern China. Apparently, because of intercept geometry and the curvature of the earth, an Alaskan site would not have a good capability against Chinese ICBMs launched from western China at U.S. east coast cities.

Beijing, as well as some Europeans, downplay or openly ridicule the notion that North Korea in particular, and rogues in general, pose a serious threat to the United States. The Chinese argue that throughout the Cold War, and even today, the United States is under a greater missile threat than North Korea could possibly pose. China questions whether North Korea could ever reach the United States with an ICBM and asks why "traditional" deterrence will not work against Pyongyang. They reject the U.S. concern that there are some countries, North Korea especially, that may not be able to be deterred.

There are other "rogues" besides Pyongyang. But because of the August 1998 Taep'odong 1 missile shot that landed 3,000 miles "down range" in the North Pacific—far enough to reach Alaska and Guam—it is North Korea that really drives the U.S. political consensus for NMD. It is surprising that Beijing has not focused its energy on removing the North Korean rationale by pressuring Pyongyang to forego further long-range missile development and deployment. This is not the place to ruminate about the degree of leverage Beijing may or may not have with Pyongyang, but it is certainly more than any other country. If Beijing was actually able to twist Pyongyang's arm hard enough to convince the North Koreans to get out of the long-range missile business, that result, along with slowly improving relations with Iran and continued UN sanctions on Iraq, could conceivably mitigate the "rogue" rationale for NMD.

Conclusion

With or without a U.S. NMD system, China has a strategic vulnerability issue it is slowly taking steps to correct through a comprehensive strategic modernization. NMD did not precipitate that modernization, but any U.S. NMD deployment will certainly affect its quantitative, and perhaps qualitative, scope.

Beijing's concerns about nuclear blackmail will almost certainly guarantee that China will attempt to stay ahead of, or circumvent, U.S. NMD deployments by eventually fielding more ICBMs than NMD interceptors. This would probably lead to some sort of Sino-U.S. understanding about the ratio of Chinese ICBMs to NMD interceptors over time, unless the overall state of Sino-U.S. relations deteriorates to the point where the United States attempts to deny China any means to retaliate against the United States by fielding a robust anti-China NMD system (if such a system was technically possible).

In informal dialogue, the Chinese frequently refer to a Chinese nuclear capability modeled on France's "Force de Frappe." What is not clear is whether this is where Beijing was headed if NMD had never appeared on the scene. This author suspects it was. An intercontinental force of largely mobile missiles would address survivability concerns and guarantee Beijing a retaliatory capability in the face of an NMD system limited to dealing with rogues if it was similar in size to the intermediate-range force that preserves a retaliatory capability against Russia. Finally, Beijing could hardly persuade the United States not to field NMD because if the United States deployed, it would constrain China's military options against Taiwan.

China has very little leverage in pursuing its anti-NMD policy. Beijing is dependent on the Russians to hold the line on an ABM Treaty modification, which paradoxically could actually make Beijing's situation worse by inspiring the United States to simply walk away from the ABM Treaty altogether. Beijing has only a faint hope its ability to mobilize world opinion will be effective in dissuading the United States from fielding an NMD system.

With Beijing's talk of an arms race, it apparently hopes the threat of a Chinese strategic buildup will be worrisome enough to Washington to cause them to rethink NMD deployment decisions. This could easily backfire and cause the United States to take advantage of its technological lead, change NMD's focus to overtly anti-Chinese, and pour resources in attempting to keep far ahead in any Beijing-Washington, offense-defense competition. Of course, given the labored and agonizingly slow pace of Chinese strategic development since 1964, it is not entirely clear that the threat of an arms "race" is entirely credible.

Beijing's best hope to arrest U.S. NMD is to somehow cause the North Korean ICBM threat to go away. Failing that, Beijing's remaining tactic may be to keep its fingers crossed and hope that, technically, NMD proves to be too big a challenge for the United States to surmount.

Notes

1. Notional NMD architecture includes:
   - Ground-based interceptors
   - Capability upgrades to existing ground-based early warning radar's in the United States, U.K., and Greenland.
   - Newly developed land based X-Band radar. The rough equivalent of fire-

control radar, which closely track incoming missiles/RV's in flight and help discriminate between missile reentry vehicle's, decoys and missile parts, so intercepting missiles can achieve a "skin-to-skin" hit.

- Battle-management and command and control installation at NORAD in Colorado Springs in order to command the NMD system.
- Space-based infrared detection of ballistic missile launches utilizing the existing DSP satellite system, and in the future the replacement Space-based Infrared System.

2. Lisbeth Gronland and George Lewis, "How a Limited National Missile Defense Would Impact the ABM Treaty," *Arms Control Today* (November 1999): 11.

3. National Intelligence Council (NIC), U.S. Central Intelligence Agency, "Foreign Missile Developments and the Ballistic Missile Threat to the United States Through 2010," unclassified summary, September 1999.

4. Over the past two and a half years the author has participated in a number of security and strategically oriented conferences, meetings, and discussions with Chinese interlocutors in official positions as well as researchers and scholars from semi-official Chinese institutes and think tanks. In virtually all cases, these encounters were on a not-for-attribution basis. This face-to-face experience has been put into context by the scholarly work and fortunate interactions I have had with serious scholars of the People's Liberation Army and their approach to nuclear weapons and strategic systems such as Paul Godwin, Iain Johnston, David Shambaugh, David Finkelstein, Bonnie Glaser, Banning Garrett, and especially Gill Bates, James Mulvenon, and Brad Roberts.

5. A draft paper by Iain Johnston, prepared for a March 2000 conference on "International Reactions to U.S. Ballistic Missile Defense" held by Stanford University's CISAC, entitled " A Compendium of Potential Chinese Responses to U.S. Ballistic Missile Defenses" includes an excellent synopsis of how China has closely tracked U.S. missile defense plans.

6. John Steinbruner, "National Missile Defense: Collision in Progress," *Arms Control Today* (November 1999).

7. Paul H. Godwin, "China's Nuclear Forces: An Assessment," *Current History* (September 1999): 260.

8. *The Bulletin of Atomic Scientists*, May-June 1999, cited in ibid., 263.

9. See for example, James R. Blaker, *Understanding the Revolution in Military Affairs: A Guide to America's 21st Century Defense*, Progressive Policy Institute, January 1997. The context in this example is toward preemption against both conventional military capability and weapons of mass destruction.

10. Adding an intercontinental bomber force to the PLA Air Force seems far fetched at this point. Sales from Russia cannot be totally discounted, although that would be a violation of START I. Most analysts credit Beijing

with plans to build additional submarines, but they must be able to elude and survive U.S. attack submarines to be considered a survivable leg of China's retaliatory force.

11. NIC, "Foreign Missile Developments," September 1999.

12. U.S. Department of Defense, "Selected Military Capabilities of the Peoples Republic of China," report to Congress, April 1997.

13. Gill Bates and James Mulvenon, "The Chinese Strategic Rocket Forces," *Bulletin of Atomic Scientists* (May-June 1999).

14. Statements of the Government of the People's Republic of China in John Lewis and Xue Litai, *China Builds the Bomb* (Stanford University Press, 1988), 241-242.

15. David Finkelstein, *China's New Security Concept: Reading Between the Lines*, a CNA Corporation Issue Paper, April 1999.

16. I am indebted to my colleague at CNA Corporation, Dr. David Finkelstein, for highlighting this point in a presentation at a recent conference on NMD sponsored by the State Department.

17. It is worth pointing out that many Russians do not believe this, knowing full well their own weaknesses and declining forces as well as declining reliability as their strategic forces age past notional service life. The U.S. government has simply not convinced them that the 5,900 warheads currently attributed to Russia could not, over the next decade, dwindle to a much lower number and still provide them with the ability to retaliate even with a limited U.S. NMD system.

Alexander A. Pikayev

Moscow's Matrix

O n April 14, 2000, in a surprising move after almost five years of inaction, the Russian Duma ratified the second Strategic Arms Reduction
Treaty (START II). According to this agreement, Russian and U.S. strategic nuclear forces are to be reduced to 3,500 deployed strategic warheads
each—almost half of the ceilings imposed by the START I Treaty. The ratification, however, is widely perceived as Moscow's attempt to intentionally
complicate possible U.S. withdrawal from the Anti-Ballistic Missile (ABM)
Treaty. The START II Treaty was ratified with amendments that make its
implementation very difficult—if not impossible—if the existing U.S.-Rus-
sian dispute over NMD deployments and the future of the ABM Treaty is
not resolved. Moreover, along with the START II ratification bill, the
Duma approved a nonbinding resolution asking the Russian president to
continue pressing for U.S. compliance to the ABM Treaty in exchange for
the START II instruments of ratification.

Russia's Security Calculations

Russia's opposition to NMD and its subsequent action on these treaties
is based on its difficult security dilemmas. There are concerns that

Alexander A. Pikayev is the codirector of the Non-Proliferation Program at the
Carnegie Moscow Center. He served as a professional staff member on the Duma
Defense Committee from 1994 to 1997.

Copyright © 2000 by The Center for Strategic and International Studies and the
Massachusetts Institute of Technology
The Washington Quarterly • 23:3 pp. 187–194.

"limited" U.S. NMD plans include deployments that could lead to a radical expansion of the system, including the capability to intercept a significant number of intercontinental ballistic missiles (ICBMs). In particular, Washington's plan includes orbiting space-based ABM sensors, which could considerably improve targeting and tracking capabilities of the potential NMD. Once effective surveillance, acquisition, targeting, and kill assessment systems are established, it would be much simpler for the United States to produce and deploy interceptors needed to cope with a large-scale missile attack. Thus, even if the number of deployed interceptors were limited by a modified ABM Treaty, it would provide Washington with significant breakout capability if it decides to abandon the treaty. In other words, deployed capability could be increased quite rapidly.

Current Russian strategic nuclear forces are powerful enough to penetrate a limited U.S. NMD. For economic reasons, however, their size will significantly decline in the future, perhaps to less than 1,000 deployed strategic warheads. Furthermore, the eastward enlargement of the North Atlantic Treaty Organization (NATO) and U.S. dominance in submarine warfare make Russian nuclear forces increasingly vulnerable to a first strike. As a result, a classic situation of instability would emerge: the Kremlin would fear that its modest nuclear forces could be considerably reduced by a first strike, and the retaliatory strike—made by the few surviving weapons—could be successfully intercepted even by a limited and relatively ineffective U.S. NMD. "Use it or lose it" incentives could threaten strategic stability.

U.S. NMD deployment together with increased capabilities to destroy Russian missiles could be sufficient to undermine Russian strategic nuclear deterrence. This would require Moscow to introduce certain countermeasures aimed at penetrating U.S. NMD. Those measures could include

- increasing overall ceilings for deployed strategic forces;
- maintaining them on a hair-trigger alert;
- re-MIRVing existing missiles and deploying decoys on them;[1]

- deploying maneuverable warheads able to escape collision with interceptors;
- resuming antisatellite programs aimed at neutralizing space-based NMD components;
- resuming routine patrol of submarines in open seas in order to circumvent the NMD system oriented to the north; and
- relying more on cruise missiles and aircraft, against which ABM defenses are only marginally successful.

On numerous occasions, the Russian military has indicated that it is developing countermeasures specifically targeting U.S. NMD. In June 1999, the Topol-M ICBM was successfully tested with a warhead capable of making "side maneuvers," aimed at avoiding collision with antimissile interceptors. Furthermore, in the autumn of 1999, authoritative military sources hinted that deploying submarine-launched ballistic missiles (SLBMs) might be considered a potential countermeasure against NMD. In November 1999 it was announced that production of SS-N-23 SLBMs would resume.

All of these measures will force Russia to increase spending on its strategic force modernization and could cause additional complications for the domestic treasury. In the near term, economic constraints would prevent Russia from engaging in an arms race in response to the U.S. NMD deployments. In the future, however, additional funding could enable Moscow to reduce strategic nuclear forces more slowly or settle for higher ceilings. A U.S. NMD might also affect the credibility of nuclear deterrence. During this decade, Russian strategic nuclear forces will be large enough to deter a first strike, but the credibility of their use could erode. Even a small NMD would reduce the opportunity to make a limited retaliatory strike, since it might be successfully intercepted.

The U.S. NMD deployments could also pose new security challenges for Russia from quite an unexpected direction—the Far East. In response to the U.S. plans to deploy NMD together with theater missile defense in the Asia-Pacific region, China has adopted a $10-billion nuclear modernization program. Reportedly, the Chinese are developing two new types of ballistic missiles—one against the United States, and the second against Russia. Beijing currently possesses only about three dozen missiles capable of hitting targets in North America, meaning they can be intercepted by even a modest NMD. In order to maintain the credibility of its nuclear deterrent, China will have to significantly increase this number, MIRV them, and consider developing sea-based deployments.

These developments would be detrimental not only for the United States but for Russia as well. The Chinese conventional weapon predominance vis-à-vis the vast but underpopulated Russian Far East is balanced by Moscow's superiority in nuclear weapons. China's nuclear buildup could erode this superiority, further weakening Russia's position in the Far East. This might force Moscow to withdraw from the 1987 Intermediate Nuclear Forces Treaty, which prohibits all U.S. and Russian land-based missiles with a range from 500 to 5,000 kilometers.

Worst Case Scenario

Although the United States and Russia have discussed ABM Treaty modification, negotiations to this point have produced little substantive progress. In January 1999, the United States requested that the Russian Federation modify the ABM Treaty in order to permit U.S. deployment of a limited NMD to protect U.S. territory from missile attacks by potential nuclear proliferators. In June 1999, then-President Boris Yeltsin agreed to bilateral talks to discuss how to maintain the ABM Treaty in the new security environment. Additionally, the United States and Russia agreed to continue talks on a new START III agreement, which would establish lower strategic nuclear ceilings for both countries than those imposed by the START II Treaty. In August 1999, the talks actually started, but they have shown little progress. Throughout this period, Russia has opposed the possibility of ABM Treaty modification. Despite growing recent speculations that the new administration of Vladimir Putin might agree to U.S. proposals under certain conditions, there is still little reason to assume that Moscow has decided to modify its position in accordance with U.S. requests.

Washington has communicated that if Russia continues to oppose the ABM Treaty modification, the United States would have to withdraw from it unilaterally. If the Clinton administration makes a decision on NMD deployment in June 2000, as expected, it could notify Russia of its intention to withdraw from the ABM Treaty as early as November 2000—six months before ground work on a new ABM site in Alaska should start. (A six-month notification is mandated by the ABM Treaty, and ABM deployment is prohibited in areas other than around the national capital or an ICBM base—neither of which is located in Alaska.)

If the United States withdraws from the ABM Treaty, the Russians have stated that they would be unable to implement START II. The START II ratification resolution mentions the ABM Treaty twice. Article 2 of the ratification bill specifies extraordinary circumstances under which Russia would have the right to withdraw in accordance with START II's Article VI. U.S. withdrawal from the ABM Treaty is specifically mentioned at the top of the list. Article 2 of the ratification bill stops short of requiring automatic cancellation of START II if the ABM Treaty is abrogated.

Conversely, Article 9 obligatorily links START II treaty implementation with the entry into force of ABM Treaty-related documents. It states that the exchange of instruments of ratification of START II by Russia will be delayed until the U.S. completes ratification of the START II Extension Protocol and the 1997 ABM Treaty Succession Memorandum together with ABM demarcation agreements. In other words, until the U.S. Senate ratifies those documents, START II would not be implemented. It should be noted that some Russian parliamentarians who assume that a Republican-dominated U.S. Senate would not ratify the 1997 agreements voted for START II ratification, hoping that it would never enter into force anyway. By doing so, they transferred the burden of the expected START II collapse to their U.S. colleagues.

Russian officials threatened to withdraw from other agreements as well. Due to economic constraints, it would be difficult for Russia to maintain strategic nuclear deployments at levels higher than those

stipulated in the existing START I Treaty. Moscow could stop implementing the agreement's intrusive verification regime, however, and
deprive Washington of the guaranteed transparency of Russian strategic
nuclear forces.

Although the Russian Ministry of Foreign Affairs have not confirmed it, some Russian experts speculate that Moscow could also withdraw from negotiations on the Verification Protocol to the Biological
Weapons Convention, currently held in Geneva, in protest.

Cooperative Scenarios

The first signs that compromise is possible emerged in early 2000 when
some Russian politicians hinted that they would use ABM Treaty modification as a bargaining chip for political support from Washington.
During a meeting between Putin and U.S. secretary of state Madeleine
Albright held in Moscow in late January, the new Kremlin leader did
not reject the idea of treaty modification nearly as bluntly as he dismissed U.S. appeals to change Russia's policy in Chechnya. Furthermore, while visiting Washington in February, the secretary of the
Russian Security Council, Sergei Ivanov, considered the transfer of the
only U.S. ABM deployment area from North Dakota to Alaska. This
can be interpreted as a positive sign because, as mentioned earlier, the
current treaty would only permit the U.S. deployment site around the
capital city or an ICBM base.

Additionally, the current Russian administration could seek a broad
deal on the ABM Treaty in exchange for debt restructuring and the renewal of International Monetary Fund (IMF) loans, sacrificing nuclear
parity for better relations with the West. Consisting of liberal reformers
associated with Anatoly Chubais and Yegor Gaidar, Putin's economic
team has prioritized Russia's incorporation into the world economy,
deemphasizing the importance of traditional security considerations advocated by the military and diplomatic establishment. In 1992, when a
similar economic team was in power in Moscow, Washington engaged
Russia in discussions on a large-scale revision of the ABM Treaty. If

concluded, these discussions would have permitted NMD deployments much more ambitious than the system currently sought by the Clinton administration.

The Kremlin recognizes that maintaining a good relationship with the West is needed to gain access to Western markets, capitals, and technologies. Such access is essential for Russia's economic recovery and modernization—clearly a national priority. Moscow also remains dependent on the West for restructuring of its foreign debt. Without it, Russia would have to spend up to 70 percent of all annual federal expenditures on debt payment over the next several years. Unlike Boris Yeltsin, however, Vladimir Putin is not universally recognized as a strong advocate of democratic reforms as displayed by his tough statements on the Chechen war. To improve its image with the West, the new Putin administration may be willing to make concessions in the arms control area, including the ABM Treaty.

In fact, the Kremlin could decide that, despite their other disagreements, the U.S.-Russian relationship is much less controversial than Moscow's current relationship with Western European countries. Moscow detected an asymmetry in Western criticism of its behavior in the northern Caucasus as European nations were more critical of Russia for human rights violations in Chechnya. It is conceivable that the Kremlin could try to revive the honeymoon in bilateral relations with Washington that flourished in the early 1990s. These considerations make it feasible that, despite the lack of practical steps to this point, Russia could agree to the ABM Treaty modification in order to establish sustainable relations with the United States. This will only evolve if Russia's initiatives are reciprocated by Washington.

Russia's room for maneuverability, on the other hand, is limited by domestic and international constraints. ABM Treaty modification might undermine relations with China, which has previously helped Moscow orchestrate an international campaign against the NMD deployments. Domestically, Vladimir Putin made his reputation as a pragmatic and tough leader by vigorously defending national interests and withstanding what was perceived as unfair international pressure on the Chechen issue. In the near term, this could help make him relatively impervious to hardliners' criticism, as opposed to Boris Yeltsin who was accused of making too many unnecessary concessions to the West. This carte blanche cannot work indefinitely, however, and Putin will have to struggle to differentiate himself from his widely discredited predecessor.

Putin will also have to take into account the national security establishment. The military seems to be united in its opposition to NMD plans. At a minimum, a relatively dovish group of officers from the Strategic Rocket Forces, formed around Defense Minister Marshal Sergeev, is institutionally suspicious of any ABM ideas. At the extreme, a more conservative faction inside the military tends to view NMD as just another Western attempt to disarm and weaken Russia. Although Putin is a strong president, he cannot completely alienate the military, especially as long as tension in Chechnya continues.

Conclusion

These factors complicate any Kremlin interest in reaching a deal with the United States on ABM Treaty modification. Therefore, it is likely that Moscow will only cooperate if the outcome is perceived to be balanced—reflecting the interests of both the United States and Russia. This thesis is supported by the dual-track tactic chosen by Russian diplomacy. Ratification of START II is considered a conciliatory gesture toward Washington. Simultaneously, conditions of the ratification were aimed at making the U.S. Senate responsible for the START II's failure if it will not ratify the 1997 ABM agreements. The timing of the ratification—a few weeks before opening the Nuclear Non-Proliferation Treaty (NPT) Review Conference in New York—supports the idea that Russia wanted added leverage over the United States in ABM Treaty negotiations.

Moscow has good reason to expect this strategy to be successful under any circumstances. If a bilateral deal on ABM Treaty modification is not achieved, Moscow can blame Washington. Alternatively, Russia can capitalize on its START II ratification to get a better deal.

In the arms control area, Russia remains interested in a new START III agreement through which it hopes to correct deficiencies of the START II Treaty. Specifically, Moscow seeks three main objectives. First, for avoiding costly production of new missiles needed to compensate those reduced under the START II, Russia asks for a lower (1,500 warheads) ceiling on strategic nuclear deployments instead of those levels (2,000-2,500) proposed by Washington. Second, Moscow wants to remove the START II ban on MIRVed ICBMs because it would be cheaper for Russia to produce a smaller number of missiles carrying several warheads each to maintain the same overall force levels.

Finally, Moscow seeks a solution to asymmetric rapid breakout capabilities. The United States can fulfill most of its START II obligations not by physically eliminating delivery vehicles, but by downloading (i.e., by removing extra warheads) from their carriers. Conversely, Russia has to physically destroy a major portion of its systems to meet their treaty commitments. If the treaty fails, the United States could quickly gain a significant advantage over Russia by returning downloaded warheads back to their missiles. This problem could be solved either by eliminating those downloaded warheads or by modifying the missile platforms to prevent their rapid return to delivery vehicles.

In the early 1990s, Russia and the United States failed to move their relationship beyond nuclear deterrence due to their preoccupation with arms control. It is important not to make the same mistake twice. Although traditional arms control remains a necessary and unavoidable tool to improve the bilateral political relationship, it is clearly insufficient to transform a Cold War rivalry into a sustainable partnership. That is why efforts should be made to complement the progress in traditional arms control with more far reaching and larger scale economic cooperation, especially in the area of defense technologies.

Note

1. A MIRV is a multiple independently targeted reentry vehicle; ICBMs with MIRVs are prohibited by START II.

Part III

Do Arms Races Matter Anymore?

Leon Fuerth

Return of the Nuclear Debate

In time, President George W. Bush's administration may release much more detail concerning its intentions for nuclear modernization, arms control, ballistic missile defense, space dominance, and the "transformation" of conventional forces.

These initiatives, though presented separately, actually relate to each other and can be best understood with reference to an organized concept of the United States' security needs moving forward into the twenty-first century. But the administration itself has announced no such overall concept. And yet, even if the administration really sees no connections between its choices about nuclear weapons and arms control, defenses and offense, and nuclear and conventional forces—even if the administration actually insists there are no connections—they do interact. It is a good thing for people to be conscious of how these interactions might work out.

The Administration's Case

The following, then, is an interpretation of what the administration appears to have in mind.

Leon Fuerth is the Shapiro Visiting Professor at the Elliott School of International Affairs at the George Washington University. He served as national security advisor to former vice president Al Gore from 1993 to 2001.

Copyright © 2001 by The Center for Strategic and International Studies and the Massachusetts Institute of Technology
The Washington Quarterly • 24:4 pp. 97–108.

• Arms control was at best a highly imperfect effort to regulate the military rivalry between the United States and the Soviet Union. In many ways, such agreements were little more than contracts allowing both sides to pursue next steps in the arms race that each had elected as desirable, arms control or not. At worst, arms control agreements may actually have channeled competition into even more dangerous technologies. Moreover, the price for these agreements was high in terms of unending squabbles about fine points, compliance, and verification—along with dismantling and inspection procedures that literally cost billions of dollars to operate.

• But by far the highest cost of arms control was that it locked the United States into the doctrine of mutually assured destruction (MAD). The objective of limiting offensive nuclear weapons was to find a way to make each side feel certain that, under even the most difficult conditions, it would always be able to destroy an aggressor. The purpose of the Anti-Ballistic Missile (ABM) Treaty was to reinforce this "security" by making it impossible for either side to develop a defense of its national territory. However, the ABM Treaty also perpetuated MAD, which was fine so long as MAD was the best arrangement both sides could envision to deter the other.

• Things are now radically different. The Cold War is over; Russia is too weak to be a threat; and, besides, relations with it are basically good. Therefore, the levels and kinds of nuclear weapons available to the United States and to Russia are no longer reasons for mutual fear. In view of this, the United States and Russia should stop trying to regulate their strategic nuclear weapons by way of explicit, formal agreements and instead rely on "understandings" informally worked out and not legally binding. Both sides would be free to shape their nuclear forces as they please; political and economic realism will assure that this translates into spontaneous deep reductions all around.

• On the other hand, the United States faces an emerging new threat from weapons of mass destruction (WMD) in the hands of countries such as North Korea or Iran. To deal with this threat, the United States needs to develop and deploy ABM weapons. The Clinton administration was working on a limited defense—the so-called national missile defense (NMD)—but its heart was never really in the program, and the design was anemic. The United States should shorten the timetable to initial deployment and aim to make the system much more powerful from the outset. The ABM Treaty prevents the United States from doing this and is therefore an obstacle to self-defense. The treaty should be abandoned if Russia will not agree to liberally rewriting it.

• Russia was ready to fight against even the last administration's very limited NMD on the grounds that it constituted a first step toward a system ultimately big enough to threaten the credibility of their nuclear deterrent. In ratifying the second Strategic Arms Reductions Talks (START II) agreement, the Russian Duma attached a condition according to which the provisions of the treaty would not be executed if the United States did not commit itself to the continuance of the ABM Treaty. The United States should not be deterred by Russian opposition. Perhaps, in time, the U.S. government can persuade Russia to accept its word that U.S. defenses are not intended to be a threat. But if not, the United States should be prepared to pull out of the ABM Treaty. Doing so will produce no untoward consequences for the security of the United States. Russia cannot afford very impressive countermeasures. Russia has threatened that, if the United States pulls out of the ABM Treaty, Russia will pull out of all existing arms control agreements, but the United States can discount that as bluster. But if this warning turns out to be real, the United States is better off without such agreements in any event and, therefore, can dispense with them.

• The United States' allies are extremely nervous about all this and are very reluctant to give the United States their cooperation. But the United States can eventually persuade them to give up their reservations and to come along with it. Washington will have to promise them protection from ballistic missiles under a U.S. or a joint defensive shield. Honoring that commitment will require that the United States explore technologies and systems that cannot in any way be reconciled with the basic logic of the ABM Treaty, but the allies will value that promise more than they value the existing system of arms control. Besides, in the last analysis, what choice do they have?

- The United States does not much care what China thinks about this or what the Chinese government's responses might be. China has a relatively small number of intercontinental ballistic missiles (ICBMs), and the United States expects them to modernize that force with or without a U.S. decision to build missile defenses. Building defenses is unlikely, therefore, to result in any increase of the Chinese nuclear threat in excess of that which we already anticipate.

- On the other hand, building ballistic missile defenses would better prepare the United States for a confrontation with China over Taiwan. The United States should not only accept that a confrontation with China is in the cards, but should act on that assumption by profoundly reshaping—"transforming"—U.S. conventional military forces.

- By its nature, the military systems needed for a full-scale transformation of U.S. conventional forces will intensify U.S. dependence on space-based intelligence and battle management systems. Space must therefore be viewed as a zone of military operations where the United States must attain dominance. The United States may even need to develop space-based offensive weapons for use against ground targets.

- In particular, the United States should attempt to develop technologies for space-based defense against ballistic missiles and, if successful, should deploy them. The fact that space-based defenses really could threaten Russia's nuclear retaliatory forces ought not to prevent U.S. action. Russia will trust the United States. Besides, given the tremendous problems besetting the Russian government, what is its recourse? Once the Russian government acquiesces to earlier

phases of development and deployment of U.S. defenses, the precedents will be set anyway.

Critique: The Yardstick of Strategic Stability

It is fairly easy to pick out some of the highly questionable assumptions
that hold this chain of reasoning together. First, there is a readiness to
gamble hugely on unproven technologies and even on technologies not
yet invented. Second, there is eagerness, even zeal, to be rid of the
ABM Treaty long before the workability of an elaborate defense system
can be estimated, much less demonstrated. Third, there is a compla-
cent view of U.S. trustworthiness, to the point where one assumes that
all the rest of the world, friends and enemies alike, have merely to hear
what U.S. intentions are, and they will be reconciled. Fourth, there is a
facile dismissal of the ability of other countries to take actions against
the United States that this country would find truly damaging. Fifth,
there is a naïve model of history that sees the United States and Russia
as having attained durable friendship, and a very dangerous corollary
that fatalistically accepts China as the next great threat. Sixth, there is
radical impatience with the difficulties of negotiating agreements. And
seventh, there is an unproven and utterly reckless belief that the United
States does not need to regard nuclear weapons, ballistic missile defenses, and space warfare as mutually interactive. The administration
may believe that a framework encompassing strategic and defensive
weapons must be accepted to mollify Russia, but it is very likely to view
that framework as a means to relax rather than to clarify linkages between offense and defense.

It is this last point that may be the most serious deficiency of all because it denies the relevance of any effort to gauge the net impact of a
complex set of proposed changes against some standard value of what is
good for the United States. There is such a standard. It is called strategic stability. One ought not to pretend that strategic stability is a scientific unit of measure. It does involve modeling and calculations at some
level, but then moves on to a heavy mixture of history, political sci-

ence, and even intuition. Despite these imprecisions, however, strategic stability offers a clear statement of what the goals of the United States should be: that its nuclear weapons and its doctrines about how and when to use them should decrease, rather than increase, the likelihood of being forced into an otherwise undesired conflict. A fundamental corollary to this definition of strategic stability is that it does not exist for any one party unless it exists for all. Hence, it cannot be imposed; it must be set in place by mutual consent.

The concept of strategic stability evolved over a lengthy period of time. Until the advent of modern arms control in the late 1960s, there was no means in place to constrain rivalry between the United States and the Soviet Union over nuclear weapons and delivery systems. Each side imputed the worst intentions to the other and reacted to every new weapons development—rumored or real—as a further proof of hostility. Consequently, each side sought to offset any perceived advantage accruing to the other. It was soon clear that, because neither side could ever allow the other to enjoy what it would regard as marked overall supremacy, the arms race might continue indefinitely in a kind of rolling stalemate.

The first Strategic Arms Limitation Talks (SALT I) treaty, signed in 1972, attempted to end this cycle, but mainly rechanneled it. Limits on the number of launchers for ICBMs perversely encouraged both sides to speed the deployment of multiple independently targetable reentry vehicles (MIRVs) on those launchers remaining. Each side watched the other deploying more and more warheads on fewer missiles. The net result was to increase a sense of vulnerability on each side. As the number of MIRVs deployed per launcher increased, and as improvements in accuracy were made, each side feared the other was acquiring the means to carry out a first strike against the other's ICBMs.

Prospective defenses against ballistic missiles added to this growing sense of insecurity, because if either side were able to effectively protect its national territory, it might be even more tempted to think of launching a first strike. To be more concrete, the idea was that one side might think that it would be able to destroy a substantial portion of the other's retaliatory force in a first strike, and then use its ABM shield to deal with the response. The ABM Treaty was negotiated to settle this fear, by denying each party the means to build the necessary shield, but it also locked both sides into a condition of permanent mutual vulnerability.

The START II agreement, signed in 1993, was a deliberate effort to break this cycle by shaping the offensive forces of both sides in such a way as to negate even the hypothetical advantages of a first strike. Both sides agreed to begin de-MIRVing their ballistic missiles, while reducing them in number. The result would be a smaller overall force but, perhaps even more importantly, a force that both sides believed would be intrinsically more stable. That is to say, there would be a balance between the nuclear forces of both sides such that neither would have reason to believe that the other could objectively benefit from launching a first strike. Defenses were to remain bounded by the ABM Treaty, which now acquired a new value: as a means to facilitate deeper reductions by reducing the fear that radically improved and expanded defenses might create a first-strike capability at a much lower overall offensive weapons level.

START II responded to three fundamental axioms about strategic stability: first, that reductions alone may not necessarily produce a better, more crisis-resistant situation; second, that the relationship between offensive forces needs to be consciously designed to produce this effect; and third, that reductions may continue to progressively lower levels, providing that (1) the resultant balance is always arranged with a view toward stability and that (2) defenses are not allowed to become a wild card.

If all this sounds arcane, it was. The possibility that either Washington or Moscow would actually think it wise to launch a first strike may have been very small. But the fear that each side felt about this was real because it was based on the actual capabilities of weapons and on a reading of human psychology. START II recognized that this fear had to be addressed through a mutually acceptable, ergo negotiated, arrangement.

Obviously, the world has changed tremendously since the days when START II was negotiated, but strategic arithmetic is the same as always. And so is human nature. Strategic arithmetic tells us that deep reductions can lead to results that damage strategic stability, if they are not worked out on a mutual basis. Unilateral reductions are a role of the dice, by comparison. Chances that things will work out for the worse are at least 50/50. And if they do work out for the worse, basic human instincts will take over: the fear of the other's intentions, based on the fear of the other's capabilities, will again acquire the power to drive events. If, at the same time, the ABM Treaty falls away so that the defensive side of the stability equation becomes completely unpredictable, paranoia about first strikes will be reestablished.

The administration argues that, because the Cold War is over, the need for arms control has disappeared. In doing so, the administration uses profound changes in the real world to rationalize old policies dressed up as new. The administration asserts complete freedom of action for the United States, including the right to dispense with the Comprehensive Test Ban Treaty (CTBT), the ABM Treaty, and any other arms control agreements that might perish along with them.

In the real world, however, attention must be paid to the interests and considerations of others if the United States is not to end up isolated and unable to marshal support for issues that matter greatly to U.S. principles and even U.S. security. Arms control remains necessary precisely in order to build durable structures for order and stability in the twenty-first century. The United States needs it to regulate and balance out strategic nuclear forces; it needs it to open a path toward progressively deeper reductions in those forces; it needs it to have the transparency and legal structure needed to dispel uncertainty and stop paranoia from putting down new roots. "Good fences make good neighbors" remains a simple truth.

Consequences: A Renewed Arms Race

Following Bush's meeting with Russian president Vladimir Putin at the G-8 meeting in Genoa, the administration is now able to test its theories with Russia. The stakes are extremely high. In the worst case, the administration's course of action can literally reignite the arms race. One should think carefully about what that would mean.

Even though the Russian government is strapped for cash, the fact is that ballistic missiles and nuclear warheads are relatively cheap (land-based systems, that is). Russia has throw-weight to spare on their existing ICBM force and could load up to maximum, something that it did not do even in the Cold War. The Russian nuclear weapons establishment still has the capacity to manufacture at arms-race levels. The U.S. weapons establishment, by the way, is drastically smaller than in the past and is in no position to compete, nor would it be for at least a decade.

So Russia could rapidly build up its inventory of online strategic warheads without fielding new missiles. That would be the obvious, brute-force response to a U.S. move that potentially threatened the credibility of Russia's nuclear deterrent in its eyes. Credibility is at least as much a matter of subjective impression as it is of force-planners' calculations. It does not matter what the United States thinks of Russia's deterrent, or vice versa; it only matters what each country thinks of itself—and in existential calculations of this sort, too much is never enough. The prompt Russian reaction could thus easily be to build up their forces.

Such a buildup would also obliterate what progress the two countries have made toward strategic stability because increasing the numbers of warheads loaded on ICBMs would progressively add to the value of the Russian land-based launchers as targets for the United States, or so Russia would reason. Now, any American may think it would be an act of insanity for the United States to contemplate a first strike, but the whole point is that our opinion does not matter: it is the opinion of the Russian side that is dispositive.

There would also be immense opportunity costs. In the atmosphere of a renewed arms race, it is unlikely that the United States would be able to make progress toward what should be its follow-on goals at this moment: START III, with lower final levels than those agreed at Helsinki; reduction of the Russian nuclear arms complex to post–Cold War size; transparency arrangements for nuclear weapons in storage; accountability for inventories of bomb-grade fissionable materials; continuity of the joint program for U.S. purchases of Russian bomb-grade uranium blended down into fuel-grade for U.S. power reactors; execution of agreements just completed for the safe disposition of plutonium; and negotiation of a treaty for the cessation of further production of bomb-grade fissionable material. In theory, one supposes, programs premised on remarkably intimate cooperation might continue even in the midst of a new arms race, but that flies in the face of any sensible reading of political and psychological reality.

To this list of costs, one should also add the possibility that Russia will act on its threat to abrogate all other arms control agreements, including perhaps the Intermediate-Range Nuclear Force (INF) Treaty, which eliminated SS-20s, ground-launched cruise missiles, and Pershing IIs aimed at the heart of Europe. Never mind, of course, that the United States will promise to protect Europe under a U.S. ballistic missile shield. Who will pay for that additional safety? The North Atlantic Treaty Organization (NATO) allies have already reduced military spending so much that they are running hollowed-out armed forces. If the NATO allies were prepared to spend billions more on defense, one would hope that the money would go first to remedy their tremendous weaknesses in conventional forces. Or is the United States supposed to foot the bill? And if so, then at what cost to the U.S. military posture?

Of course, it might be that Russia is simply too short of money to take any of these steps, but that does not mean reconciliation with U.S. behavior. On the contrary, it would inspire a slow-burning desire to even the score. At some point, sooner or later, Russia would have its chance. It is folly to imagine that the history of Russia as a great power has been written and sealed.

As for China, its resources may limit it only to modernization in forms it was already pursuing. In that case, China may deploy road-mobile ICBMs that are harder to target, and push forward until it has the technology to MIRV these, to maximize the chance of overwhelming a U.S. defensive shield. China is, however, a country whose gross domestic product (GDP) grows at about 8 percent a year and will not lack for means for much longer. Thus, one should not ignore the possibility of a major expansion of Chinese ballistic missile forces. Meanwhile, the United States will have built into the Chinese political system a deepening conviction that the United States is an implacable enemy. The United States will therefore be building momentum toward confrontation that could unleash the nuclear war it was fortunate enough to avoid with the Soviet Union.

A final word about our allies. In the end, faced with an atmosphere of inevitability, and the choice of resisting the United States to the point of severely damaging alliances, U.S. friends may swallow their objections and acquiesce. If this happens, however, it will be yet another galling example for the allies of their dependence on the United States and of a style of U.S. leadership they consider both arrogant and reckless. If a new arms race does materialize, the consequences for relations between the United States and its allies will be disastrous.

A Constructive Alternative

All this having been said, there are some valid elements in the administration's position. It is possible to stipulate that (1) the proliferation of weapons of mass destruction and the means to deliver them to the United States represents a potential, important oncoming threat; (2) if these threats continue to develop, it would be appropriate for the United States to have developed and, as necessary, deployed a proportionate, limited defense; and (3) deeper reductions of nuclear weapons than those provided for in the START II agreement are acceptable and desirable.

But there are critical qualifications. Those qualifications should be the organizing issues of the national debate the United States needs the Congress to undertake. This debate would be most meaningful in Congress. From the congressional perspective, possible elements of a constructive alternative are:

- Given a choice between defensive technologies that require a reasonable modification of the ABM Treaty and more aggressive technologies that require the treaty's abrogation, the United States should prefer the former. Such a choice exists. It is the NMD system, whose development commenced under the last administration.

- The United States should explicitly avoid developing technologies that can be scaled up to threaten to neutralize the entire Russian nuclear deterrent. Space-based interception of ballistic missiles is such a technology and should not be on the U.S. agenda.

- The United States should explore technologies for attacking ballistic missiles during boost phase, using land- or sea-based interceptors. However, these technologies should be viewed as hedges in case of the appearance of second-generation ballistic missile delivery systems in the hands of rogue states (e.g., systems MIRVed or with penetration aids). Moreover, the United States should offer to develop such systems jointly with Russia.

- The United States should resist an effort to rush to deploy an improvised boost-phase defense. Haste is unnecessary and, notwithstanding what the administration is likely to say in support of such defenses, they are in fact technologically immature and present very serious issues of crisis stability.

- Vigorous work should continue on theater ballistic missile defenses, up to and including deployment. However, the U.S. Congress should refuse to fund work on theater defenses that would violate the memorandum of understanding on succession to the ABM Treaty signed with Russia in 1997, which established an upper limit for the performance of theater ballistic missile interceptors.

- Any proposal for deeper reductions of nuclear weapons than those agreed at Helsinki (2,000–2,500) must be preceded by a thorough review of the implications for U.S. security and must be accompanied by testimony from the Joint Chiefs of Staff (JCS) as to military sufficiency under existing guidance. The deeper the proposed cut, the more imperative it is to be sure that what the military says truly reflects their private judgment, as opposed to the political line one can expect to hear from the Pentagon's civilian leadership.

- Unilateral reductions certified by the JCS as militarily sound could be considered, particularly if the case can be made that savings are important for other military applications. Such recommendations should be preceded by persuasive arguments concerning stability, including an assessment of how different end-states for the United States and Russia might influence perceptions of stability. Finally, Congress should not fund such reductions unless the administration either has worked out thorough arrangements for mutual verification with Russia, in binding form, or has presented a convincing case for why the United States should have no concern regarding the disposition of hundreds of Russian strategic nuclear warheads. There is no need to rush into unilateral reductions. Patience should rule.

- The dollar costs of a ballistic missile defense must be convincingly presented, along with the means for financing them. Trade-offs between developing defenses and paying for the "transformation" of our conventional military forces must be presented clearly and discussed. The U.S. government should not agree to a missile defense project with open-ended costs, to be paid for either at the expense of military readiness or modernization/transformation.

- We should not follow an artificially accelerated timetable, or one that deliberately moves to destroy the ABM Treaty simply to explore whether one technology or another is likely to work.

- If, after thoroughly testing technologies that are candidates for deployment, after getting the best cost estimates possible, and if the efforts of rogue states to proliferate continue, the United States should be prepared to deploy. At that juncture, if Russia—having been thoroughly consulted beforehand—still objects and has been unwilling to work out an amendment to the ABM Treaty, the United States would be obliged to let national interest govern its actions, notwithstanding Russian views. The U.S. government should use the intervening time to make similar efforts to talk through these issues with China. As a nonsignatory to the ABM Treaty, China has no say in its fate, but every effort should be made to enter into a serious strategic dialogue with China.

- Despite the administration's announced intention not to seek ratification of the CTBT, Congress should refuse to fund new programs for nuclear weapons development or testing. Congress should, however, be prepared to spend any reasonable amount on stockpile management in order to assure the viability of the U.S. reserve. It should also make clear that legal restraints on funding for testing will expire if another of the CTBT's original nuclear state signatories were to start testing.

- Whether or not an NMD system is deployed, Congress should both demand and support a comprehensive program to combat proliferation and to protect the U.S. homeland against the possible infiltration of weapons of mass destruction, which could turn out to be a vulnerability as great, if not greater than, exposure to any future threat of ballistic missile attack by a rogue state.

- Given the potential expense of an NMD system of even the most modest proportions, the overall impact on the availability of funds for modernizing conventional military forces needs to be assessed. The United States will continue to need conventional military forces with balanced capabilities for dealing with a wide range of contingencies.

These, then, could be the outlines of a responsible political stance in the face of steamroller tactics from the administration, and they could also, ultimately, be the basis for an emerging compromise. Those who take the lead in this debate may be characterized as lacking vision. On the contrary, they will be looking out for all of us.

Keith B. Payne

Action-Reaction Metaphysics and Negligence

O n May 1 of this year, President George W. Bush called for a new strategic framework, one allowing the United States "to build missile defenses to counter the different threats of today's world" and encouraging "further cuts in nuclear weapons."[1] The president's initiative signals Washington's first truly significant departure from its Cold War strategic policy.

Despite dramatic changes in the international system, for eight years the United States has perpetuated the main themes of U.S. Cold War strategic policy. It embraced the Anti-Ballistic Missile (ABM) Treaty, and thereby the 1960s' deterrence concept of mutually assured destruction (MAD), as the basis for U.S.-Russian strategic relations and arms control negotiations. Correspondingly, the United States perpetuated the legalistic, adversarial strategic arms control process that characterized the Cold War. When the central organizing principle of negotiations is to keep mutual capabilities for nuclear annihilation codified, prospects for political amity are limited. This process was incompatible with the new realities of the post–Cold War landscape, precluding any significant, new strategic arms agreement during the Clinton administration.

Keith B. Payne is president of the National Institute for Public Policy, editor in chief of *Comparative Strategy*, and adjunct professor in the Security Studies Program at Georgetown University.

Copyright © 2001 by The Center for Strategic and International Studies and the Massachusetts Institute of Technology
The Washington Quarterly • 24:4 pp. 109–121.

As described, the new strategic framework will include the possibility of U.S. unilateral nuclear reductions, in conjunction with the deployment of ballistic missiles defenses (BMD). The president's readiness to leave behind Cold War deterrence concepts and arms control processes is clear.

Obviously discarded, for example, is the belief that has been at the heart of U.S. Cold War arms control policy since the 1960s: that strategic missile defense must undermine deterrence stability and preclude nuclear arms reductions. As several critics of U.S. missile defense have rightly noted, "The SALT I and II negotiations were premised on the assumption that limitations on strategic offensive forces would not be possible without extensive constraints on strategic defenses."[2] Bush's call for both nuclear force reductions and missile defense deployment poses a direct challenge to this foundation of Cold War thinking.

Much of the arms control establishment was in high dudgeon following the president's speech. Great resentment greeted his challenge to Cold War–vintage sacred cows and conceptual shibboleths. Missile defense opponents again repeated the SALT I–era assertion that U.S. BMD deployment can only lead challengers to add to their offensive ballistic missile capabilities, thereby overshadowing U.S. defenses and leaving the United States more threatened than it was prior to building the defense. The bottom line of this 1960s-era argument, of course, is that the United States should not start this "action-reaction" process by deploying national missile defenses. As Yogi Berra said, "It's like déjà vu all over again."

The supposed certainty of an action-reaction cycle in response to U.S. missile defense has been so popularized during the previous decades that the charge is asserted gravely as if gospel with every new BMD debate. The only change in today's version of this prediction from its 1960s roots is that Russia is no longer identified as the only potential challenger sure to respond to U.S. defenses with an offensive missile buildup. China, North Korea, and others are now similarly certain to be driven to an unbeatable offensive reaction.

For example, a former senior official in the Clinton administration warned recently that, although the United States cannot perfect missile defense technology, "[e]ven if it were possible, the program would motivate a response from adversaries that would inevitably offset the defense."[3] A recent commentary in the normally staid *Business Week* confidently predicted that, in response to U.S. missile defense, "China ... is bound to expand its arsenal. It certainly won't stand by and let its small retaliatory capability be blunted by our defense system."[4] A joint publication by the Federation of American Scientists, the Natural Resources Defense Council, and the Union of Concerned Scientists similarly asserts that U.S. missile defense "will almost certainly spur China to compensate by building more missiles, both to overwhelm the defense and to make this capability evident to the United States."[5] Now, even North Korea will surely follow this action-reaction cycle: "North Korea can be expected to step up the development and production of long-range ICBMs, inevitably with multiple warheads."[6] Worse yet, according to a former U.S. State Department official, "With China increasing its missiles, India and Japan, and then Pakistan, would follow suit, inciting a worldwide arms race."[7] Such confident predictions understandably scare those who believe they reflect more than just hackneyed speculation.

Debunking the Myth

What should one think of this mechanistic prediction that U.S. BMD deployment will cause potential foes to add to their offensive missile arsenals that, in turn, will increase the missile threat to the United States and instigate a "worldwide arms race"? Its strength is its elegance. The logic could not be simpler: if we build defenses, opponents will not accept a diminution in their capability to threaten the United States with ballistic missiles. They will react by building more offensive missiles, thereby restoring their threat. Everyone understands this model of the arms race. In fact, so widespread is the belief in its predictive power that some refer to the action-reaction arms race cycle as the "first law of nuclear politics."[8] For decades it has been employed as such by opponents of missile defense.

The political nature of that use is often reflected in its inconsistency. The danger of missile defenses instigating an action-reaction arms race, if real, should apply as much to defenses against tactical- and theater-range missiles as to defenses against long-range missiles. Yet, its proponents typically level the charge nearly exclusively against the latter. Indeed, some frequently call for theater missile defenses as the "first priority" alternative to defenses against long-range missiles. In this case, when defenses against shorter-range offensive missiles are couched as the preferred alternative to strategic defenses, the great concern about instigating an action-reaction arms race curiously disappears.

As a political polemic, the argument that strategic missile defense will cause an arms race has an enormous advantage: for any specific future case, no one can demonstrate in a scientific sense that the contention is total nonsense. It deals with predictions of an opponent's behavior. Thus, no one can "prove" that U.S. defenses will not initiate an action-reaction cycle. The prospects for such a cycle may be quite limited for a host of reasons, and those who continue to assert that U.S. defenses surely will lead to an arms race are likewise limited in their capacity to predict the future. These facts, however, typically do not reduce the absolute certainty with which many opposed to missile defense predict an arms race. They are, after all, simply restating what by now is a well-known "law" of international relations.

The elegance of the action-reaction arms race model and its constant repetition apparently overshadow the fact that, as a basis for actually predicting opponents' behavior, it is highly speculative at best. The notion that it represents a law of international relations would be laughable if the subject were not serious. The use of this model for years against missile defense is evidence of the unfortunate fact that, if a vapid assertion is made loudly, often, and by influential voices, it can become accepted wisdom, even a law. Mistakenly believing that a crude action-reaction model of the arms race is a law guarantees misplaced confidence in predictions based on it.

MIT professor George Rathjens, an early "discoverer" of the action-reaction arms race model as applied to U.S. missile defense, has long since acknowledged its significant limitations.[9] Unfortunately, that acknowledgement has not stilled others' hubris in the use of that model during U.S. missile defense debates, including the current one. For example, in a recent article aptly entitled, "Don't Know Much about History," Stephen Schwartz claims that the action-reaction model was reflected "at every key juncture in the Soviet-American competition." Therefore, says Schwartz, no one should doubt that the Chinese now will "respond to a U.S. missile defense system by deploying additional weapons."[10] This grave prediction, of course, is supposed to close the question.

Beyond the telltale, selective use of the action-reaction arms race charge, what is wrong with it? In principle, nothing is amiss with the observation that one can trace some decisions to deploy or to upgrade forces to an action-reaction dynamic. This type of interaction to some extent certainly appears to have shaped U.S. strategic bomber programs and Soviet air defenses during the Cold War—the strengthening of Soviet air defenses spurred the modernization of U.S. strategic bombers. The problem, however, is that numerous other factors typically drive decisions about the forces a country will—or will not—develop and deploy. The Cold War action-reaction model has been elevated to a law or maxim despite the fact that it may be only partially in play, or be wholly irrelevant, to many armament decisions. When many factors can determine decisions about force acquisition, confident predictions based on a single, possible dynamic are likely to be misleading.

Although extreme caution should accompany any prediction of an arms race based on the action-reaction model, we are constantly treated to frightening predictions of absolute certainty: China and North Korea will respond to U.S. defenses with a buildup of offensive missiles, and U.S. defenses will not be capable of coping with these new offensive forces. Two very specific predictions are imbedded in this mantra, and neither is certain. First, challengers will respond in a particular fashion, in this case by adding to their offensive missile arsenals. Second, that reply will overcome U.S. missile defenses.

This latter part of the mantra is akin to Stanley Baldwin's famous dictum, "The bomber will always get through." In a recent French repudiation of U.S. missile defense goals, President Jacques Chirac took Baldwin's maxim, broadened it, and made it even more definitive: "[In the] struggle between sword and shield, there is no instance in which the shield has won."[11] Consequently, according to this simple logic, defense is hopeless. Foes simply will overwhelm U.S. missile defenses by adding to their offensive missile arsenals in response.

The Historical Record

From the late 1960s to the present, the first-order response to U.S. missile defense initiatives by political opponents has been to assert this logic with confidence, pointing to all historical evidence as proof. The supposed historical proof of the "inevitable" superiority of the offense, however, is nonsense. Defensive measures have frequently, and for long stretches of history, dominated the offense. Athens's defensive walls, for example, precluded a bloody invasion by Sparta in the Peloponnesian War. The defensive walls of Constantinople provided security for nearly a thousand years. British air and naval defenses shut down the planned Nazi invasion of the British Isles, Hitler's "Operation Sea Lion." Of course, Karl von Clausewitz considered defense in general to be the stronger form of warfare. Obviously, the lethality of nuclear weapons would necessitate extremely effective defenses if comprehensive protection for cities against a large-scale ballistic missile attack by a peer challenger were the goal. This, however, is not the declared U.S. goal, and whether powerful new defensive technologies, such as "exotic" beam weapons, will make this type of defense possible in the future is not known; but it hardly can be ruled out as if by some inevitable law of history. Historical evidence supports neither the assertion that offense must dominate defense nor the argument that an action-reaction arms race cycle is inevitable. In fact, predictions based on the action-reaction model have often proven to be far different from the subsequent course of events.

That model, for example, provided much of logic behind the 1972 ABM Treaty. Opponents of missile defense claimed at the time that an action-reaction arms-race dynamic "is precisely what fuels the arms race"[12] and that "the action-reaction phenomenon, with the reaction often premature and/or exaggerated, has clearly been a major stimulant of the strategic arms race."[13] The typical prediction, therefore, was that U.S. BMD deployment would stimulate a "new round in the arms race," but that the limitation of BMD by the ABM Treaty would provide the basis for precluding the further buildup of Soviet offensive missiles. U.S. "inaction" with regard to missile defense would, it was argued, lead to Soviet "inaction" vis-à-vis additional offensive missile capabilities.

The logic of the action-reaction model in this regard was elegant: if the United States built missile defenses, the Soviets would deploy unbeatable additional offensive missile capabilities in response, leaving the United States no more secure following its deployment of defenses. In contrast, if the United States forewent missile defense, the Soviets would have no incentive to add to their offensive missile forces, and negotiated offensive limitations could go forward. BMD opponents contended that, in the absence of "destabilizing" U.S. missile defenses, the Soviets could agree to offensive missile limitations, and the action-reaction cycle would be broken.

This supposed linkage between U.S. missile defense and Soviet incentives to build new offensive capabilities, based on the action-reaction arms-race model, was clearly a primary rationale for the ABM Treaty. As Henry Kissinger stated at the time:

> By setting a limit to ABM defenses, the [ABM] [T]reaty not only eliminates one area of dangerous defensive competition, but it reduces the incentive for continuing deployment of offensive systems. As long as it lasts, offensive missile forces have, in effect, a free ride to their targets.[14]

Subsequent developments, however, were the reverse of the BMD opponents' confident predictions, demonstrating the fragility of the action-reaction model. In the absence of U.S. missile defense, the Soviet Union pursued the greatest buildup of strategic offensive missile capabilities in history. The number of deployed Soviet intercontinental ballistic missile (ICBM) warheads increased from 1,547 in 1972 to 6,420 in 1985, and Soviet submarine-launched ballistic missile (SLBM) warheads increased from 497 in 1972 to 2,307 in 1985.[15] Foregoing missile defense hardly checked the Soviet Union's incentives to expand its missile capabilities. In fact, they increased by orders of magnitude following the signing of the ABM Treaty. As Harold Brown, President Jimmy Carter's defense secretary, concluded in 1979, "When we build, they build; when we stop building, they nevertheless continue to build."[16]

Clearly, factors unrelated to U.S. missile defense and unaccounted for by the action-reaction model drove Soviet decisions regarding the buildup of its offensive missile capabilities powerfully. Reality dashed sanguine U.S. expectations, based fully on the action-reaction model, of Soviet offensive moderation following the ABM Treaty's signing; the model proved hopelessly inadequate as the basis for these predictions. Indeed, according to Colonel General Nikolai Detinov, a key player in Soviet arms control policy throughout the period, the Soviet leadership never accepted U.S. logic in this regard. Rather, Washington's proposal for an ABM treaty came as a "pleasant surprise" because it allowed Moscow to devote resources fully to its planned buildup of ICBMs. Consequently, as William Odom concludes in his unparalleled study of the Soviet military, "Thus the ABM [T]reaty appeared to have allowed a considerably larger number of offensive nuclear weapons in the Soviet arsenal than there would have been without it."[17] The ABM Treaty actually facilitated the Soviet ICBM buildup. This outcome, of course, was the reverse of what BMD opponents had predicted with such confidence.

Nevertheless, when President Ronald Reagan set in motion the next great missile defense debate with his 1983 Strategic Defense Initiative, missile defense opponents again predicted with absolute certainty the same frightening action-reaction cycle. "The Soviet Union would be certain to respond, by developing countermeasures and increasing its offensive forces to ensure that the U.S. defense could be penetrated."[18] Furthermore, again, they asserted that the ABM Treaty was necessary for success in offensive force reductions by arguing that

> limits on missile defenses are the necessary base for negotiated limits on offensive strategic missiles. ... The ABM Treaty is even more critical today, as the focus of negotiation shifts from limitations to reductions in strategic arms. It is clear that there will be no strategic

arms reduction (START) agreement unless the ABM Treaty is maintained, and limits on defenses will be even more essential as the United States and the Soviet Union negotiate subsequent agreements for deeper reductions.[19]

As four former senior officials warned at the time, "Star Wars, in sum, is a prescription not for ending or limiting the threat of nuclear weapons, but for a competition unlimited in expense, duration and danger. ... [I]t is possible to reach good agreements, or possible to insist on the Star Wars program as it stands, but wholly impossible to do both."[20]

Subsequent developments, however, again proved the inadequacy of the action-reaction model and the hubris of predictions derived from it. On October 5, 1991, in the context of a relatively robust U.S. missile defense program and congressional endorsement of BMD deployment in the Missile Defense Act of 1991, Soviet president Mikhail Gorbachev announced, "We are ready to discuss U.S. proposals on nonnuclear defensive systems. We propose to study the possibility of creating a joint system to avert nuclear missile attack with ground- and space-based elements."[21] Shortly thereafter, at the June 1992 Washington summit, President Boris Yeltsin and President George Bush agreed to a START II framework for nuclear force reductions, including the elimination of ICBMs with multiple warheads; simultaneously, they agreed to work toward cooperation on global missile defenses. The subsequent Ross-Mamedov talks made surprising progress toward this goal until derailed by the Clinton administration in 1993. Most importantly for this discussion, this progress was made while Russia and the United States successfully concluded START negotiations that would, for the first time in history, lead to agreed reductions in strategic offensive forces.

Complexity Is Reality

Once again, the action-reaction model proved to be completely inadequate as a basis for prediction. Following the signing of the ABM Treaty, the promises of missile defense opponents based on the model went unrealized, and the actual course of events moved in a dramatically different direction. Reality this time brought simultaneous progress toward missile defense and offensive reductions, the reverse of what BMD opponents had starkly and confidently predicted in the late 1960s and in the 1980s. The inadequacy of the action-reaction model as employed by most BMD opponents has been increasingly manifest for decades; those who now continue to repeat confident promises derived from it appear to be engaging in strategic negligence.

Why have missile defense critics been so wrong in their predictions? In short, numerous factors drive armament decisions, and the simplistic action-reaction formulation does not account for most of them.[22] For example, the theory ignores such basic factors as:

- competing foreign policy goals and defense requirements,
- inter- and intraservice rivalries,
- bureaucratic politics,
- the specific character and style of political and social systems,
- electoral politics,
- resource availability or limitations,
- organizational momentum, and
- technological innovation/limitation.

Even highly personal and idiosyncratic factors can drive armament decisionmaking. Adolf Hitler, for example, canceled the V-2 program on the basis of a bad dream he had about the missile. Only the combined efforts of Albert Speer and Wernher von Braun got the program back on track.

When observers ignore these potentially significant factors in favor of a simplistic rendition of the action-reaction model, grossly inaccurate predictions likely result. Such factors, singularly and in combination, have frequently produced patterns that bear no resemblance whatsoever to the crude action-reaction model typically expressed by missile defense critics. They can lead to action-inaction, inaction-reaction, and noninteractive armament decisions.

For example, Soviet heavy-bomber capabilities did not develop in accord with the action-reaction model. Neither the significant buildup of

U.S. national air defense throughout the 1950s and 1960s, nor their virtual elimination in the 1970s, drove the Soviet heavy-bomber threat in this fashion. No apparent, great Soviet strategic bomber buildup corresponded to the U.S. defensive buildup, nor did dramatic change follow U.S. elimination of its strategic air defenses. In other words, no action-reaction cycle occurred. In fact, the most obvious Soviet strategic bomber modernization programs that did occur—the Bear G, Bear H, and the Blackjack—came after the United States no longer had an appreciable strategic air defense capability.

Since the late 1990s, the United States has been on an obvious track toward some form of BMD, as numerous Russian officials have noted. Yet, Russian offensive ballistic missile capabilities are in the process of a relatively rapid drawdown, not an action-reaction buildup.

Of course, perfectly logical and understandable reasons for these deviations from a simplistic action-reaction cycle exist. In 1960, for example, Nikita Khrushchev made missiles, not bombers, the centerpiece of Soviet nuclear strategy. The Soviet Union never produced heavy strategic bombers in significant numbers; it focused instead on heavy ICBMs. More recently, the collapse of the Soviet Union and Russia's economic difficulties have limited (but not eliminated) Moscow's capability to deploy new offensive missile capabilities. That such factors can be significant to armament decisions is, of course, the point.

Cautious Predictions

Following Bush's announcement of a new strategic framework, which includes missile defense, commentators reissued dire predictions about the action-reaction arms race sure to follow. They point with supreme confidence to a crude action-reaction model as if it were a law of international relations, offering predictions that exclude the many other dynamics that frequently underlie armament decisions. These current predictions reflect no deeper apparent appreciation of the actual complexity of armament decisionmaking than have similar past predictions, and they are no more likely to be accurate.

Are China, North Korea, and other rogue states likely to react to U.S. missile defenses by undertaking an unbeatable offensive-defensive missile competition, as now is claimed with such certainty? Any answer, of course, is speculative, and humility should govern all efforts to anticipate future foreign decisionmaking.

Nevertheless, some basis exists for expecting that the mechanistic action-reaction model will not apply here any more than it has in celebrated cases of the past. As two prominent specialists on the Chinese military have observed, for example, no one can understand China's force structure decisions using such a crude model. "Rather, an understanding of such variables as domestic political, technological, historical, and cultural factors provide[s] far greater insight and predictive capacity about the drivers that shape China's doctrinal and force structure decisions."[23] The significance of these variables, of course, is not unique to China, which is why the action-reaction arms race model is so broadly inadequate.

Notably, China has been in the process of improving its ICBM force for years, possibly since the 1970s. For more than a decade, Chinese officials have clearly intended to replace or supplement China's reported current ICBM arsenal of approximately 20 operational DF-5As with the introduction of the DF-31 and DF-41 ICBMs now in development and (in the case of the DF-31) undergoing testing.[24]

U.S. missile defense plans may of course affect China's ICBM improvement programs, but multiple reasons for Chinese offensive missile modernization have long been in play in the absence of U.S. defenses. These reasons apparently include the natural process of updating old systems with newer ones; the requirement for greater ICBM force survivability and flexibility; and movement toward a Chinese nuclear doctrine that calls for "limited, counterforce, warfighting capabilities" as the basis for deterrence and coercion across a wide range of contingencies, including intrawar deterrence.[25] China is already well on the road toward modernization of its offensive missile force, at least in part for logical reasons ignored by the action-reaction model.

In addition, an action-reaction arms race with the United States in the high-technology realm of missiles versus BMD would seem to be unattractive to China, North Korea, or any other rogue state. These countries have other plausible areas of potential strength where competition with Washington might seem more fruitful: the willingness to absorb civilian and military losses; to accept risks; to impose draconian measures on the civilian population (as Mao put it, China's capacity to "eat bitterness"); to stay the course in a bloody regional conflict; or, in China's case, to put masses of population under arms.

Many commentators suggest that the U.S. development of offensive warhead technology in the 1960s helped move the Soviet Union away from its nationwide ABM aspirations for fear of an unwinnable offensive-defensive competition with the United States. China's or North Korea's expectations of a serious U.S. commitment to missile defense may lead them away from ICBMs as a basis for dealing with Washington. Can such an "action-inaction" cycle initiated by U.S. BMD be predicted with absolute confidence? No. Such an outcome, however, is not obviously less likely than the arms race promised anew by BMD opponents; and it may be more so. A serious effort at understanding the full panoply of factors likely to animate decisions in this regard should precede any confident predictions. Positing action-reaction as a law, of course, relieves any need for such understanding.

A starting point in this examination is the fact that the U.S. annual defense budget is more than eight times larger than the annual Chinese defense budget and more than 250 times larger than the North Korean defense budget.[26] Meanwhile, the U.S. government appears to have such a large, prospective budget surplus that the debate in Washington has been over how much money (more than a trillion dollars) should be returned to the taxpayer in the form of tax cuts. In contrast, North Korean defense spending takes place amid recent and widespread starvation, skyrocketing infant mortality, and plunging life expectancy. These conditions are not conducive for starting an arms race with the United States in any traditional meaning of the phrase.

A relatively high-tech competition with the United States involving the significant exploitation of space and technologies in which the United States excels would seem an unlikely road for these countries. In this arena, the United States is in a class by itself. The Soviet Union, with its enormous capabilities, ultimately concluded that it could not compete adequately with the United States in these areas. Are we now to believe that China and North Korea will choose to pursue a race that so plays to U.S. strengths? To paraphrase Br'er Rabbit: Please don't throw us in that brier patch.

Dismissing the possibility of some form of Chinese or North Korean offensive reaction to U.S. missile defense obviously is beyond what evidence can bear. Nevertheless, given the conditions described above, and the manifest inadequacy of the action-reaction model, the current crop of gravely repeated predictions that U.S. missile defense can only lead to an unbeatable buildup of Chinese or North Korean offensive missiles and a "worldwide arms race" should be given about as much credence as tarot card reading or some other metaphysical fortunetelling. Self-serving, and occasionally coached, Chinese and North Korean statements that they will respond in just such a fashion hardly constitute proof to the contrary.

In conclusion, a national review should be underway concerning the U.S. strategic framework most appropriate for contemporary security, including the role for BMD. Such a review, in fact, was long overdue. This national debate about BMD, however, will not be the first. Our awareness of the past four decades should discipline the predictions that are and are not now accorded credibility. During the first great BMD debate of the late 1960s, the inadequacy of a simplistic action-reaction arms-race model was not yet blatantly obvious; neither was the misleading nature of confident predictions based on it. Now the opposite is true. The time to move beyond metaphysics and negligence has arrived.

Notes

1. "Text of President Bush's Speech," *New York Times*, May 1, 2001, www.nytimes.com/aponline/national/01, accessed May 1, 2001.

2. Thomas K. Longstreth, John Pike, and John Rhinelander, *The Impact of U.S. and Soviet Ballistic Missile Defense Programs on the ABM Treaty* (Washington, D.C.: National Campaign to Save the ABM Treaty, March 1985), p. 4.

3. Jan Lodal, "Pledging 'No First Strike': A Step Toward Real WMD Cooperation," *Arms Control Today* 31, no. 2 (March 2001): 6.

4. Stan Crock, "It's Rocket Science—And That's Not Good," *Business Week,* May 14, 2001, p. 64.

5. Bruce Blair et al., *Toward True Security: A U.S. Nuclear Posture for the Next Decade* (Cambridge, Mass.: UCS Publications, 2001), p. 10.

6. Walter Pincus, "The First Law of Nuclear Politics: Every Action Brings Reaction," *Washington Post,* November 28, 1999, p. B2.

7. Craig Eisendrath, "Missile Defense System Flawed Technically, Unwise Politically," *Philadelphia Inquirer,* May 23, 2001.

8. Pincus, "First Law of Nuclear Politics," p. 2.

9. See George Rathjens, Abram Chayes and J. P. Ruina, *Nuclear Arms Control Agreements: Process and Impact* (Washington, D.C.: Carnegie Endowment for International Peace, 1974), p. 1.

10. *Bulletin of the Atomic Scientists* (July/August 2001), p. 11.

11. Justin Vaisse, "French Views on Missile Defense," *U.S.-France Analysis,* April 2001, 3, www.brook.edu/fp/cust/analysis/missd.html, accessed May 9, 2001.

12. Senate Committee on Armed Services, *Authorization for Military Procurement, Research and Development, FY 1970,* 91st Cong., 1st sess., 1969, p. 1233 (testimony of Herbert York).

13. George Rathjens, "The Dynamics of the Arms Race," *Arms Control Readings from Scientific American* (San Francisco: W. H. Freeman and Co., 1973), p. 181.

14. Senate Committee on Armed Services, *Military Implications of the Treaty on the Limitation of Anti-Ballistic Missile Systems and the Interim Agreement on Limitation of Strategic Offensive Arms,* 92 Cong., 2d sess., 1972, p. 121 (statement by Henry Kissinger).

15. See John Collins and Peter Glakas, *U.S./Soviet Military Balance, Statistical Trends, 1970–1982,* 83-153 S (Washington, D.C.: Congressional Research Service, August 1983); John Collins and Bernard Victory, *U.S./Soviet Military Balance, Statistical Trends, 1980–1987,* 88-425 S (Washington, D.C.: Congressional Research Service, April 15,1988), pp. 11, 15.

16. Arms Control and Disarmament Agency, *The Soviet Propaganda Campaign Against the U.S. Strategic Defense Initiative* (Washington, D.C.: Arms Control and Disarmament Agency, 1986), p. 8.

17. See William E. Odom, *The Collapse of the Soviet Military* (New Haven: Yale University Press, 1998), p. 71.

18. Matthew Bunn, *Foundation for the Future: The ABM Treaty and National Security* (Washington, D.C.: Arms Control Association, 1990), p. 6.

19. Ibid., p. 7.

20. McGeorge Bundy et al., "The President's Choice: Star Wars or Arms Control," *Foreign Affairs* 63, no. 2 (Winter 1984/85): 273, 277.

21. "Full Text of Statement Made by President Mikhail Gorbachev on Soviet Television on 5 October," TASS, October 5, 1991, in FBIS, *Daily Report: Soviet Union*, October 7, 1991, pp. 2–3.

22. For an early and still useful discussion of this point, see Colin S. Gray, *The Soviet American Arms Race* (Lexington, Mass.: Lexington Books, 1976), pp. 12–55.

23. Bates Gill and James Mulvenon, "The Chinese Strategic Rocket Forces: Transition to Credible Deterrence," in National Intelligence Council, Federal Research Division, Library of Congress, *China and Weapons of Mass Destruction: Implication for the United States*, November 5, 1999, CR 99–05 (April 2000), p. 12.

24. Ibid., pp. 35, 46–48.

25. Ibid., pp. 47–55.

26. See Center for Defense Information, *Fact Sheet Last of the Big-Time Spender: U.S. Military Budget Still the World's Largest and Growing*, May 1, 20001, www.cdi.org/issues/wme/spendersFY02.html, accessed May 14, 2001.

Bruno Tertrais

Do Arms Races Matter?

"**A**rms racing," technically, may have begun as early as the moment when mankind started to rely on military equipment to wage war. In the last century, however, technology pushed the concept to previously unknown levels. The British-German naval arms race was arguably the first modern one, with the *Dreadnought*-type ships as the ultimate weapon. The drive for the atomic bomb, and later the fusion bomb, were typical examples of races in which the goal was to develop the weapon before the adversary did (Adolf Hitler's Germany in the former case, Joseph Stalin's Soviet Union in the latter).

Since the Cold War, the understanding of the term "arms race" has become rather loose and extensive. The general media now tends to equate it with any substantive development, progress, or buildup in weapons acquisition, but it takes two to compete. Thus, the more restrictive definition Colin Gray gave in 1971 would probably be more useful: "Two or more parties perceiving themselves to be in an adversary relationship, who are increasing or improving their armaments at a rapid rate and restructuring their respective military postures with a general attention to the past, current, and anticipated military and po-

Bruno Tertrais is senior research fellow for strategic studies at the Paris-based Fondation pour la Recherche Stratégique (FRS). Until September 2001, he was special assistant to the director of strategic affairs at the French Ministry of Defense.

The Washington Quarterly • 24:4 pp. 123–133.

litical behavior of the other parties."[1] Gray's definition omits the alac-rity and out-of-control connotations suggested by the term "race." In this general framework, the development of ballistic and nuclear weap-ons, the so-called weapons of mass destruction that have the most im-portant strategic and political implications, now best exemplify arms races.

Of the two types of arms races, Type-I races, as one may call the first type, are legitimized by strategic actions. Several variants of Type-I races exist, depending on their respective main drivers. One variation stems from counterforce strategies, as demonstrated during the 1970s and 1980s debate on the MX and Midgetman missiles, which were supposed to close a "window of vulnerability" opened by the alleged Soviet capa-bility to exert a disarming first strike on U.S. intercontinental ballistic missiles (ICBMs). Another stems from the existence of defenses; the classic "sword vs. shield" phenomenon fuels this variation. The develop-ment of multiple independently targetable reentry vehicle (MIRV) war-heads by the United States is a combination of both variants: the MIRV program was largely, though not solely, the result of perceived Soviet de-fensive and offensive build-ups. Concerns of "escalation dominance" drives yet another variation, as exemplified by the Intermediate-Range Nuclear Force (INF) controversy of the late 1970s and early 1980s, when Western allies were concerned that the Soviet Union could threaten Eu-rope with limited nuclear strikes without the North Atlantic Treaty Or-ganization (NATO) being able to respond in kind.

Symbols and politics drive Type-II arms races, not the mechanics of force ratios and the offense/defense calculus. To a large extent, this phenomenon existed during the Cold War. In his history of the first 50 years of the nuclear age, McGeorge Bundy concludes, "The decisions leading to massive and varied deployments have been dominated by the conviction in each government that it could not tolerate the nuclear superiority of the other."[2]

Clear distinctions between the two types are obviously difficult to make, and these two processes often work simultaneously. For instance, the so-called bomber gap and missile gap (arguably created in part by bad or distorted intelligence) are examples where both dynamics—strategy and politics—were at work.

Some analysts have placed the very existence of the action-reaction processes in ballistic and nuclear weapons acquisition in doubt. Some have emphasized the responsibility of the intrinsic dynamics of the military-industrial complex and suggested that the potential adversaries' arsenals are often, deliberately or not, exaggerated to justify a weapons program.[3] Indeed, strategic weapons procurement decisions often involve organizational routines and domestic political factors that have little to do with strategic analysis per se. Defense Secretary Robert McNamara seems to have based his 1962 decision to procure 1,000 ICBMs, for example, much more on the need for compromise between the White House and the Pentagon than on strict nuclear planning rationales. At the other end of the political spectrum, conservative analyses have vigorously challenged the very idea of arms racing and suggest that such an expression unduly places an equal burden of political responsibility on the potential aggressor and on the defender.[4]

Do Arms Races Matter?

Discarding the existence of action-reaction phenomena in strategic weapons procurement is nevertheless difficult. The MIRV programs of the nuclear powers, for example, seem to be a typical case in point. As an in-depth study of the issue argues, "[Although] the claim that MIRV was solely a reasoned response to perceived and anticipated Soviet activities can certainly not be sustained, to deny the existence of this dimension of the decision-making process for MIRV is to miss completely one of the central themes of the strategic weapons drama of the 1960s."[5] The question is whether this phenomenon deserves to be qualified as arms racing, with its connotations of irrationality and brinkmanship. The most important debate, however, is probably less about whether strategic competitions and action-reaction phenomena should be called arms races than about whether they are negative and even dangerous.

Do arms races cause wars? This classic international relations question is almost a century old. After World War I, scholars and politicians were tempted to label the extraordinary military buildup that developed between 1870 and 1914 as a major cause, if not the major cause, of the conflict. Subsequent historical studies, however, have shed considerable doubt on this theory.[6] Moreover, arms racing may in fact have positive aspects. NATO's 1979 decision to deploy Pershing-2 and ground-launched cruise missiles (GLCMs) in response to the Soviet Union's deployment of SS-20s and Backfire bombers, which undoubtedly was part of an action-reaction process, made the "zero option" and the INF Treaty possible. When competition spirals out of control, states may feel that engaging in a dialogue to control it is in their common interest—thereby creating an atmosphere conducive to a better understanding of the other party. In other words, to the extent that arms races create arms control, and arms control fosters confidence-building, then arms races ultimately can have a positive effect. Some policymakers and analysts have posited that massive U.S. defense spending and the "Star Wars" program brought the Soviet Union to its knees. That claim rests on shaky grounds and is heavily disputed.[7] British historian Sir Michael Howard makes a more convincing argument, suggesting that arms racing can in fact be "almost a necessary surrogate for war."[8]

Certainly, such analyses are generally made after the fact. Historical analysis is quite different from policy recommendations for the present. Arms racing may be recognized as a positive development after the possible danger is discarded, but encouraging or welcoming arms racing on the premise that it may eventually have a positive outcome would be imprudent and perhaps even foolish. Assuming that arms races, even if they do not cause wars, may encourage the forces that drive countries toward war, perhaps to a point where conflict becomes possible, is not unreasonable. Arms races may fuel existing rivalries and foster perceptions of aggressiveness. A recent study on "strategic personalities" noted, "The expensive and aggressive Anglo-German naval race ... played a key role in further souring the Anglo-German relationship and contributing to their eventual slide into hostility and the outbreak of the First World War."[9] Returning to the INF example, the Soviet Union became genuinely concerned by U.S. missile deployment policies to the point of misreading the NATO *Able Archer* 1983 exercise as possible preparations for imminent attack.

Thus, arms racing remains a dubious and controversial concept, charged with emotional undertones. How relevant is it in the post–Cold War geopolitical environment? In the second half of the twentieth century, strategic competition was essentially an East-West phenomenon. The real strategic competition of the first decades of the twenty-first century will involve Asia (in this article, "Asia" excludes the Middle East). How meaningful is the concept of arms racing in Asia? This problem has two dimensions.

The Potential for Asian Arms Races

Bilateral competition exists among regional actors in Asia, but should that qualify as arms racing? Regarding China and India, and India and Pakistan, there is no evidence of arms racing of the sort that existed during the Cold War in these two situations. All three countries have adopted rather modest nuclear doctrines, each of them calling, in reality if not in declared intentions, for what is usually called "minimum deterrence": a capability that is limited to the possibility of inflicting unacceptable damage on the adversary, generally understood as focusing on countervalue targets, such as population centers. The level of Chinese, Indian, and Pakistani strategic forces that each country desires does not appear to be dependent on the numbers of ballistic and nuclear weapons that their adversaries have or may have eventually. Some "internal arms races," or competitions between various domestic entities, reminiscent of similar processes during the Cold War, may also exist in Asian countries (particularly in Pakistan). If China, India, and Pakistan are increasing their strategic arsenals, however, they act primarily to reach or maintain a level of sufficiency and ensure minimal deterrence in all possible circumstances, not to achieve superiority and not to sustain war-fighting nuclear doctrines. Moreover, missile defenses and counterforce strategies, arguably two of the main drivers of the East-West arms race of the Cold War, are absent in these three regional nuclear actors. A combination of budget limitations, lessons learned from the history of the Cold War, and a desire to be recognized as "legitimate" nuclear powers are probably at the root of their behavior.

Some dynamic processes exist in the region, however, by which one state, mostly for political reasons, imitates or responds to the actions of another. Initiation of the Pakistani Ghauri missile program was partly a reply to the Indian Prithvi program (with an interesting symbolic dimension insofar as those two names appear to have been chosen for names of former conquerors of the other's territory). In 1998 the Pakistani test of a Ghauri missile, which reduced the "strategic depth" that India had traditionally enjoyed, contributed to Delhi's decision to engage in a series of nuclear tests. The Pakistani nuclear explosions were obviously a response to the Indian ones—Islamabad engaging in one-upmanship by announcing one more test than India, certainly for political more than technical reasons. The Chinese, Indian, and Pakistani programs, however, evolve at a very slow pace. There is no rush to deploy missiles and nuclear weapons, and the three countries seem to have adopted delayed-reaction postures, with emphasis on survivability rather than on first-strike options.

Two other Asian adversaries are developing strategic capabilities: North and South Korea. For a decade, Pyongyang has been developing its No-Dong and Taepo-Dong missiles. More recently, Seoul has engaged in the development of a Hyonmu missile with a 300-kilometer range (the Missile Technology Control Regime's limit), with a green light from the United States. Yet, the two countries are not really engaged in an arms racing process. North Korean programs are slow to develop and have a multiplicity of strategic, political, and economic rationales that exceed the situation on the peninsula. South Korea, for its part, responds extremely cautiously to North Korean ballistic programs. It has refused to consider acquiring missile defenses to protect its territory, and its missile program remains very limited.

Two cases of possible Type-I arms racing in Asia remain. They involve the declared intention of Japan and Taiwan to acquire missile defenses—Tokyo, mostly because of the progress of the North Korean missile program; and Taipei, because Beijing appears to pile up dozens of missiles every year in the coastal regions of mainland China. Some action-reaction processes, real or anticipated, are at work here. The prudence observed by the United States and its friends and allies, as far as the deployment of defenses is concerned, however, indicates that talk of an arms race would be an overstatement.

The Potential for Global Arms Races

A second dimension exists in the dynamics of strategic relations between the three recognized nuclear powers that have a role in the region: the United States, China, and Russia. Classical Type-I arms races become possible because two of the three actors are known to have counterforce strategies and have or plan to have ballistic defenses covering the capital region (Russia) or their whole territory (the United States, with a program largely justified by an Asian missile threat).

Could a new arms race between the United States and Russia occur because of the deployment of U.S. missile defenses? Current Russian defense resources do not allow for a renewal of the competition that existed during the Cold War. For political reasons, Moscow will try to maintain apparent parity, and it will seek to retain the capability to inflict considerable damage on U.S. territory in a worst-case scenario. That effort may involve re-MIRVing some of its ICBMs, but this process would qualify more as a slowdown of the disarmament process—and as measures to limit the natural attrition of Russian forces—than as arms racing.

What about China? Certainly, here lies one of the most pressing concerns of Western policymakers and observers: that the declared U.S. intention to deploy robust missile defenses may prompt China to increase the number of its strategic nuclear weapons dramatically. U.S. official estimates indicate that a tenfold expansion of the Chinese strategic nuclear arsenal is possible.[10] Given the importance of U.S. strategy in Beijing's strategic calculus, Beijing is likely ready to take the necessary measures to maintain its "don't mess with me" (i.e., minimum) deterrent capability vis-à-vis the United States. Given the uncertainties about the U.S. missile defense program, China probably has the means to ensure that the United States could never be confident that it is protected against any significant Chinese strike. Most analysts agree that, although U.S. missile defenses will affect the pace and scope of Chinese modernization that has been on track for a long time, it will not affect the existence of the modernization but may, at its worst, make it "more unpredictable."[11] Beijing has a long historical record of developing strategic programs very slowly; the Chinese leadership may be wary of entering into a competition that it may perceive—whatever the reality—as having been lethal to the Soviet Union. Thus, for many reasons, China is likely to "jog" with rather than race with the United States.[12]

Finally, the Bush administration's missile defense program is intended to intercept handfuls of incoming missiles, not hundreds. The extinction of the Anti-Ballistic Missile (ABM) Treaty would no more trigger a new arms race than it limited the Cold War's arms race (if the ABM Treaty had closed the possibility of an offensive/defensive race, it channeled the superpowers' competition toward the offensive side).[13]

These analyses produce a few conclusions.

- Asian countries have not engaged in arms racing of the sort that existed during the Cold War, although the countries strategically compete among themselves. Claims of the existence of a "nuclear reaction chain" do reflect a reality.[14] The links between the Chinese, Indian, and Pakistani nuclear programs, for instance, are historically well proven. Asian arms races, however, to the extent that they exist, are mostly slow processes fueled by political rivalries and of a qualitative rather than quantitative nature, especially as far as ballistic missiles are concerned. They qualify as Type-II arms racing rather than Type-I. As a former Pentagon official argued, "It is a bunch of loosely coupled arms races, and our past has been dominated by one very large arms race. ... People need to stop living in the past."[15]

- The conditions do not exist for a new arms race involving the United States, Russia, and China. Neither Russia nor China has the means or the will to race in the way that the Soviet Union and the United States did during the Cold War. Moscow and Beijing will only seek to maintain their current ability to strike the United States, not compete for the best missile or the highest number of warheads.

- Some links do exist between Asian arms racing and global arms racing involving the five recognized nuclear powers. Notably, because "China's nuclear identity is both global and Asian,"[16] it stands at the juncture of Asian and global strategic dynamics. There is a logical abyss, however, between this idea and the belief that a mechanical process exists whereby an increase in the Pakistani nuclear weapons arsenal would automatically trigger a rise in the Indian one, instigating a Chinese decision to augment its own forces, and eventually leading Moscow to build up its own forces—or vice versa.

Why We Should Care and What Can Be Done

The negative effects of strategic competitions tend to be exaggerated, and the very notion of arms racing in Asia should be handled with care. For these reasons, the inclination of key U.S. policymakers to take intellectual shortcuts of the sort mentioned above—suggesting that the U.S. national missile defense program could lead to "many more nuclear weapons in China, prompting a buildup in India and Pakistan, thus increasing the likelihood that any conflict between them would involve nuclear weapons"[17]—is regrettable.

Still, Western policymakers and analysts would be wise to avoid adopting a benign approach to Asian strategic arms competitions for several reasons. First, the contests are happening in a context of acute tensions on the continent, carrying the risk of armed clashes and even war between nuclear-armed adversaries in at least the three critical areas of Kashmir, the Korean Peninsula, and the Taiwan Strait. Second, an increase in the number of Asian nuclear weapons may, if only marginally—but here again, low probability is balanced by high consequence—increase the risk of accidental or unauthorized detonation, especially if one state in the region collapsed. Third, although disarmament as a general principle is certainly not the key to development, the increase in procurement budgets that must accompany any arms racing would, in some countries already facing a critical budgetary situation (e.g., Pakistan), divert potential resources that could otherwise be used for more immediate, basic population needs. Fourth, the augmentation of ballistic missile ranges means that Asian strategic arsenals will cover an increasingly wide part of the globe—eventually putting, for instance, the Middle East and Europe technically at risk from distant countries. Fifth, the development of Asian strategic arsenals might have some spillover effects on the Middle East (in Iran, for instance). Sixth, Asian strategic growth will also make Western nuclear states and Russia more prudent on nuclear disarmament.

What is needed is a limit on both arms racing and the possible negative consequences of existing and forthcoming strategic competitions.

- To prevent serious arms racing in Asia, China, India, and Pakistan should maintain the current "opacity policy" about their nuclear capabilities and numbers. Certainly, a lack of reliable information about the potential adversary, and unsatisfactory intelligence, can fuel arms races. Transparency, however, is certainly no recipe for dampening competition, as shown by the history of the Cold War. This argument is especially valid regarding public transparency in Asia, where it is possible to say without cultural prejudice that a premium is often placed on "face-saving." Such transparency would likely fuel domestic political pressures to "catch up" with one country or the other, whereas the current opacity policy observed by the Asian nuclear actors acts as a buffer against such pressures, reducing what a journalist once called the "lust to be first."[18] In other words, give opacity a chance.

- The United States and China must embark on a serious strategic dialogue—more than short trips by U.S. officials visiting Beijing to explain rationales for U.S. missile defense. This communication should involve an in-depth dialogue on conceptions of deterrence and defenses and the role of nuclear weapons. The United States should overtly recognize that China's nuclear force is legitimate and take steps, to the extent possible, to ensure that U.S. defenses will not drastically affect China's nuclear forces. Some missile defense concepts—such as sea-based boost-phase defenses—can provide assurance to Beijing that U.S. systems could not intercept ICBMs stationed in the Chinese heartland. For its part, China should accept the U.S. desire to protect itself against limited ballistic attacks by regional powers. The goal, even if distant, of such talks (and hardly separable from the achievement of some kind of *modus vivendi* on the issue of Taiwan) would be a grand strategic bargain in which Beijing would limit the growth of its nuclear arsenal in exchange for a guarantee that U.S. defenses will not be able to negate the Chinese deterrent. Granted, this understanding could only be an unverifiable declaration of principles, but its political value would be very significant.

- Rather than attempting to roll back Asian nuclear capabilities, the goal of the West should be dampening the risks that local arms races may create. In other words, if the West cannot make Asia a nuclear weapon–free zone (assuming that it should), it should try to make it, as much as possible, a nuclear risk-free zone. A culture of mutual knowledge and lessening distrust must be established in a region where the sequels of twentieth-century conflict are still very much present. Informal meetings, seminars, and other various tools of second-track diplomacy are as important, if not more, here than technical gimmicks (such as hotlines which often exist but are not used in times of crisis). Finally, Russian and U.S. arms control experts and former officials should help Asian countries draw lessons from the strategic competitions of the Cold War.

Arms racing is a powerful political concept but a sloppy analytical tool. Yet its inadequacies are no reason for complacency about the dynamics of today's new strategic competitions in Asia and among other major powers. The study of these phenomena and the quality of strategic debate would gain by discarding the arms racing metaphor, which may act as an intellectual lens that unduly simplifies the complex dynamics of the twenty-first century strategic environment.

Notes

1. Aaron Karp, *Ballistic Missile Proliferation: The Politics and Technics* (Oxford: SIPRI/Oxford University Press, 1996), pp. 14–15.

2. McGeorge Bundy, *Danger and Survival: Choices about the Bomb in the First Fifty Years* (New York: Vintage Books/Random House, 1990), p. 586.

3. Herbert F. York, "Controlling the Qualitative Arms Race," *Bulletin of the Atomic Scientists* 29 (1973): 4–8. Herbert F. York, "Deterrence by Means of Mass Destruction," *Bulletin of the Atomic Scientists* 30 (1974): 4–9.

4. Albert Wohlstetter, "Is There a Strategic Arms Race?" *Foreign Policy* 15 (summer 1974): 3–20; Albert Wohlstetter, "Rivals, But No 'Race,'" *Foreign Policy* 16 (fall 1974): 48–81.

5. Ted Greenwood, *Making the MIRV: A Study of Defense Decision Making* (Cambridge, Mass.: Ballinger Publishing, 1975), p. 97.

6. Patrick Glynn, *Closing Pandora's Box: Arms Races, Arms Control, and the History of the Cold War* (New York: Basic Books/HarperCollins, 1992), chap. 1; Colin S. Gray, *House of Cards: Why Arms Control Must Fail* (Ithaca and London: Cornell University Press, 1992), pp. 44–46.

7. Frances Fitzgerald, *Way Out There in the Blue: Reagan, Star Wars and the End of the Cold War* (New York: Simon & Schuster, 2000), pp. 473–475; Gordon R. Mitchell, *Strategic Deception: Rhetoric, Science, and Politics in Missile Defense Advocacy* (East Lansing: Michigan State University Press, 2000), pp. 87–88.

8. Michael Howard, *The Causes of War and Other Essays* (London: Unwin Paperbacks, 1983), p. 21.

9. Caroline F. Ziemke, Philippe Loustaunau, and Amy Alrich, *Strategic Personality and the Effectiveness of Nuclear Deterrence* (Institute for Defense Analyses/Defense Threat Reduction Agency, IDA Document D-2537, November 2000), p. 90.

10. Stephen Lee Myers, "Intelligence Report Says U.S. Missile Defense May Stimulate China," *New York Times*, August 10, 2000.

11. Li Bin, "The Effects of NMD on Chinese Strategy," *Jane's Intelligence Review* (March 2001): 49.

12. Brad Roberts, *Nuclear Multipolarity and Stability* (Institute for Defense Analyses/Defense Threat Reduction Agency, IDA Document D-2539, November 2000), p. 19.

13. Glynn, *Closing Pandora's Box*, p. 268.

14. Joseph Cirincione, "The Asian Nuclear Reaction Chain," in *Nuclear Tensions in a New Era* (Washington, D.C.: Carnegie Endowment for International Peace/Foreign Policy, 2000).

15. Annapolis Group to President George W. Bush, memorandum, "Policymakers Views on Addressing the Nuclear Threat," May 2001, p. 12.

16. Roberts, *Nuclear Multipolarity and Stability*, p. 31.

17. Senator Carl Levin (D–Mich.), speech to the National Defense University, May 11, 2001, in Carnegie Endowment for International Peace, *Proliferation Brief* 4, no. 12, June 5, 2001, www.ceip.org.npp.

18. Mitchell, *Strategic Deception*, p. 81 (quoting James O. Goldsborough).

Leon Sloss

The New Arms Race

The term "arms race" is a figure of speech widely used during the Cold War to reduce a complex strategic interaction into terms that a large audience could comprehend. The phrase conjures an image that was quite accurate when the United States and the Soviet Union were the two principal racers, developing and deploying new nuclear weapons and delivery systems at a rapid pace. The major currencies of the old arms race were missiles, bomber aircraft, and nuclear weapons. The race was between two competitors, roughly equal in nuclear capability, who strove mightily to maintain that equality—plus a little edge. The future plans of the other party were never entirely transparent, and a tendency to assume the worst existed.

This old nuclear arms race is over and unlikely to be reborn in the foreseeable future. Today, the new security environment could be termed a new arms race, but it is very different from the competition of the Cold War era. Few recognize the new arms race as such yet because both the competitors and the currencies of competition have changed. This new arms race involves several countries and a variety of weapons. Although the United States has superior military capabilities, competitors are seeking ways to offset that superiority. The new arms race requires a different U.S. strategy toward arms control and force planning.

Leon Sloss is a consultant specializing in nuclear strategy and arms control.

Copyright © 2001 by The Center for Strategic and International Studies and the Massachusetts Institute of Technology
The Washington Quarterly • 24:4 pp. 135–147.

Contemporary Nuclear Debates

The Old and the New

Exploration of the factors underlying the arms race that took place during the Cold War provides a basis for understanding the current system. Of the seven major drivers of the old arms race, many are not present today, while others have changed radically.

GEOPOLITICS

The Soviet Union posed a major military threat to Western Europe (and Japan to a lesser extent), and the United States helped its allies defend against this threat. The collapse of the Soviet Union, the demise of the Warsaw Pact, and severe economic and social problems within Russia have radically changed that threat. The Russian Army—now withdrawn from Central Europe—is a shadow of its past glory, unable to end warfare in Chechnya and unable to pay its troops.

STRATEGY

The United States, facing superior Soviet conventional forces in Central Europe, relied heavily on a strategy of deterrence, based on the threat of massive retaliation with nuclear weapons. Today, the United States is militarily superior to any likely adversary and therefore has much less need to make nuclear deterrence central to its strategy. Contemporary threats are characteristically more conventional and asymmetrical, and the United States will have to meet them on that level. Nuclear weapons still have a role to play, particularly to deter the use of weapons of mass destruction. No one, however, has yet clearly defined that role.

DIPLOMACY

During the Cold War, the United States committed its nuclear forces to protecting its allies from attack and nuclear blackmail and hence discouraged the proliferation of independent nuclear capabilities. Although the need for reassurance remains, nuclear weapons play a lesser role in diplomacy due to changes in threats and in U.S. nonnuclear capabilities relative to major potential adversaries. U.S. allies, who saw nuclear deterrence as a mixed blessing, now want to push nuclear planning into the background.

ECONOMICS

In the early 1950s, when Western allies decided not to match Soviet conventional strength in Europe, the reasoning was basically economic. The West possessed the potential economic and manpower resources to match Soviet conventional military strength, but the cost would have been very high, and the West chose instead to increase its dependence on nuclear weapons. This decision freed resources for investment in the recovery of Europe and economic expansion in the United States. Today's security challenges demand major changes in U.S. military forces, but budgetary pressures within the military establishment are drawing resources from strategic nuclear programs, not toward them.

TECHNOLOGY

In the period from 1950 to 1980, changes in the technologies affecting nuclear deterrence were dramatic. Nuclear warheads shrank in size as well as weight, and missile accuracy improved dramatically. As a result, deploying multiple warheads on a single missile became possible. Both sides deployed these weapons and strove to defend against them, and competition intensified. Today, new military technology exists, but little of it affects strategic nuclear weapons. The United States, in the belief that current nuclear systems are adequate, is not developing new weapons or delivery systems, but rather seeks to extend the life of existing strategic systems. This situation is very different from the 1960s and 1970s, when the United States was developing and deploying new nuclear warheads and delivery systems regularly.

MOMENTUM

The engine for designing and producing strategic weapons, once ignited, was difficult to stop. Massive establishments arose in the United States and the Soviet Union to support each government's penchant for nuclear expansion. Today, that dynamic is reversed. The governments are reducing nuclear stockpiles to devote resources to higher priority needs, and the industries that support them are shrinking.

UNCERTAINTY

Lack of transparency about the military plans and intentions of the other side often led to "worst case" planning. Today, areas of uncertainty remain (e.g., the number of nonstrategic nuclear weapons in Russia and their intended role), but far more contact between the United States and Russia exists through a variety of official and unofficial channels, and transparency has increased. No one need rely on "worst case" assumptions.

New Security Concerns about Russia

Security issues between the United States and Russia remain, but they are different from those of the past. Despite threats—such as Russian president Vladimir Putin's response to U.S. antiballistic missile (ABM) deployment—that contain more bluff than substance, no issues with Russia are likely to generate an arms race of the sort seen in the past.

Russia has renewed its emphasis on nuclear weapons in its overall defensive strategy, but Russian leaders have explained this action as a response to the decline in Russian conventional capabilities.[1] No one can ignore Russia's thousands of nuclear weapons, large stockpiles of weapons-grade material, and functioning production base that continues to produce new long-range missile systems.[2] These capabilities seem inconsistent with a shrinking strategic nuclear force. Some policymakers attribute these trends to bureaucratic inertia. Others believe that nuclear weapons provide a means for Russia to continue to assert its great-power status. Still others see more sinister Russian intentions. Given the large nuclear force that remains, possibilities exist for nuclear blackmail of Russia's neighbors. Deterioration of both morale and discipline in Russia's armed forces has also raised concerns about a nuclear accident or unauthorized use. Although these issues should concern U.S. planners, none are likely to fuel a new nuclear arms race. Russia cannot afford it, and the United States has other uses for its substantial, but still limited, defense resources.

The greatest concern for U.S. security policy in the near term is Russia's potential contribution to nuclear proliferation. Russia has nuclear weapons, delivery systems, personnel, and facilities that exceed their current needs. Most Russian nuclear scientists, engineers, and soldiers live in poverty, and the temptation to sell inactive weapons and the knowledge to operate them to the highest bidder is great. The United States has been working, through the Cooperative Threat Reduction program and other means, to reduce the pressures and incentives to transfer Russian nuclear weapons and technology to third parties. Although the program has had many difficulties and attracted political criticism, continued efforts to discourage the diffusion of Russian nuclear capabilities are essential to U.S. security. After all, the potential threat of arms competition comes from the recipients of those nuclear weapons, not from Russia.

A long-range strategic concern is the potential for closer political-military collaboration between Russia and China. On July 16, 2001, Russia and China signed the "Sino-Russian Treaty of Good-Neighborly and Friendly Cooperation." Its security implications are unclear. Chinese officials say the treaty will not touch upon military cooperation.[3] Russia's need to sell military equipment in order to generate cash and China's need to modernize its military forces, however, create a common interest that could broaden if the states—one on the rise and the other on the decline—begin perceiving the United States as a common enemy. Granted, the long, ill-defined border between China and Russia, among other issues, has been the scene of clashes between the two in the past. Nevertheless, closer Russian-Chinese collaboration, particularly if directed against the United States and its Asian allies, could have very significant strategic consequences. The situation requires careful U.S. monitoring and skillful diplomacy with both parties.

Missile defense remains a major issue between the United States and Russia. Although Russian concerns about U.S. plans are exaggerated, they are genuine. Russians view a U.S. national missile defense (NMD) as a potential threat to their deterrent capabilities, but given Russia's economic weakness, the possibility that U.S. missile defense could spark a major new arms race with Russia is more rhetoric than reality.

Russian fears of U.S. missile defense stem as much from political as from military considerations. Russia knows that the United States has the technology and the resources to develop a major missile defense program, and they do not wish to be seen as incapable of matching the U.S. effort. Yet, Russia has also demonstrated a keen interest in missile defense in the past and forged well ahead of the United States in deploying missile defense capabilities during the Cold War.[4] In recent months, they have shown interest in a cooperative missile defense effort in which they would participate as equal partners and possibly obtain business for their floundering defense industry. Such a program would be a promising way to defuse Russian opposition, and U.S. officials should explore this option further.

Russia is likely to remain economically weak and socially unstable for many years, making an "old fashioned" arms race unlikely. Indeed, the current environment is ripe for expanded, if wary, U.S.-Russian cooperation on a variety of fronts, particularly on curbing proliferation and expanding stability in Europe. In the longer term, a new arms race cannot be entirely ruled out but seems unlikely. The United States can protect itself against this unlikely contingency by maintaining a solid nuclear research and development and production base as well as testing capabilities that it could expand rapidly, should the need arise. Not only would this course provide a hedge against Russian reconstitution of its nuclear forces, it would also be a powerful deterrent to such action.

The New Arms Race—A U.S. View

The new arms race features a diverse cast of characters racing to arm with modern weapons. In many cases, a regional threat is the stimulus to arms competition. Some states arm to offset U.S. military superiority, which they could view as an obstacle to their regional ambitions.[5] From the U.S. perspective, its main competitors in this new race are China, North Korea, Iran, and Iraq, but others could emerge in the future. These states present potential threats to U.S. forces, allies, the homeland, and interests abroad and are actively acquiring conventional high explosives, nuclear weapons, and biological and chemical weapons to compete with the United States. They are also expanding the delivery systems for these weapons, including ballistic and cruise missiles, aircraft, ships, and state-sponsored terrorists. Cyberwarfare against U.S. information systems and communications presents a new dimension of vulnerability because of heavy U.S. dependence on electronic systems to manage and transmit information. The United States views the new arms race in this manner, but the competition is truly multipolar, and each participant has its own perspective on the race.

A full understanding of the new arms race requires a detailed, country-by-country analysis that exceeds the scope of this article. Generally, though, all of these states have ambitions to be major powers within their region. A small elite that controls power within the society dominates all, and this elite can channel resources to military programs without regard to the needs or desires of its citizens. All perceive the United States as an obstacle to their ambitions and seek to counter what they believe to be U.S. dominance in their backyard.

Why should the United States view these circumstances as an arms race if it is superior in military capabilities to any other nation? Races are not always among equals, and the underdog often will seek victory through guile rather than by brute force. Although the new arms race has one dominant military power—the United States—several states with far less military power but with large ambitions could counter U.S. interests. Knowing they cannot match the United States in total military power, they attempt to develop asymmetric strategies and supporting capabilities that are within their means. These strategies could present the United States with significant challenges in the future, including the prospect of attacks on U.S. territory.

One reason that these smaller states believe that an asymmetric strategy may be successful is that U.S. military superiority may not translate into tactical superiority at the point of attack. History is replete with examples of an inferior force concentrating its force in a local operation, creating a momentary superiority, and thereby winning the battle. In the Persian Gulf War, although the United States and its allies ultimately prevailed against Iraq, it took many months to assemble the necessary force in the region to carry out Operation Desert Storm. If Iraq had been able to deter that buildup—with a credible nuclear or biological threat, for example—the coalition might not have assembled a superior force on the battlefield.

A significant asymmetry could arise when the adversary has a higher stake in the outcome of a conflict and therefore would be prepared to accept higher risks and greater casualties. For example, if China believed that Taiwan was possibly slipping from its grasp and about to become an independent state, it would be willing to take very large risks and pay a very heavy price to prevent this event. The United States has an implied commitment, recently made somewhat more concrete by President George W. Bush, to assist Taiwan if China uses force to change the political status quo.[6] A successful Chinese attack on Taiwan would have immense consequences for future security in Asia and worldwide and thus would engage very important U.S. interests. Nevertheless, China may perceive that its stake in the outcome of Taiwan's actions is higher than the U.S. stake and that the prospect of major damage to U.S. forces, allies, or cities would deter the United States from intervening.

A Multipolar View of the Arms Race

Although the United States tends to focus on threats to U.S. interests, other participants in this multipolar arms race also play a role. Without a doubt, their perceptions are critically important to how an arms race would erupt.

CHINA

China's dominant security objective is to prevent Taiwan from asserting its independence. If China must use force to achieve this objective, it will; under that scenario, it will attempt to deter U.S. intervention. China also has broader interests and concerns and will seek in the long term to expand its influence in Asia. In this context, China views the United States as a major competitor. China shares a 3,000-mile border with Russia and, despite its neighbor's internal political and economic problems, China cannot ignore the potential threat of Russia's extensive nuclear arsenal. To its south, China watches India and Pakistan emerge as nuclear states, a situation complicated by border disputes between India and China in the past.

With these varied interests and concerns in mind, China has been modernizing its military forces. In its nuclear modernization, China has emphasized short-range theater missiles that threaten Taiwan. China has also long had a modest long-range missile force that provides a proportional deterrent to U.S. intervention, much as the French *force de frappe* did against Russia. China is modernizing this force and has threatened to expand it in response to deployment of a U.S. missile defense.

Whatever it does, China is not likely to seek numerical parity with the United States, but will take whatever steps it believes necessary to maintain a minimal deterrent. These stages could involve deploying more missiles, developing a missile with multiple warheads (multiple independently targetable reentry vehicles, or MIRVs), deploying penetration aids to offset a U.S. defense, or some combination of these measures. China also is likely to use deceptive basing (e.g., concealment and mobility) to complicate U.S. targeting of its nuclear forces. No one could characterize any of these actions as an arms race in the Cold War sense because China's defense programs are based on their own goals and strategic priorities. Any U.S. actions that appear to stimulate a Chinese response, however, will have reverberations among China's neighbors, particularly India and Japan. From China's perspective, it is at the vortex of a complex multipolar competition.

SOUTH ASIA

India and Pakistan are both developing nuclear weapons and seeking modern means of delivery. Neither India and Pakistan have ambitions to race with the United States, but the impact of their nuclear competition is not limited to South Asia. As already noted, China must be concerned with an Indian buildup, particularly because India has cited the nuclear threat from China as a major rationale for its program.[7] To make matters more complex, if China believes that a U.S. missile defense will adversely affect its deterrent capability and responds to this presumed threat with an expansion of its own long-range nuclear forces, India and Russia may perceive an increased threat to themselves.

How India will perceive an expansion or modernization of China's long-range nuclear forces is unknown, but given India's expressed sensitivity to the Chinese threat, one cannot assume that New Delhi will treat changes in China's programs as merely a response to Washington's moves. If India responds to a perceived new threat from China by modifying its forces, will Pakistan be far behind? The United States has another major stake in this regional race because Pakistan has become a potential source of military assistance to other Muslim states, which might present a new threat to Israel.

NORTH KOREA

The Democratic People's Republic of Korea (DPRK) has long sought to dominate the Korean Peninsula and possesses a large army that seriously threatens the south and the U.S. forces stationed there. For years, the modern and competent South Korean (ROK) military force, the presence of some 35,000 U.S. troops in South Korea, and the prospect that the United States might use nuclear weapons if the south was attacked have deterred the DPRK. Following the impressive demonstration of U.S. air power in the Persian Gulf War and in the Balkans, the likelihood that the United States and the ROK would rapidly achieve air superiority in any conflict with the DPRK, offsetting any advantage that the North Korean army might achieve on the ground, is also a deterrent.

North Korea is producing and has tested a medium-range missile that threatens U.S. and ROK forces in the south as well as U.S. bases in Japan. The DPRK also is developing a longer-range missile that could reach the United States, and some believe it possesses one or two nuclear weapons.[8] Today, the North Korean nuclear program appears to be on hold, but only due to intense international pressure and inducements. North Korea is also credited with "probable development" of chemical weapons and a research program on biological weapons.[9] The United States and South Korea, as well as Japan, China, and Russia, are closely watching all of these developments.

IRAQ

Iran and Iraq are competitors in the Persian Gulf and have waged a war in which one party and/or the other used chemical weapons. Iraq demonstrated in 1990 that it has designs on the oil resources of its neighbors, Kuwait and Saudi Arabia. It also seeks ways to offset Israeli power and influence in the region, and Israel—as when it attacked and destroyed the Osirak reactor in 1981—clearly views Iraqi plans to develop nuclear capability as a security threat. Saddam Hussein believes that the United States is a major obstacle to his ambitions and will do whatever he can to offset U.S. power and influence in the future. Prior to the Persian Gulf War, Iraq was developing nuclear weapons and had purchased Scud missiles.[10] Iraq also had a chemical weapons stockpile and an active biological weapons research and production program that it is now attempting to restore.[11]

IRAN

As a result of the Persian Gulf War, Iran may have a temporary lead in the competition for dominance in the region. Tehran, however, realizes that Iraq is striving to restore its military power. Thus, this regional competition is likely to continue, with each side developing and deploying more sophisticated weapons. In a different sense, Iran also sees Israel as a competitor with far superior military force and with nuclear weapons. Iran's efforts to acquire long-range missiles and to develop a civilian nuclear reactor that could produce weapons-grade nuclear material in the future are a part of their arms competition with Iraq, but also a possible means to offset the acknowledged military superiority of Israel. Iran is credited with a probable chemical weapons program and with the research and possible production of biological agents.[12] Furthermore, the U.S. Department of State has cited Iran as a major training ground for terrorists.[13] Although Iran's ambitions are focused on the Middle East and the Persian Gulf, Iran undoubtedly has drawn the same lessons as others from the Persian Gulf War: a state that wants to control its destiny must have a capability to deter or thwart U.S. intervention.

Implications of the New Arms Race for U.S. Policy

For the past several months, U.S. planners have seriously studied the strategic and force requirements necessary to deal with the radically new security environment. One has only the broadest hints about what will emerge from the current Pentagon reviews. Certain broad principles about what will be needed, however, seem clear.

A NEW CHALLENGE FOR U.S. SECURITY POLICY

Nations that have regional ambitions will seek to deter the United States from intervention in their backyards. They cannot accomplish this task by developing superior overall force and will instead develop asymmetrical strategies involving deception; surprise; concentration of superior force at the point of attack; the threat of chemical, biological, and/or nuclear weapons; and cyberattacks to deter U.S. intervention. The United States must be prepared not only to deter regional aggression, but also to prevent the aggressor from deterring the United States' freedom of action.

A NEW APPROACH TO PLANNING DETERRENCE

When nuclear weapons dominated deterrence, the Strategic Air Command (now STRATCOM) and the European Command became the focal point for planning the deterrent and targeting nuclear forces. If nonnuclear forces are to dominate our future deterrent posture, however, and if the deterrent must be tailored to each specific country that poses a potential threat, the planning system must change. Major responsibility for planning a combined conventional, nuclear, and defensive posture and strategy should rest with regional commanders in chief (CINCS) and their planning staffs. STRATCOM remains the repository of expertise in nuclear planning and targeting, and decisionmakers must find a way to meld that expertise with the practical knowledge and responsibilities of the regional CINCS.

A Holistic Approach to Defense

The ballistic missile threat to the United States is a real, but not the only, threat.[14] Aircraft cruise missiles and remotely piloted vehicles can be used to deliver nuclear, chemical, and biological weapons. A few experts working thousands of miles from a target could easily infiltrate such weapons into the United States. A total defense policy must consider all of these threats. NMD will be part of the mix, but what share of the defense pie should it consume? Although the United States could afford such a program if its leaders deem it to be important, opportunity costs could mean slighting defenses against other threats as well as relations with our allies.

A New Approach to Arms Control

The ABM Treaty and the Strategic Arms Reduction Talks (START) process belong to another era, when the United States and the Soviet Union were in an intense race and when mutual assured destruction was at the heart of U.S. strategy. Some argue that the START process has become an impediment to nuclear force reductions and that the ABM Treaty is an obstacle to a needed missile defense, but the United States cannot walk away from these Cold War arms control treaties without major diplomatic repercussions. Furthermore, although the U.S.-Russian strategic dialogue has improved, the need for expanding transparency with respect to strategic programs remains. For example, the United States is uncertain of the implications of Russia's changing strategic doctrine and has little idea how many nonstrategic nuclear weapons remain in Russia; conversely, Russia is obviously concerned with U.S. plans for an NMD system.

To address these mutual concerns, both sides must develop a new regime that focuses less on counting the number of deployed nuclear weapons or the power aperture product of radar and more on mutual assurance and transparency. The United States and Russia would lay their future plans for strategic weapons and defenses on the table, and each side would have an opportunity to question the other's plans and indicate their reservations. A written agreement, but not necessarily a treaty, would incorporate mutual understandings and concerns. The agreement would establish a mechanism through which either party could challenge apparent changes in the other party's programs and plans and would oblige the parties to meet and consider any challenge promptly.[15]

At the same time, engaging China in a meaningful strategic dialogue to develop a mutual understanding of strategic plans and programs is equally as critical. Although such a dialogue seems very difficult, it seemed impossible in 1960 that the United States could develop such an exchange with the Soviet Union; and yet a dialogue did develop, largely through the arms control process. That dialogue led to a tacit mutual understanding about the dangers of nuclear war, which was a critical element in maintaining stability through a series of Cold War crises. Formal arms control negotiations that now seem so out of date for dealing with Russia can possibly provide a means for engaging China. Given the stakes involved, continuing to develop such a dialogue is worth the effort.

SOME PRINCIPLES TO BUILD ON

It will take some time to think through the strategy and force requirements and address the radically new situation described above, and much debate in this country and abroad is likely. The outcome of that debate is uncertain, but several broad principles seem clear. First, the United States needs to develop a more comprehensive approach to deterrence that looks beyond nuclear weapons to include nonnuclear forces and a variety of defenses. Second, the United States must tailor deterrence strategies and postures to each potential adversary. Third, the United States will no longer rely as heavily on nuclear weapons for deterrence as it did in past confrontations with the Soviet Union. At least for some years, dominant U.S. conventional capabilities will provide the cutting edge for deterrence. Fourth, nuclear weapons, although a much smaller element in the new deterrent scheme, will still play an important role in deterring the use of weapons of mass destruction by others, a role that must be more clearly defined. Finally, defenses also will contribute to deterrence by making the prospect of a successful attack less likely, and they can limit damage if deterrence fails and the attack occurs. Melding all of these elements into a new deterrent posture will be a major challenge. It requires new, imaginative thinking; and one must cast aside outdated paradigms, including the twentieth-century image of an arms race. It no longer exists.

Notes

1. Ian Traynor, "Russia Raises Nuclear Threat against the West with New Defense Strategy," *Guardian*, January 14, 2000.

2. International Institute for Strategic Studies, *The Military Balance, 1999–2000* (October 1999), pp. 106–107; Nikolai Sokov, "Nuclear Weapons and Russia's Economic Crisis," *Policy Memorandum No. 43* (Monterey Institute of International Studies, November 1998).

3. Peter Baker and John Pomfret, "China Leaders in Moscow to Sign Pact," *Washington Post*, July 16, 2001, p. A9.

4. For a provocative analysis of Soviet missile defenses and the ABM Treaty, see William T. Lee, *The ABM Treaty Charade: A Study in Elite Illusion and Delusion* (Washington, D.C.: Council on Social and Economic Studies, 1997).

5. David L. Grange, "Asymmetric Warfare: Old Method, New Concern," *National Strategy Forum Review* (winter 2000).

6. "We would do whatever it took to help Taiwan defend itself." President George W. Bush, statement on ABC Television's Good Morning America, April 26, 2001.

7. *India Today*, July 1998 (quoting Prime Minister Atal Bihari Vajpayee).

8. Federation of American Scientists, *Nuclear Forces Guide*, www.fas.org/nuke/

guide/dprk/nuke, accessed March 4, 2000.

9. Center for Nonproliferation Studies, Monterey Institute of International Studies, *Chemical and Biological Weapons: Possession and Programs Past and Present* (June 23, 2001) (hereinafter *Chemical and Biological Weapons*).

10. David Albright and Khidir Hamza, "Iraq's Reconstitution of Its Nuclear Weapons Program," *Arms Control Today* (October 1988).

11. *Chemical and Biological Weapons.*

12. Ibid.

13. *Patterns of Global Terrorism 2000* (Washington, D.C.: U.S. Department of State, April 30, 2001); Phillip T. Reeker, acting spokesman, and Edmund J. Hull, acting coordinator for global terrorism, U.S. Department of State, briefing on report release, April 30, 2001.

14. Report of the Commission to Assess the Ballistic Missile Threat to the United States, July 15, 1998 (known as the Rumsfeld report).

15. For a fuller description of this idea, see Leon Sloss and Benson Adams, "Arms Control Needs Overhaul," *Naval Institute Proceedings* (February 2000).

Part IV

Is Arms Control Dead?

Harold Brown

Is Arms Control Dead?

O n the evening of January 22, 1961, while snow still lay on the ground in Washington from a storm that had nearly disrupted the presidential inauguration two days earlier, a group met at the Metropolitan Club at the invitation of John J. McCloy, whom the newly inaugurated president had designated as his advisor on arms control and disarmament. After dinner, McCloy asked the advice of each of those present on how to organize the executive branch for those issues and, specifically, where to lodge the function of arms control and disarmament. Later that year, acting on McCloy's conclusions, President John Kennedy created an independent agency, instituted in 1962 as the Arms Control and Disarmament Agency (ACDA). Nearly 40 years later, in 1999, that agency was dismantled and its functions incorporated into the Department of State.

Does the end of ACDA signal the demise of arms control? Certainly it could be argued that arms control is very sick. Last year the U.S. Senate rejected the Comprehensive Test Ban Treaty (CTBT). The Russian Duma has failed to act favorably on the second Strategic Arms Reduction Treaty (START II) several times since it was signed in 1993. Russia cited its need for troop deployments in the Caucasus to crush the

Harold Brown is a counselor and trustee at CSIS and is a partner at Warburg, Pincus & Co. Brown served as secretary of defense from 1977 to 1981. He wishes to thank Daniel Rankin for contributing to this article.

revolt in Chechnya as the basis for its violation of the treaty that limits conventional forces in Europe. The Clinton administration seeks a revision of the Anti-Ballistic Missile (ABM) Treaty of 1972 on the basis of a looming missile threat from North Korea and a potential one from other rogue states. Congressional Republicans consider the administration's proposed ABM deployment and corresponding revisions in the treaty inadequate. Many urge complete withdrawal from the ABM Treaty on the basis that it was entered into with a now-defunct partner, the Soviet Union. India and Pakistan continue to develop nuclear weapons and ballistic missiles; they have not adhered to any agreement that would deny them this option. Compliance with the Missile Technology Control Regime by some U.S. allies is questionable. The Wassenaar agreement that succeeded the earlier Coordinating Committee for Multilateral Export Controls Agreement, directed at depriving Communist countries of Western military technology, has proven more difficult to enforce because it is aimed not only at the former Soviet states but also at states about whose threatening nature the industrialized signatories of Wassenaar disagree. Finally, China, an emerging military power (emerging more slowly than political and journalistic rhetoric suggests), is a participant in few arms control agreements.

Nonetheless, Russian and U.S. nuclear delivery systems continue to be dismantled under the original START. Chemical and biological warfare agreements do limit (though not eliminate) those threats. The parties to the Conventional Forces in Europe Treaty have worked to adapt it to changed borders. U.S. funding continues to buy surplus Russian fissionable material and to support nonweapons research by Russian scientists and engineers who might otherwise be producing weapons for rogue states. From this point of view, arms control is preferable to the alternatives and is making progress. But which assessment is correct?

The end of the Cold War has encouraged American political leaders, analysts, strategic-military thinkers, and pundits in general to conclude that the United States won the arms race against the Soviet Union. By extension, many conclude that it could win any future one that may develop in competition with an emerging China, a possible resurgent

Russia, or any rogue state. They may be right, but there are dangers in a path that begins with the belief that arms control is therefore irrelevant. That suggests the utility of arms control has not disappeared.

For one thing, the pro-armaments rhetoric in the Congress has not been accompanied by a nearly commensurate increase in the level of funding and is even less likely to be so in the future. Our European and Japanese allies will not go along with a U.S. national security policy that does not include an arms control component. Although the threat of a massive thermonuclear attack on the United States is gone and deterrence worked for four decades, the spread of weapons of mass destruction to terrorist states and nonstate groups, even if only as a counterdeterrent to possible U.S. actions against them, is real. Active defense and preemption are important and legitimate responses on the part of the United States, but renouncing arms control agreements gives up what is also a valuable tool to deal with such threats—specifically, allied cooperation in inhibiting proliferation by preventing technology transfers, which is heavily dependent on an arms control regime. The tension between these conflicting responses is a challenge to national security policy. Absent a U.S. arms-control policy and corresponding initiatives, the field would be left to pressures by other countries and by nongovernmental organizations that often aim their initiatives at dismantling weapons systems of special value to the United States. An example is the treaty to ban land mines; it would delegitimize the defensive mine system on which the United States and South Korea rely for protection against a North Korean invasion. Therefore, an earlier, more proactive U.S. leadership role in arms control, working with our allies and others, is needed to ensure that U.S. interests are preserved.

Some proponents of arms control think of the process as an end in itself, a way of reversing a trend toward self-reinforcing, arms-driven political conflict. Many opponents see arms control as a trap, lulling the United States to sleep in the face of real threats, as a false substitute for military strength and political will. They expect the United States to be out negotiated or fear that others will cheat while the

United States will be constrained, even beyond the formal limits of agreements, by lawyers and by congressional pressures.

In a given case, either may be right. However, in my view, conflicting political goals and strategies drive arms competitions, not the reverse. Arms control is, therefore, a useful tool in managing such conflicts rather than a cure. There is, in fact, a zero-sum component to arms control agreements, with each participant trying to constrain others to the maximum extent possible while minimizing the constraints that apply to itself. U.S. negotiators can be out negotiated if they are unskillful, but there are benefits and one must remember that the real goal for the United States is neither to engage in, nor to avoid, arms control agreements but to enhance our security.

Arms control can do this by limiting the size and/or nature of military threats. Moreover, predictability can help enhance security; bounding the uncertainties about behavior of other players does improve U.S. security. The verification provisions of arms control agreements, despite the usual protests about their imperfections, assist national means of verification. It is worth accepting some limits on U.S. weapon systems and on some operational deployments, of the sort found in confidence-building measures, in order to limit threats to the United States and to reduce our uncertainties about what others will do. These favorable effects of arms control on U.S. security explain the frequent support (surprising to arms control opponents) by senior military officers, including the Joint Chiefs of Staff.

So arms control is an integral component of national security. Each proposal needs to be weighed in context with other factors—military capability, diplomatic conditions, and the long-term effect on political behavior of all the players—in order to decide on the proper policy. To either dismiss arms control out of hand or blindly pursue it, however, is ill advised. In that light, here are some specific judgments.

Because the CTBT will be observed by the United States even in the absence of Senate ratification, by Republican and Democratic presidents alike, and because the effect of undetected cheating by others will not be different whether the United States ratifies or not, the Senate should ratify the CTBT. If a serious concern develops about the reliability of the U.S. nuclear stockpile (despite sophisticated computer simulations and nonnuclear experiments), a future president could invoke "Supreme National Interest" provisions and order testing.

So long as Russia abides by START II, and irrespective of Duma ratification, the United States should negotiate further reductions in strategic delivery systems. Reducing the number of strategic warheads by half would eliminate as many warheads from a potential Russian attack as would a 50-percent-effective ABM. But that does not deal with the threat of attack by a rogue state or from an accidental launch. A technically effective and cost-effective ABM deployment responsive to the size, geography, and sophistication of the threat is therefore justified. To that end, amendment of the ABM Treaty to allow a very limited national missile defense (NMD) deployment should be negotiated. In the face of a substantial probability of proliferation of weapons of mass destruction to nations that are geographically nearer to Russia than to the United States, Russia should have an interest in such modifications to the treaty, especially if given suitable incentive. The diplomatic environment for such negotiations will be tricky, because that environment will need to be shaped as well with our European and Asian allies and with China, even though they are not parties to the treaty. In any event, it would be a bad mistake to withdraw from the ABM Treaty without going through a serious attempt at amendment. Actual deployment should start with theater ballistic missile defense currently permitted under the ABM Treaty, while working with Russia on NMD amendments and interpretations.

Confidence-building measures should be pursued. The negotiations leading to the conventions on incidents at sea with Russia and with China are successful examples. Such measures are especially important to improve regional security, as in, for example, the Middle East, Korea, and the Asian subcontinent.

Some easing of strategic offensive force readiness has already taken place and more is possible. However, large-scale separation of warheads from delivery systems would require days—or possibly months—to reconstitute in the event of an attack. That level of unpreparedness would, in itself, prove a temptation to some to attack and is therefore an unjustified increase in vulnerability.

When McCloy got around to me at that January 1961 meeting, I was then director of the Lawrence Livermore Laboratory and had no idea that within weeks I would be asked to become a senior Department of Defense (DoD) official. The others were horrified when I suggested—more than half seriously—that the best place to locate arms control within the U.S. government was in the DoD, because it could be integrated with weapons system planning and military policy there. It was an impractical suggestion—the words "fox in the hen house" come to mind. But, without DoD support, or at least acquiescence, arms control tends not to go very far. Conversely, some of the most important arms control initiatives have come from thoughtful civilian and military leaders in the DoD who know that, though arms control does not substitute for military capability, it can limit threats.

Because arms control is an integral and valuable tool for national security, informed national security officials will support it and use it. Even more important than DoD acquiescence is strong White House, and specifically presidential, support and leadership. Every president beginning with Truman and Eisenhower has indeed pursued arms control at some point during his administration—Nixon, Ford, Reagan, and Bush, no less than Kennedy, Johnson, Carter, and Clinton. Future presidents will continue to do so, whatever the rhetoric during a presidential campaign, and whether a separate agency, such as ACDA, exists or not. Arms control will be a part of U.S. foreign and defense policy because it can and does enhance our national security. Arms control is not dead.

James Schlesinger

The Demise of Arms Control?

Is arms control dead?—certainly not if its proponents recognize and adapt to the altered world in which we now live. Alternatively, if we fail to adapt and instead pursue arms control objectives derived from a bipolar world or reflecting naïve, universalist assumptions, arms control will be useless and, at times, counterproductive.

The proper objective for arms control is to increase international stability and, more directly, the security of the United States and its allies. It should not be, as its most eager supporters advocate, simply to reduce armaments.

The central feature of classic arms control agreements was that the United States and the Soviet Union could enhance mutual stability and thus their own security by agreeing to limit certain categories of (destabilizing) armaments, providing such agreements could be verified. Thus, overall international stability would be enhanced. The risk, of course, was that achieving or preserving the agreement might become an end in itself and that such painful questions as compliance or whether the agreement actually enhanced stability would be overlooked.

James Schlesinger is a counselor and trustee at CSIS. He is also senior adviser to Lehman Brothers and chairman of the MITRE corporation. He was secretary of defense from 1973 to 1975 and secretary of energy from 1977 to 1979.

Copyright © 2000 by The Center for Strategic and International Studies and the Massachusetts Institute of Technology
The Washington Quarterly • 23:2 pp. 179–182.

Even during the Cold War, the presupposition of bipolarity was pressed by some further than it should have been, as if the United States and the Soviet Union were alone in the world. Some advocates, for example, tended to forget the simple fact that U.S. forces provided extended deterrence for U.S. allies in Europe—and, in a somewhat more benign context, in northeast Asia. Thus, the generally bipolar world was complicated by the need to take third parties into account. In that bipolar world, many arms control issues could be viewed in terms of duopoly—in that only the United States and the Soviet Union had significant capabilities, and thus the task was one of negotiating with, and scrutinizing the behavior of, one's principal adversary.

But the Cold War is now over; the Soviet Union is gone. Advanced weapons capabilities have spread and will further spread to other parties. Thus, the analogy for arms control has now shifted from duopoly to cartel—in which the behavior of numerous other parties must be watched and preferably controlled. This is a far more demanding task. History teaches us that smaller participants in cartel agreements frequently enter those agreements with no intention to comply in the long run (and frequently not even in the short run). They enter into the cartel agreement to restrict the behavior of others, to draw advantages for themselves, and with every intention, to put it bluntly, to cheat early. In the history of cartels, incidentally, it has normally been the leader that has born the principal burden of complying with the agreement. For that reason, it is particularly incumbent upon the leader to be wary at the outset regarding the details of the agreement.

Consider the goal of nonproliferation. What we have seen in the last half-century is that proliferation cannot be prevented—but it can successfully be slowed. Indeed, compared with the fears expressed in the 1950s and 1960s, the spread of nuclear weapons has been remarkably slow. (It might have been even slower if the United States, priding itself on its openness and its eagerness for declassification, had not so generously spread around information on how to design and produce nuclear weapons).

Given the metaphor of the cartel, the necessary target for arms control is to constrain those who desire to acquire nuclear weapons. A Luxembourg or even a Germany may have no inclination to exploit an arms control agreement as a cover for cheating, but others will have that simple objective. A general agreement imposes no restraint on a North Korea or an Iraq. They will be constrained by direct pressure or by direct action, if they are to be constrained at all. For rather different reasons, an India or an Israel is not going to be constrained by a general agreement. To believe otherwise is to embrace the quixotic notions of the Kellogg-Briand Pact.

Thus the question of enforceability becomes more difficult as it becomes more central. Sometimes, difficult tradeoffs must be made. In 1994, the United States chose to ignore the clear violations of North Korea and its obligations under the Non-Proliferation Treaty to the International Atomic Energy Agency—in the hope that it might be able to "freeze" North Korea's nuclear development. Sometimes, arms control agreements are little more than pious hopes with little capacity (or even intent) to achieve enforcement. Today there are 10 to 15 nations aggressively seeking chemical or biological weapons, many of them unconstrained by their obligations under the Chemical Weapons Convention or Biological Weapons Convention. Detection or verification is simply too difficult. Indeed, in the case of the Biological Weapons Convention there simply is no enforcement mechanism.

The upshot is that we fool ourselves if we believe that general agreements impose substantial barriers to those determined to acquire new capabilities. But arms control objectives can be obtained through direct pressure—rather than through a general agreement—or, as the case of Israel and the Osirak reactor may suggest, through direct action. For those who would argue that, in a world of sovereign equals, such action violates national sovereignty, one should point to the recent rhetoric regarding Serbia. If we have embraced the right to trample on sovereignty in the name of human rights, surely we must be prepared to consider similar action to prevent a rogue nation from acquiring a nuclear capability (something that is detectable).

Of course, the issue of sovereignty goes to the heart of the presumption of universalism that forms the basis of many recent arms- control agreements. That all sovereign nations are equal is an axiom among international lawyers—if not among practicing politicians. Nonetheless, this legal concept should not be allowed to obscure fundamental realities.

The fiction of equality among sovereign nations underlays the recent controversy over the Comprehensive Test Ban Treaty (CTBT). The negotiators of that treaty sought to be faithful to the principle of equal treatment of all nations, but could do so only by ignoring the basic realities. Thus, they presumed that the testing regime should be the same for both weapon states and non-weapon states. In the quest to constrain weapons development, it is presumed that the testing regime should be the same for the United States and, for example, Luxembourg. Thus, the testing regime becomes the same for nations that have no nuclear weapons, for those that have nuclear weapons but are most unlikely to have to envisage circumstances in which they must be used, and for states that must maintain the readiness of their nuclear arsenal. Such a regime might be acceptable to the last category of states for an extended period, but cannot be accepted in perpetuity.[1] For a number of reasons, too lengthy to be developed here, complicated devices like nuclear weapons, composed of thousands of parts, cannot remain untested for extended periods—without confidence in the reliability of those weapons diminishing. Thus, over time, the total cessation of testing implies gambling with the effectiveness of the deterrent. Computer modeling—even good computer modeling—is no substitute for testing. (For many, the inevitability of the decline of the reliability of the nuclear stockpile was a bonus and possibly an objective of a test ban).

When presented with the CTBT, all members of the Senate would have to judge for themselves how much risk over time they were prepared to accept. The majority of the Senate ultimately concluded— quite properly in my judgment—that gambling with the efficacy of the U.S. deterrent was not something that they were prepared to ratify, given the unique position of the United States in the world today. Not knowing how the strategic scene might change over 20, 30, or 40 years, the majority were unwilling to gamble with the reliability of the U.S. nuclear deterrent.

Perhaps a regime of no testing would have been acceptable if the United States were a normal country with a normal foreign policy. But the United States has drifted to, been pushed to, or seized the role of international sheriff and arbiter. So long as it accepts the heavy commitments that role implies and so long as uncertainties regarding the longer-run strategic scene exist, the United States cannot accept the same testing regime as nations prepared to forego the acquisition of nuclear weapons or nations whose deterrents are essentially there for show.

The quixotic pursuit of universality, which ignored both the long-run necessity of testing for serious nuclear weapon states and the distinct role that the United States plays in the world, has meant that the opportunity was lost to craft a testing regime that would have imposed some restraint on proliferation without imposing a long-run decline in the reliability of crucial nuclear weapons stockpiles.

The conclusion is simple. General arms-control agreements, if they are to be successful, must be grounded in the realities—including the reality of different roles and requirements for different states. Otherwise, such agreements will come apart on a Procrustean bed, which essentially denies that such differences exist—and must be dealt with. Thus, the future of arms control will depend on the willingness of our negotiators to shed obsolescent ideas—and to find more imaginative ways for limiting the spread of arms in a greatly altered environment.

Note

1. When questioned on the test ban by the White House in 1993, I indicated that, while I was not a fan of the test ban, the two ingredients that could not be part of such a ban were permanence of the treaty and zero yield. It is perhaps unnecessary to remind this audience that those two features were ultimately included in the proposed treaty presented to the Senate.

Brad Roberts

The Road Ahead for Arms Control

How is arms control likely to evolve? Will arms control grow more important to the national security of the United States or less so? Will growing numbers of states seek arms control to enhance international stability or reject it as unreliable? These are perennial questions. They are gaining new currency at the end of the 1990s as major elections loom in the United States, Russia, and elsewhere.[1]

The first post-Cold War decade seems to have raised more questions than it has answered about the future of arms control. Its purpose has drifted in U.S. policy circles while the international community has been uncertain about where it might be headed. Its process over the last decade has been determined largely by momentum, a momentum that appears to be dissipating. That decade began in promising fashion for arms control. The long-running U.S. debate between its advocates and opponents had given way to broad consensus about the utility of arms control to manage the end of the U.S.-Soviet confrontation. The 1990s also brought a host of possibilities for arms control in the new bilateral U.S.-Russian relationship. Additionally, the end of the Cold War led to a new, nearly global consensus that proliferation challenges re-

Brad Roberts is a member of the research staff at the Institute for Defense Analyses in Alexandria, Va. He also serves as chairman of the research advisory council of the Chemical and Biological Arms Control Institute. From 1987 to 1995 he was editor of *The Washington Quarterly*. The views expressed here are his own and should not be attributed to any of the institutions with which he is affiliated or their sponsors.

Copyright © 2000 by The Center for Strategic and International Studies and the Massachusetts Institute of Technology
The Washington Quarterly • 23:2 pp. 219–232.

quired substantial improvements to the nuclear, biological, and chemical (NBC) weapons control regimes.

But the promise of arms control so evident at the beginning of the decade is not so evident today. Some of the most important possibilities for deep nuclear reductions have proven difficult to capture. Waiting for Russian ratification of the second Strategic Arms Reduction Treaty (START II) is like "waiting for Godot," and the Clinton administration's decision not to pursue further agreements until START II was ratified has meant that the 1990s passed without formal negotiations on new measures. At the same time that bilateral approaches have receded in importance, multilateral approaches have multiplied and gained international prominence. But it has also proven difficult to turn the desire for a stronger global treaty regime on NBC weapons into reality.

Moreover, the political energy in Washington devoted to arms control has receded almost as quickly and dramatically as the Soviet threat. A large measure of the available energy has been spent on what might politely be called "reengineering" of the arms control process within the U.S. government, as both the Departments of State and Defense have reorganized to deal with the arms control agenda. Arms controllers have been asked to do more with less (some would even prefer that they do less with less). The broad centrist commitment to arms control so evident a decade ago has been replaced by something more familiar: a replay of the old debate between the two extremes, between those who believe arms control is not in the national interest and those who see it as an unalloyed good, as the right and necessary work of any decent nation. Political gridlock in Washington has deepened, with the Senate holding a growing number of treaties hostage—or killing them outright, as in the case of the Comprehensive Test Ban Treaty (CTBT). Not surprisingly, congressional involvement in the arms control process has brought partisanship with it and a growing willingness to exploit national security issues for domestic political gain.

So what next? In speculating about the role of arms control over the next decade, most experts in the arms control community anticipate that momentum will continue. By and large, they tend to predict an expanding writ for arms control, through the broader and more effective implementation of existing regimes and the accretion of new instruments. The future they envision is a fairly linear projection of the past, though with some bumps along the way to be sure. But the future may prove rather different from this caricature. Momentum alone may not propel the process much further. The bumps may turn out to be rather severe and the writ of arms control may well contract.

The central thesis of this short article is that down the arms control road are some big forks. The years ahead are not likely to be business as usual, as these forks are probably closer than many believe. There is little to suggest that the analytical community has either thought through the nature of the necessary choices to come or assessed the types of security environments that might be encountered down one path or another. Without a clearer sense of the alternatives, the United States is likely to find it difficult to know which direction to choose when a fork appears.

The road ahead consists of three paths. The first is the path to continued strategic reductions. The second is the path to a stronger global treaty regime. The third is the path to restored compliance by noncompliant states. Of course, the paths also intersect. It is therefore useful to explore the synergies among them. This approach helps to bring into better focus the long-term viability of arms control and the basic U.S. strategic choices.

The Future of Strategic Reductions

The first fork lies on the path of strategic reductions. In the U.S. arms control community it is still widely assumed that a continued progression of nuclear reduction and deemphasis as well as a widening scope for strategic arms control lies ahead. How often is the question "What is the future of arms control?" framed by wondering what START III will look like? To be sure, arms controllers appreciate the many bumps on the START path, but for most it is simply a given that the bilateral reductions process between Washington and Moscow will continue to serve as the backbone of arms control for decades to come. As of winter 2000, many experts in Washington seem to believe that the process will get back on track as soon as presidential elections in the two countries restore a measure of predictability and initiative to the bilateral political dialogue. Many also hold to the view that some point of compromise will be found whereby the Russians agree to modify the Anti-Ballistic Missile (ABM) Treaty in a way that allows the United States to proceed with national missile defense (NMD) deployments without unilaterally abrogating the treaty. Such an agreement seems likely only if Moscow decides to proceed with the START process.

But START II may well be dead; indeed, START may be dead. There are many hints of this already in Russia.[2] The Russian military and political leaderships have reemphasized the role of tactical nuclear weapons in their military strategy. Russian force structure planning is dictated increasingly by budgetary factors and technological obsolescence rather than by arms control considerations. Former president Boris Yeltsin made explicit threats to target the West with strategic rocket forces and even to make first use of nuclear weapons to punish members of the North Atlantic Treaty Organization (NATO) for its actions in Kosovo. Russian experts have also made it clear that U.S. national missile deployments may cripple bilateral agreements on offensive forces, except possibly in a narrow set of circumstances.

Moreover, it is not at all clear that the political will exists in Moscow to compromise with Washington on the ABM Treaty. Nor is it clear that any deal that might be struck between negotiators would be accepted by the Russian Duma. From the Russian perspective, the world has changed profoundly since the Soviet negotiators were last tempted to strike such a deal a decade ago. There is a widespread conviction in Moscow that the United States has exploited its unipolar status to Russia's disadvantage, not least by expanding NATO eastward and making war against a Russian ally in Kosovo. Why, then, should Moscow do Washington's bidding by helping it to secure a strategic advantage?

How might Russia depart from START? Russian experts have offered a variety of scenarios. Sergei Kortunov has described one possibility, in which Moscow no longer decides to pursue a parity-based nuclear relationship with the United States and to turn its nuclear planning "eyes" to potential nuclear adversaries nearer to its periphery.[3] Sergei Rogov has described another possibility, a decision to seek common cause with Beijing in an antihegemonic alliance based in part on Sino-Russian nuclear cooperation.[4]

But even if Washington and Moscow renew their political commitment to the bilateral U.S.-Russian strategic reductions process, the future of deep reductions is going to be determined in part by China, a factor that barely plays today. China has had a unique nuclear posture until now, depending on very low numbers of not particularly survivable strategic weapons backed by a relatively small nuclear infrastructure. But China also has rising concerns about the viability of its nuclear deterrent and especially about the survivability of assured second-strike capabilities in light of the advances in Western conventional weapons and the emergence of a host of nuclear problems around its periphery.[5]

What kind of a strategic relationship is possible among the three major nuclear powers? Is a trilateral version of mutually assured destruction possible or desirable? Who is willing to accept parity with whom? How might U.S. deployment of missile defenses, both theater and national, impact the force structure preferences of Russia and China? Indeed, what does the Sino-Russian leg of the triangle look like? How deeply unsettled would the world be by a sharp decline in Russian offensive forces, a robust increase in Chinese offensive forces, and some movement by the United States to a limited NMD?

As the U.S. arms-control community begins to ponder these questions, it typically turns to the strategic vocabulary of old. To think strategy is to think nuclear is to think deterrence. Never mind that deterrence is a language of enemies, and the big three may be adversarial but show no signs of actively planning to launch all-out wars of societal annihilation against each other. Never mind that the strategic nuclear dimension is increasingly likely to be defined by complex and ambiguous relations of offense and defense. For China to come fully into the conceptual picture of the U.S. arms-control community will likely require a good deal of intellectual homework in the period ahead.

So what are the forks in the strategic reductions path ahead? The arms control process seems certain to pause for at least a year or two, as governments in Washington and Moscow remake themselves and settle on new policy directions. It may well have stopped entirely, if Russia opts to move in a novel and independent direction, and/or if China cannot be brought in. Alternatively, strategic arms control may lurch in an entirely new direction, with an agreement encompassing China, and perhaps France and Britain as well. Reductions by the United States and others seem likely to continue, at least for a while, though perhaps not as part of a formal process. Perhaps the least likely path ahead is the incremental and linear movement through a series of bilateral START measures leading later rather than sooner to virtual denuclearization by the the five permanent members of the United Nations Security Council, the P-5.

The Future of the Global NBC Treaty Regime

The second fork lies on the path of the nonproliferation regime. Many in the U.S. arms control community see continued progress toward strengthening the larger regime by making incremental improvements to each of its components and by bringing a larger number of states within the regime. Indeed, the 1990s began with a major push in this direction. The end of the Cold War made new things possible, and the Persian Gulf War made new things necessary.

Since then, negotiation of the Chemical Weapons Convention (CWC) concluded and the treaty entered into force. The Nuclear Non-Proliferation Treaty (NPT) was extended indefinitely at the review and extension conference in 1995. The International Atomic Energy Agency has gained new rights to conduct special inspections, with the promise of more to come. And negotiators have been at work on a monitoring and compliance protocol for the Biological and Toxin Weapons Convention (BWC). These myriad activities all suggest that the international community is committed to strengthen the regime and that the result has been good progress.

But appearances may prove deceptive. NPT extension was won with a lot of arm twisting and there is ample evidence to suggest that a significant portion of the member states are sufficiently dissatisfied with the pace of nuclear arms reductions (or, more precisely, Article VI performance) of the nuclear weapon states to consider extraordinary measures. Concerns about the long-term viability of the regime were accentuated by the subsequent emergence of India and Pakistan as de facto nuclear weapon states, and the apparent ineffectiveness of the regime in preventing this and of the major powers in reversing it.

The U.S. Senate's rejection of the CTBT magnifies these concerns. The Senate's decision focused primarily on the treaty's impact on the reliability of the deterrent and focused hardly at all on the international consequences of rejection. Those consequences could yet prove very significant for the future of the NPT regime. U.S. rejection raises a big question about the fate of the CTBT. It unavoidably raises the question about the likelihood that the nuclear weapon states will ever live up to their obligations in the NPT and about the reductions process more generally. It raises a question about whether or how Washington intends to lead the effort to secure the nuclear peace. And it raises yet another question about the commitment of the United States to multilateral processes. Answers to these questions await a new administration in 2001.

In the meantime, the spring 2000 NPT Review Conference will bear the brunt of these grievances and unmet expectations. It is likely to raise profound questions about the regime, as many of those opposed to indefinite extension act to express their opposition to U.S. moves by distancing themselves somehow from the function of the regime. One plausible scenario would see a dozen or so especially aggrieved states opt to "pause" their membership in the NPT, whether at the review conference in 2000 or in 2005. At the very least, growing friction over the NPT regime is likely to have a deleterious impact on the effort to engage these states to strengthen the NBC treaty regime more generally by signing up to specific new measures.[6]

Similarly, implementation of the CWC has not gone smoothly.[7] Initial entry into force was delayed by the failure of the principal chemical weapons possessors—the United States and Russia—to act in timely fashion on ratification. Initial implementation has been hampered by the collapse of their bilateral agreement to jointly resolve their chemical weapons problems outside of the framework of the multilateral convention and also by the prolonged U.S. delay in passing the necessary implementing legislation. The U.S. ability to lead in The Hague, the site of the Organization for the Prohibition of Chemical Weapons, has been impaired by ambivalence in Washington about the merits and viability of the regime, and indeed about the United States' stake in combating the proliferation of chemical weapons through arms control approaches.

The effort to strengthen the BWC has also proven more difficult and time consuming than many had anticipated.[8] Technical and operational factors have been important, as negotiators have found it difficult to find treaty-based mechanisms sufficient to monitor and enforce compliance that are not detrimental to other interests, including the protection of commercially-sensitive information. But political factors have also been important, including deep divisions between the nonaligned states and the West, and even within the Western group itself.

What can we know today about the path ahead between now and the year 2005? The 2000 Review Conference for the NPT is likely to be fractious. This, combined with proliferation developments in South Asia and elsewhere, is likely to lead to a more fundamental debate between now and the 2005 Review Conference about the long-term viability of the regime. At that time, CWC implementation will enter a new phase, as the 10-year destruction period gives way to extended monitoring and rising debate about hold outs, drop outs, and delayed implementation by Russia (and perhaps the United States). In 2005, the BWC is likely to have some new protocol, which has been opened for signature by states parties but has actually been ratified by a relatively small number of the states of special concern to the regime—in other words, a two-tiered system.

What departures are possible? Collapse of the regime over the coming decade certainly appears unlikely. But the alternative may be something as troubling in its own right.[9] If the effort to strengthen the global treaty regime is widely perceived to have lost its momentum, an increasing number of countries are likely to position themselves for a rapid material response to a collapse of the regime. As latent capabilities are increasingly shaped into virtual weapons programs, there will be a heightened risk of rampant proliferation in response to some catalytic event. Absent such an event, we may well find ourselves in a world in which the writ of arms control appears broad but its actual effect is quite circumscribed.

The Looming Crisis of Confidence

The third fork lies on the path of treaty implementation. A major crisis of confidence in arms control is brewing.[10] That crisis has its seeds in the so far incomplete efforts to restore Iraq and North Korea to full treaty compliance. It grew a bit with nuclear developments in South Asia and that challenge to the regime. If the arms control architecture is shown to be incapable of dealing with extant noncompliance, the entire edifice may come tumbling down.

Let us not write off the possibility of success in either Iraq or North Korea. But let us also consider the consequences of failure. The Iraqi and North Korean cases have emerged as tests of the United Nations (UN) Security Council—which, after all, is final arbiter and enforcer of the global treaty regime. The Security Council has not yet failed this test; but its interim grades are not encouraging. Its effectiveness has been hindered by the absence of strategic consensus among its permanent members—and by continued doubts about Russian and Chinese compliance with their own arms control obligations (not least the BWC). Successful resolution of the situations in Iraq and North Korea (and of the BWC problems in Russia and China) could go a long way to sustaining the viability of arms control.

But Russian and Chinese voices, along with many others, are quick to argue their case for how U.S. actions have impaired the ability of the Security Council to protect the global treaty regime. They would argue that the problems confronting the Security Council's enforcement role are exacerbated by U.S. disinterest in CWC implementation and compliance, its corruption of the UN Special Commission on Iraq (UNSCOM) process through the introduction of independent spying activities, its reluctance to fulfill its part of the Agreed Framework with North Korea, its hard line in BWC negotiations, its failure to pay long-tardy dues to the UN, and its obvious executive-legislative gridlock on arms control.

The perception is growing that the Security Council has been proven incapable of delivering arms control compliance. It derives from the fact that the Security Council has not managed to restore compliance even when chips are down—when noncompliance has been proven, as in the cases of Iraq and North Korea—and when it has explicitly committed itself to serve as the final arbiter of compliance disputes, as its members have agreed in each of the treaty regimes. If this perception grows unchallenged, there would likely be repercussions well beyond the arms control domain. The perception that the major powers are paper tigers could unleash a new wave of proliferation by states that wish either to contest their guarantees or to protect themselves from such challengers with something more tangible than a guarantee of doubted viability. Alternatively, the perception of the major powers as tougher tigers who can be counted upon to fall out among themselves could generate proliferation pressures of its own.

In short, there is a crisis of confidence brewing about the enforceability of the treaty regime, a crisis magnified by the politics of collective security. Confidence restored would have a salutary effect on arms control by demonstrating the efficacy of the regime and the reliability of the system to protect the security of its adherents. Confidence lost would have a highly damaging effect by demonstrating that arms control is worth nothing more than the paper on which it is written. To be sure, not all countries would be immediately concerned about the loss of confidence in the enforceability of the treaty regime. After all, many states have signed these treaties and adhere to them because they had no interest in banned weapons in the first place. But there is a large and growing number of countries that have foresworn certain categories of weapons on the bet that a cooperative approach to international security would do more for their national security than unilateral reliance on mass destruction weapons. For those countries, the viability of the regime is critical, and they watch its functioning carefully, regularly questioning whether to revisit their original decision. The degree to which these states develop hedging strategies against the collapse of the regime ought to be an excellent indicator of the health of the regime.

The path ahead, then, for the compliance issue is very unlikely to be more of the same. Muddling through for nearly a decade has not resolved the problem. Sooner rather than later, success will be necessary or failure will be assumed.

Understanding Synergies

These three paths run along the same road. Thus there are synergies among them. How might they play out over the next decade?

The positive synergies should not be discounted. Continued or even accelerated strategic nuclear reductions, whether of the two (the United States and Russia), three (plus China), or five (all of the *de jure* nuclear weapon states), could have quite a positive impact on the politics of NPT implementation. Strengthening the global treaty regime could help to reinforce the commitment to arms control approaches more generally in Washington, Moscow, Beijing, and elsewhere. Success in dealing with compliance challenges in Iraq and North Korea could dampen proliferation fears more generally.

But the potentially negative synergies are numerous. Collapse of the bilateral U.S.-Russian agenda probably does not preclude new modes of negotiated restraint in a trilateral or P-5 context, though of course we have no notion of how to navigate from here to there, nor of how to incorporate defenses into a new tripolar or multilateral arms-control architecture. Collapse of the bilateral process could have a very negative impact on the multilateral treaty regime, accelerating the collapse of the NPT consensus, reinforcing growing international fears about collapse of the chemical and biological regimes, and eroding the viability of multilateral institutions. Absent a bilateral process between Washington and Moscow, one must also wonder how much political interest could be mustered in the multilateral processes—after all, the 1990s were not reassuring in this regard. Collapse of the multilateral treaty regime could weaken the bilateral impetus to further reductions. If treaty implementation does not weather its crisis of confidence, the political will to carry forward the bilateral and multilateral agendas seems likely to wane.

From Crisis to Collapse?

It would be hyperbole and overstatement to deem arms control to be in crisis today. But the obstacles on the road ahead appear to be quite substantial and, moreover, to have commanded relatively little thought or preparation from policymakers. Let us consider for a moment the possibility that arms control might collapse and that the treaties as such will be formally abrogated by a significant number of states. What then? Does this actually matter to the United States? There are at least three good reasons to think that it would.

First, the collapse of formalized restraint would come at a time of unprecedented diffusion of the technologies, materiel, and expertise to make weapons of mass destruction (WMD). More than ever before, developed and developing countries possess the indigenous capabilities necessary to produce these weapons and to do so relatively quickly. A rush to break out, to turn latent capabilities into deployed ones, would likely prove deeply unsettling within regions and, given the concomitant proliferation of long-range delivery systems, across them as well. Such a process would sorely test the Ken Waltz proposition that "more is better"[11]—that proliferation would be stabilizing. It is difficult to conceive that a more robust and overt competition in NBC armaments at the interstate level would not also spillover to the nonstate level, increasing the likelihood that terrorists would gain access to the necessary technologies, materials, and expertise to conduct attacks with WMD.

Second, the proliferation of WMD to more states, and the quantitative and qualitative improvements to those capabilities that would follow, would pose new military operational challenges to the United States. It is one thing to prepare for a world in which a handful of states possess banned weapons produced in the basement and untested in war. It is another to prepare for a world in which many states have not fission but fusion weapons, not handfuls of chemicals but arsenals full, not a bit of anthrax but a diverse arsenal of bioengineered organisms, as well as a proven arsenal of precision delivery systems. Protecting U.S. interests abroad and guaranteeing the security of others is likely to prove far more difficult.

Third, a collapse of arms control would likely prove politically unsettling to Americans. It would signal to many the abrupt termination and abject failure of the nation's historic mission to create an international system based on the rule of law and political consensus, and the drift toward a dog-eat-dog world, in which the dogs—and their terrorists—can inflict mass suffering in the United States. At the very least, there would likely be a domestic political price to be paid by those who permitted this to come to pass.

The Leadership Agenda

Surveying this landscape from the vantage of the end of the first post-Cold War decade, what basic strategy choices confront the United States? One is to let the entire edifice of arms control collapse. This is certainly tempting for those who believe that the United States can be protected from the perturbations of an unstable world by two wide oceans (and a stout missile defense). But the costs associated with this choice could be considerable. Our world would be changed in ways harmful to U.S. interests. Moreover, U.S. credibility would be deeply questioned internationally. Having led the international effort to construct this regime, and then having walked away from it, our partners in this effort would certainly question the wisdom of following the United States on its next crusade.

Another option is to start from scratch. This has an analytical appeal—let us set out to construct an arms control regime as if there were no Cold War inheritance. Certainly in U.S. debates over the ratification of the CWC and CTBT, the strengthening of the BWC, and revisions to the ABM Treaty, there is a strongly held view among some U.S. experts that the deal that was struck to achieve a certain outcome in an international negotiating process can readily be set aside in favor of some new deal that these experts somehow find more preferable. But it is not by accident that treaties end up as they do; it is not for lack of effort or wisdom that each and every aspect of these treaties does not match perfectly U.S. preferences—negotiation, after all, is about give and take. Walking away from these existing instruments in the hope of constructing something better would likely leave us with nothing at all. Think Humpty Dumpty here. To start from scratch means to allow arms control to collapse and to then try to use the wreckage as the foundation for something analogous. There is again the question of why others would want to follow the United States down this path.

A variant of the start-from-scratch option is to construct regional arms control regimes as replacements for a collapsed global regime. There has been a good deal of enthusiasm for regional arms control over the last decade and some progress regions formalizing such approaches in some regions.[12] But in the nuclear domain, mechanisms such as the agreement between Argentina and Brazil to abandon their nuclear weapons programs and, more broadly, those such as the Treaty of Tlatelolco have depended to a significant extent on their complementarity, both politically and operationally, with the NPT.[13] They have also depended a bit on the expectation that the major powers would be able to cooperate under UN Security Council auspices to deal with particularly egregious instances of noncompliance. It is far from clear that the circumstances that would lead to an effort to construct multiple regional substitutes for the global treaty regime are the circumstances that would allow those regional mechanisms to function effectively.

The third basic strategic option for the United States is to work with what it has and to make improvements where it can. At the bilateral level, this means continuing to work with Moscow to sustain and formalize the nuclear reduction process. At the multilateral level, this means continuing to work in multilateral venues to implement and strengthen the existing regime—and to deal effectively with extant problems of noncompliance.

If the new administration chooses to embrace this option, how might it operationalize that commitment? Put differently, what does it mean to lead the process and the community over the next decade to a world in which arms control is a reliable instrument of national security and international stability? The road ahead and three paths along it suggest something about the leadership agenda. We must know where we want to go on each of those paths—which directions best serve the U.S. national interest and the interests of the larger international community. This is not a business for platitudes, for it requires hard choices on the hard problems that others would call too hard to solve. But leadership requires more than hard choices on hard problems. To lead, others must want to follow. This requires close collaboration with our partners and listening when they want to move the dialogue in ways not always welcomed in Washington. Implementing those choices requires creating and sustaining political coalitions. Leadership also requires brokering the necessary domestic consensus in support of unpopular steps. It requires paying attention, rather than engaging only episodically. It also requires that self-accepted commitments be honored.

This arms control agenda affords leadership opportunities for many countries, especially within the existing treaty regimes and their associated implementing bodies, but the opportunities are especially salient for the United States. Without Washington playing its proper and necessary role, it seems unlikely that others can pick up the slack adequately to navigate the difficult challenges ahead.

Conclusion

The place of arms control in U.S. national-security strategy and its continued relevance to the evolving global strategic landscape cannot be taken for granted. Indeed, it should not be taken for granted. Times are changing, and it is right and necessary to ask what arms control strategies best suit U.S. interests.

In the first decade after the Cold War, arms control did not play out as many expected when the decade began. Today, we face a number of forks in the arms control road. Conceivably, the efforts to reduce nuclear risks, strengthen the global NBC regime, and deal with compliance challenges will continue to move forward more or less as anticipated by arms control advocates. But alternative possibilities cannot be ignored, and partial or complete failures in one or another of these efforts could have significant implications. In the decade ahead, continued muddling through on the inherited arms-control agenda seems unlikely as momentum is clearly attenuating. A collapse of the arms control process is by no means out of the question. The actual consequences of a collapse of one of the three main arms control paths would depend directly on how it collapsed and crosscutting synergies. But collapse could well change our world in fundamental ways, by making a global power-projection strategy prohibitively risky and by making friends and allies abroad reluctant to follow U.S. initiatives.

If arms control is to play some constructive role in managing the international security environment of the next decade, care must be taken to navigate our way down the right forks on the road ahead. This means setting aside the inherited debate about arms control as doing Good versus doing Evil and getting on with the necessary new debate about the utility of specific instruments and approaches in light of new requirements.

Notes

1. An earlier version of this essay was presented to a conference on "Entering the New Millennium: Dilemmas in Arms Control," April 16-18, 1999, at Sandia National Laboratory and was subsequently published in the conference proceedings. See James Brown, ed., *Entering the New Millennium: Dilemmas in Arms Control* (Albuquerque, N.M.: Sandia Corporation, 1999).

2. Alexander A. Pikayev, *The Rise and Fall of START II: The Russian View,* Work-

ing Paper No. 6, Global Policy Program (Washington, D.C.: Carnegie Endowment for International Peace, September 1999).

3. Sergei Kortunov, "Russian Nuclear Policy After the Cold War," in James Brown, ed., *Arms Control Issues for the Twenty-First Century* (Albuquerque, NM: Sandia Corporation, 1997), 147-172.

4. Sergei Rogov, "The Ballistic Missile Defense Challenge: Consequences of National Missile Defense for Strategic Arms Control Regime," in Brown, ed., *Entering the New Millennium*, 185-204.

5. For more on China's nuclear posture and nuclear future and the implications of its modernization program for U.S. policy, see Robert Manning, Ronald Montaperto, and Brad Roberts, *China, Nuclear Weapons, and Arms Control: A Preliminary Assessment* (New York: Council on Foreign Relations, forthcoming).

6. See "Damage Assessment: The Senate Rejection of the CTBT," *Arms Control Today* 29, no. 6 (September/October 1999): 9-14.

7. "The CWC at the Two-Year Mark: An Interview with Dr. John Gee," *Arms Control Today* 29, no. 4 (April/May 1999): 3-9.

8. For more on this process, see the periodic reports of the Project on Strengthening the Biological and Toxin Weapons Convention and Preventing Biological Warfare, at Bradford University, UK, as posted on their website at <http://www.brad.ac.uk/acad/sbtwc/prgeneva/bw-prgeneva.htm>.

9. Michael Barletta and Amy Sands, eds., *Nonproliferation Regimes At Risk* (Monterey, Calif.: Center for Nonproliferation Studies, 1999).

10. Therese Delpech, "Restoring Compliance," in James Brown, ed., *New Horizons and New Strategies in Arms Control* (Albuquerque, N.M.: Sandia Corporation, 1998): 379-388. See also Brad Roberts, "Revisiting Fred Iklé's 1961 Question: 'After Detection, What?'" in Amy Sands and Michael Moodie, *The Arms Control Compliance Challenge* (Alexandria, Va.: Chemical and Biological Arms Control Institute, forthcoming).

11. Kenneth N. Waltz, *The Spread of Nuclear Weapons: More May Be Better*, Adelphi Paper No. 171 (London: International Institute for Strategic Studies, 1981). See also Scott D. Sagan and Kenneth N. Waltz, *The Spread of Nuclear Weapons: A Debate* (New York: Norton and Co., 1995).

12. Michael Moodie, "Multilateral Arms Control: Challenges and Opportunities," in James Brown, ed., *Challenges in Arms Control for the 1990s* (Amsterdam: VU University Press, 1992), 71-82. See also Jayantha Dhanapala, ed., *Regional Approaches to Disarmament: Security and Stability* (Geneva: UNIDIR, 1993).

13. John R. Redick, Julio C. Carasales, and Paulo S. Wrobel, "Nuclear Rapprochement: Argentina, Brazil, and the Nonproliferaton Regime," *The Washington Quarterly* 18, no. 1 (winter 1995): 107-122.

Thomas Graham

Strengthening Arms Control

International security and the conduct of war have changed dramatically during the last hundred years, perhaps more than in any previous century. One constant in the second half of this century, however, has been the relationship between international security and nuclear weapons. Throughout the Cold War and since, nuclear weapons and arms control have been central components of security discourse and are likely to remain so for the foreseeable future.

While for much of the Cold War, arms control[1] was principally focused on managing the bilateral superpower relationship and capping the arms race, the actors involved and the focus of arms control efforts have broadened to include an increasing number of states and nonstate actors. This article examines the continuing relevance as well as the multilateralization of arms control by exploring the prevailing trends in arms control and analyzing its current condition.

Ambassador Thomas Graham Jr., president of the Lawyers Alliance for World Security, served as the special representative of the president for arms control, nonproliferation, and disarmament from 1994 to 1997 and led U.S. government efforts to achieve a permanent Nuclear Non-Proliferation Treaty (NPT) prior to and during the 1995 Review and Extension Conference of the NPT.

The Washington Quarterly • 23:2 pp. 183–196.

Baby Steps in the Cold War

Preliminary nuclear-arms-control efforts focused on proposals that placed all atomic energy under international control and offered states access to nuclear technologies for peaceful purposes under international safeguards. Initially the key nuclear states agreed to place atomic energy under the control of the United Nations (UN), which ultimately led to the June 1946 Baruch Plan, a U.S. proposal to transfer to the UN exclusive ownership and management of the entire fuel cycle. The Plan was never implemented, but it set the stage for President Dwight Eisenhower's 1953 Atoms for Peace proposal, which similarly relied on international control of atomic materials and technology to prevent the spread of nuclear weapons. Both efforts assumed that offering states access to the benefits of peaceful nuclear energy under international supervision would prevent them from pursuing research into military applications. Superpower agreement on these and similar proposals proved elusive. Nuclear weapons began to play an even greater role in defense policies, and the focus of arms control began to shift from the internationalist nature of Atoms for Peace and the Baruch Plan to the bipolar process that would characterize arms control for much of the Cold War.

Efforts by Eisenhower later in the 1950s to reduce the U.S. defense budget and at the same time protect the European allies from Soviet aggression helped make proposals for international control of nuclear technology impractical. During this period, it became U.S. policy to use the overwhelming nuclear advantage it enjoyed over the Soviet Union to deter conventional attack. In a January 1954 speech to the Council on Foreign Relations, Secretary of State John Foster Dulles enunciated what would become known as the "massive retaliation" posture. He stated that, in the event of a new communist aggression, the United States would "respond vigorously by means and at places of our choosing" and that that retaliation would be undertaken "instantly" and "massively" against the centers of communist power.

Soviet advancements in nuclear and missile capabilities prompted a shift in Western policy to a "flexible response" posture in the 1960s. In

1974, Secretary of Defense James Schlesinger described flexible response as "a series of measured responses to aggression which bear some relation to the provocation, have prospects of terminating hostilities before general nuclear war breaks out, and leave some possibility for restoring deterrence." Flexible response required the development of new types of weapons and larger arsenals. Coupled with the need to maintain an effective nuclear deterrent, this meant that both sides rapidly expanded their strategic nuclear arsenals during this period, prompting an arms race. By the end of the decade each country had more than 20,000 warheads and sufficient delivery systems to destroy the other's military facilities and industrial infrastructures many times over.

OFF AND RUNNING

Arms control efforts in the 1970s succeeded in stabilizing the U.S.-Soviet nuclear arms race. The 1972 Anti-Ballistic Missile (ABM) Treaty prohibited the deployment of a nationwide missile defense by either the United States or the Soviet Union and, as amended in 1974, limited each side to one ABM deployment site with one hundred interceptors. By limiting the amount of defenses either side could deploy, the ABM Treaty made strategic offensive arms limitation possible. If strategic defenses were not limited, and one nation could deploy an effective nationwide defense against a missile attack, the other would be forced to build larger arsenals to overwhelm those defenses and thereby maintain a credible deterrent. Moreover, if one nation had an effective nationwide defense, it might be perceived as more inclined to initiate a first strike with the expectation that the remaining arsenal of the undefended opponent would be insufficient to penetrate the defensive shield, thereby creating an unstable situation.

The ABM Treaty allowed the superpowers at one and the same time to limit their arsenals and to preserve mutual deterrence. The SALT (Strategic Arms Limitation Talks) agreements in 1972 and 1979 placed limits on the numbers of intercontinental ballistic missile (ICBM) launchers, submarine-launched ballistic missile launchers, and heavy bombers. While the limits essentially were not lower than the numbers of these delivery vehicles that existed at the time and required few actual reductions, the SALT agreements were successful because they capped the strategic nuclear missile race, "structured" the U.S.-Soviet strategic relationship, and paved the way for the arms reductions of the 1980s and 1990s.

In the 1987 Intermediate Nuclear Forces (INF) Treaty, the United States and Soviet Union agreed to eliminate an entire class of nuclear weapon delivery systems for the first time. Pursuant to the INF Treaty, all deployed and nondeployed missile systems with ranges between 500 and 5,500 kilometers were destroyed. The 1989 Conventional Armed Forces in Europe Treaty, which arguably ended the Cold War, cut conventional force deployments in Europe to low, equal levels. Finally, the Strategic Arms Reduction Treaties (START I & II) signed in 1991 and 1993 reduced the number of each side's deployed strategic warheads—from 12,000 to 6,000 under START I and 3,500 under START II, should it come into force.

These agreements were not reached in a vacuum. Arms control negotiations benefited from improved superpower relations during the so-called détente period in the 1970s. The INF and START treaties might not have been possible without this relaxation of tensions that took place as the Cold War came to an end. Moreover, effective arms-control agreements were possible only after the capacity of the states to verify compliance with the agreements improved, first by satellite surveillance and later by negotiated on-site inspection arrangements. Nevertheless, the agreements reached during and immediately after the Cold War significantly reduced nuclear arsenals and were crucial elements of U.S. security. By stabilizing the arms race and providing a framework for U.S.-Soviet dialogue, bilateral, Cold War-era arms control efforts contributed greatly to international peace and stability.

Contemporary Arms Control

The end of the Cold War shifted the conceptual framework for national and international security dramatically. The bipolar world order was replaced with a new, less-understood world filled with shifting strategic interests, different and more-diffuse threats, and uncertainty about the proper means of confronting them. The roles of arms control and of negotiated U.S.-Russian strategic reductions remain central to international security, and are likely to for the foreseeable future, but new actors are playing increasingly vital roles. In a word, arms control is becoming increasingly multilateral. The new model for nuclear arms control in the twenty-first century is one of cooperation between a number of governments, intergovernmental organizations and nongovernmental organizations (NGOs).

THE NONNUCLEAR WEAPON STATES

Multilateral arms control is not new. The centerpiece of efforts to prevent the spread of nuclear weapons is the 1968 Nuclear Non-Proliferation Treaty (NPT), which now has 186 states parties. Under the NPT, 181 nonnuclear weapon states parties to the treaty have pledged never to develop or otherwise acquire nuclear weapons and to submit to international safeguards intended to verify compliance with this commitment. In exchange, these states were promised unfettered access to peaceful nuclear technologies, and the five nuclear-weapon states—the United States, Russia, United Kingdom, France, and China—pledged in NPT Article VI to engage in disarmament negotiations aimed at the ultimate elimination of their nuclear arsenals. This central bargain—nonproliferation in exchange for nuclear arms reductions and eventual nuclear disarmament—is the foundation upon which the NPT regime rests.

The NPT was completed during the Cold War, but it and nonproliferation in general have become the principal focus of arms control in the post-Cold War era. Political leaders, experts, and scholars the world over have identified proliferation rather than war among the nuclear powers as the most important threat to international security. As President Chirac of France, Prime Minister Blair of the United Kingdom, and Chancellor Schroeder of Germany noted in a recent opinion piece published in the *New York Times,*

As we look to the next century, our greatest concern is proliferation of weapons of mass destruction, and chiefly nuclear proliferation. We have to face the stark truth that nuclear proliferation remains the major threat to world safety.[2]

The increasing importance of nonproliferation efforts has similarly increased the importance of a healthy and viable NPT regime. When the treaty was indefinitely extended in 1995, the states parties also agreed to an associated consensus agreement called the Statement of Principles and Objectives for Nuclear Non-Proliferation and Disarmament. This statement was intended to strengthen the regime and, in effect, at least politically if not legally, provide the conditions for the extension of the treaty. The Statement of Principles and Objectives pledged the NPT states parties to work toward eight primary objectives. These included universalization of NPT membership, a reaffirmation of the Article VI commitments of the nuclear weapon states to pursue in good faith measures related to eventual nuclear disarmament, and the completion of the Comprehensive Test Ban Treaty (CTBT) by the end of 1996. The Statement of Principles and Objectives also called for the commencement of negotiations for a fissile material cutoff treaty, efforts by the nuclear weapon states to reduce global nuclear arsenals, and the encouragement of the creation of new nuclear-weapon-free zones. An enhanced verification system and further steps to assure the nonnuclear weapon states against the use or threat of use of nuclear weapons (otherwise known as "negative security assurances") were also called for.

The 1995 Review and Extension Conference also negotiated a strengthened review process that included the conduct of NPT Review Conferences every five years and Preparatory Committee (PrepCom) meetings in each of the three years prior to the Review Conferences. The agreement establishing this new process stipulated that the PrepComs would meet to consider "principles, objectives, and ways ... to promote the full implementation of the Treaty, as well as its universality, and make recommendations thereon to the Review Conferences." The agreement further notes that the Review Conferences should look forward as well as back, stating that,

They should evaluate the results of the period they are reviewing, including the implementation of undertakings of the States parties under the Treaty, and identify the areas in which, and means through which, further progress should be sought in the future.

Together, these provisions require the states parties to the NPT to meet almost annually to discuss substantive issues relevant to the treaty, including progress toward meeting the goals in the Statement of Principles and Objectives. This is a significant change from the previous, quintennial structure in place prior to the 1995 Review Conference. In effect, as part of the agreement to make the NPT permanent, the nonnuclear weapon states were given greater ability and opportunity to address concerns about progress by the nuclear weapon states toward fulfilling their half of the NPT's basic bargain. Thus, the enhanced NPT review process has contributed to the multilateralization of arms control by adding nearly annual oversight of treaty-related issues by a conference of 186 nations, 181 of which are nonnuclear weapon states.

The role of nonnuclear weapon states in multilateral arms control is not limited to the NPT regime. More than 110 nations have signed international agreements establishing nuclear-weapon-free zones in Latin America, Africa, the South Pacific, and Southeast Asia. Collectively, these treaties in effect prohibit the development, storage, deployment, or placement by any other means of nuclear weapons on the land area of the Southern Hemisphere. By their nature these regimes distribute the responsibility for preventing the proliferation of nuclear weapons among the nonnuclear weapon states themselves, thus promoting the multilateral-ization of arms control.

Nonnuclear weapon states are playing greater roles in other regional arrangements as well. For example, several nonnuclear members of the North Atlantic Treaty Organization (NATO), most notably Canada and Germany, have encouraged the North Atlantic Alliance to review its policy regarding the potential first use of nuclear weapons, with the ultimate objective of the consideration of an Alliance adoption of a no-first-use policy. At the Washington Summit in April, largely as a result of these efforts, NATO opened the door to such a review. The Washington Summit Communiqué states in paragraph 32:

> In light of overall strategic developments and the reduced salience of nuclear weapons, the Alliance will consider options for confidence and security-building measures, verification, nonproliferation, and arms control and disarmament ... The Council in Permanent Session will propose a process to Ministers in December for considering such options.

At an April 24 news conference, Canadian foreign affairs minister Lloyd Axworthy confirmed the willingness of NATO "to have a review initiated" of its nuclear weapon policies. Axworthy added,

> It's a message that the prime minister took to certain NATO leaders ... I think we have now gained an acknowledgement that such a review would be appropriate and that there would be directions to the NATO Council to start the mechanics of bringing that about.

Leading up to the December Ministerial, however, some believed that certain members of the Alliance were seeking to exclude the no-first-use issue from the agenda of the review, prompting Axworthy to renew his campaign. In a December interview, he noted that "it's just absolute insanity that we would not focus on this matter. I find it very disturbing." He pledged to use the Ministerial to push for a formal Alliance review of its nuclear-weapon-use policy. As a result of his efforts, the communiqué agreed upon by NATO foreign ministers that month announced that NATO "decided to set in train" the process agreed to at the Washington Summit and "review Alliance policy options in support of confidence and security building measures, verification, nonproliferation, and arms control and disarmament." The no-first-use issue was not specifically excluded from the review and likely will be addressed.

In another example of increased initiative by the nonnuclear weapon states, the foreign ministers of Brazil, Egypt, Mexico, Ireland, New Zealand, Slovenia, South Africa, and Sweden in June 1998 simultaneously released a joint statement calling for a new agenda for nuclear disarmament. In November 1998, this group minus Slovenia, which has come to be known as the New Agenda Coalition, submitted to the UN

General Assembly a resolution calling for such an approach. While the nuclear weapon states and their allies have voted against similar nuclear disarmament resolutions in the past, all of the nonnuclear-weapon state members of NATO except Turkey abstained on the New Agenda Coalition Resolution in 1998, resisting heavy pressure from the NATO nuclear weapons states to vote against the resolution. On a second, similar draft resolution in November 1999, all but two nonnuclear weapon state members of NATO, including Turkey, abstained. Incidentally, while two of the newly admitted NATO members voted against the resolution, the third, the Czech Republic, resisted heavy pressure and joined the remaining nonnuclear members in abstaining. These abstentions demonstrate that nonnuclear weapon states are committed to nonproliferation and disarmament and that so-called "middle power" states have begun to assert themselves to urge greater progress on arms control and disarmament.

MULTILATERAL ORGANIZATIONS AND NONGOVERNMENTAL GROUPS

As the role of the "middle powers" and other nonnuclear weapon states continues to grow, so too does that of multilateral arms control, nonproliferation, and disarmament institutions. Forums such as the UN First Committee provide arenas for nations to exchange views on a variety of issues and air disputes among members. The International Atomic Energy Agency, which includes 126 nations among its membership, plays an important role in verifying compliance with nuclear nonproliferation commitments, a role enhanced by the recent completion of stronger verification protocols as agreed upon in the 1995 Statement of Principles and Objectives. The UN Security Council has played a greater enforcement role in recent years, as demonstrated by its pivotal role in instituting the disarmament of Iraq and in convincing North Korea to rescind its stated intention to withdraw from the NPT in 1993 and remain a party to the treaty.

The multilateralization of arms control has broadened the role of responsible NGOs. NGOs are rapidly becoming more involved in the arms control, nonproliferation, and disarmament work of the UN and other international organizations. A July 1998 report by the UN secretary general noted that in 1948, only 41 NGOs were granted consultative status by the UN. Today, there are more than 1,550 NGOs registered by the UN, though not all of these groups do arms-control-related work. In terms of cooperation with NGOs, the UN Department for Disarmament Affairs is among the organization's leading departments. The work of these NGOs has not gone unnoticed. Three arms-control-focused NGOs—International Physicians for the Prevention of Nuclear War (IPPNW) in 1985, the Pugwash Conferences on Science and World Affairs in 1995, and the International Campaign to Ban Landmines in 1997—have been awarded the Nobel Peace Prize. Another NGO, Médecins Sans Frontières, received the award in 1999.

In this age of reduced secrecy and enhanced access to information, NGOs can do more than ever before to promote nuclear nonproliferation and disarmament because they operate with fewer of the restraints that can hinder governments. For example, in the late 1980s, when the question of verifying a comprehensive test ban treaty was a great concern, the Natural Resource Defense Council was granted access to the Soviet Union's nuclear test site, something that had been considered out of the question for years for the U.S. government.

By conducting, organizing, and sponsoring informal exchanges involving representatives of governments and nongovernment entities, NGOs can help break down barriers between governments. Such exchanges provide participants with avenues for exchanging or discussing ideas in an informal forum that lacks the baggage of government-to-government negotiations. These efforts can be used to develop informal agreements that can be formalized once the political climate between the parties involved is right. In the interim, such exchanges provide channels of communication that might not otherwise exist between governments and can help to foster discussions aimed at identifying mutual areas of concern. Now and in the future, these efforts will likely play an important role in developing a wide variety of confidence-building measures and other efforts that improve interstate relations.

NGOs also have an important role to play in the negotiation of multilateral arrangements. In some instances they may be able to help level the playing field during international treaty negotiations. Larger nations can often exert greater influence over arms control negotiations simply because of the size of the delegation that they can afford to send and the depth of expertise available to them. At treaty negotiations, the U.S. delegation, for example, will typically include legal, military, scientific, technical, and political expertise specific to the subject under consideration, while some smaller states may only send a handful of negotiators. NGOs can help by enhancing the access of smaller states to expertise and information. For years, Canada went so far as to include an NGO representative on its disarmament and nonproliferation delegations. At the NPT review conferences, the Conference on Disarmament, the UN First Committee, and other multilateral forums, it is increasingly common for NGO representatives to address the delegates, and NGOs often arrange delegate briefings on the margins of meetings.

At the national level as well, NGOs are playing greater roles. U.S. government officials from time to time consult with nongovernmental organizations on various policy issues and initiatives. In certain circumstances, they can also be effective in mobilizing public support for arms control and nonproliferation measures. Efforts to promote U.S. ratification of the Limited Test Ban Treaty in 1963 benefited from public outrage over the public health and environmental impact of atmospheric testing, due to a great extent by studies circulated by Physicians for Social Responsibility. Another more recent example was the NGO campaign, subsequently in partnership with Canada, to produce a treaty banning landmines. In this case, more than a thousand NGOs from some 60 nations organized under an umbrella group called the International Campaign to Ban Landmines which utilized the Internet and other modern communication technologies to coordinate a campaign directly engaging national governments and the international media. In the Information Age, the ability of NGOs to produce and disseminate information in order to mobilize public support is magnified by the reduced cost and enhanced speed of communication. The Internet has made it possible for organizations to provide information to countless people from all corners of the globe and increased the ability of NGOs to communicate with other NGOs and governments. As the Information Age continues to dismantle barriers between peoples and governments, NGOs have an enhanced ability to contribute to policymaking debates, become more effective advocates of nonproliferation and disarmament, and play a greater role in the policymaking process.

Is Arms Control Still Relevant?

While the mechanisms, rationale, and tangible benefits of arms control are somewhat different today than during the Cold War, arms control continues to be, and will certainly remain for the foreseeable future, essential to U.S. and international security. During the Cold War, the gravest danger to the United States was nuclear war with the Soviet Union and accordingly arms control was principally designed and intended to curb that threat. The Soviet Union has vanished but nuclear weapons remain the principal threat to the United States, only today the danger is the spread of nuclear weapons around the globe. Nuclear tests by India and Pakistan in May 1998; heightened existing concern about nuclear weapon programs in Iran, Iraq, North Korea, and elsewhere; and anxieties that unilateral deployment of a nationwide missile defense by the United States could prompt a renewed nuclear arms race involving the United States, Russia, and China demonstrate that the dangers of nuclear weapons have broadened in the last decade. The threat that additional states with which the United States has poor or strained relations, or even subnational groups such as terrorist organizations or religious cults, could acquire these weapons has reinforced the relevance of arms control, nonproliferation and disarmament efforts.

The ongoing debate surrounding the question of whether the United States should unilaterally deploy a national missile defense (NMD) against missile attack from so-called rogue states, which as currently envisioned would require violation of or withdrawal from the ABM Treaty, underscores the continued relevance of arms control. Proponents of NMD deployment have argued that the ABM Treaty is a Cold War relic which reflects outdated thinking on security and that the United States needs to prepare itself to meet new and emerging missile threats. NMD opponents, on the other hand, argue that the technology may not ever exist to deploy an effective defense against incoming missiles and that any state technologically capable of developing ICBMs would be able to develop countermeasures designed to defeat a U.S. NMD system. As French president Chirac noted in December 1999,

> If you look at world history, ever since men began waging war, you will see that there's a permanent race between sword and shield. The sword always wins. The more improvements that are made to the shield, the more improvements are made to the sword.

Even an absolutely effective defense against incoming missiles would not protect the United States from the dangers of nuclear attack from a more likely delivery means, such as cruise missile, light aircraft, boat, truck, or even backpack. Additionally, unilateral NMD deployment would likely terminate nuclear disarmament efforts, lead to a new nuclear-arms race, and greatly increase the risk of widespread nuclear proliferation.

NMD opponents contend that the net effect on U.S. national security would be harmful as a result of the instability derived from the renewed nuclear arms race. Senior officials in Russia, China, and the NATO allies have expressed in recent months their concerns in this regard. Chirac noted that missile defense systems

> are just going to spur swordmakers to intensify their efforts ... China, which was already working harder than we realized on both nuclear weapons and delivery vehicles for them, would of course be encouraged to intensify those efforts, and it has the resources to do so ... India would be encouraged to do the same thing, and it, too, has the resources.

In a November 1999 letter to President Bill Clinton, then-President Boris Yeltsin remarked that unilateral U.S. deployment of a NMD system "would have extremely dangerous consequences for the entire arms control process." Russian defense minister Sergeyev, too, has stated publicly that unilateral U.S. NMD deployment would do "unacceptable damage to the reduction of strategic offensive weapons."

A middle ground between these seemingly irreconcilable viewpoints could possibly be found in arms control. It may be possible for the United States and Russia to agree to reductions in strategic nuclear arsenals to levels below those proposed for START III, perhaps even as low as one thousand for each side. In exchange, the ABM Treaty could be amended in a manner that preserves the viability of the treaty but allows the deployment of a system that would protect against rogue state missile threats by permitting the deployment of perhaps one hundred interceptors at each of two sites. Instead of unilaterally deploying an NMD system to protect the United States against the threat of nuclear attack—a "fortress America" approach—the United States should adjust to the new shape of international security and cooperate with Russia, France, and China to promote peace and security. Rather than trying to go it alone, it is in the interest of the United States to work to strengthen international arms control, nonproliferation, and disarmament structures designed to keep nuclear weapons away from potential aggressors. Today and in the foreseeable future, this is a principal role for arms control.

Prospects for the Future

Despite the fundamental changes in arms control, nonproliferation, and disarmament discussed above, however, efforts to prevent the spread of nuclear weapons cannot succeed without dedicated commitment from the nuclear weapon states. Recent events suggest that this commitment may not be as strong as it should be and the NPT regime as a result is under siege. The October 1999 rejection of the Comprehensive Test Ban Treaty (CTBT) by the U.S. Senate, the suggestions to change unilaterally the ABM Treaty to deploy an NMD, the stalled START process, and last year's nuclear tests by India and Pakistan underscore the perilous condition of the NPT regime. Without serious efforts by the international community, specifically the nuclear weapon states, to bolster the regime in the short term, there is a very real possibility that the NPT could begin to unravel in the next five to ten years. The question is, how can the arms control, nonproliferation, and disarmament regime be revitalized and the NPT regime preserved?

It may be desirable for the NPT states parties to agree to an additional Statement of Principles and Objectives at the 2000 NPT Review Conference as part of an agreement to diffuse widespread disaffection and criticism at the conference. In such an understanding, the nonnuclear weapon states would pledge to refrain from acting in a manner that would question the NPT regime at and after the 2000 Conference and the nuclear weapon states would agree to pursue specific additional steps prior to the 2005 Review Conference. These could include good faith efforts to bring the CTBT into force, to universalize no-first-use policies among the nuclear weapon states or establish legally binding negative security assurances for NPT nonnuclear weapon states parties, to maintain the viability of the ABM Treaty, and to pursue reductions in U.S. and Russian nuclear arsenals to a level well below proposed START III levels. Three of these four suggestions are, or are close to, current government policy. Under such an agreement, if sufficient progress, or at least a good faith effort, is perceived to have been made toward fulfilling these commitments, the 2005 Conference would reaffirm the fundamental international commitment to the NPT. Otherwise, support for the NPT regime might begin to erode after the 2005 Conference.

If the NPT regime is reaffirmed at the 2005 Review Conference, the nuclear disarmament process could continue. After 2005, the United States and Russia could agree to a comprehensive transparency regime, a limit of 500 nuclear tactical warheads for each, and a subsequent limit of 1,000 total nuclear weapons for each of the United States and Russia. This in turn could lead to the establishment of a five-power nuclear disarmament process with three main objectives:

- A reduction in U.S. and Russian nuclear arsenals to residual levels in the low hundreds.
- A reduction in Chinese, French, and British nuclear arsenals to levels below 100.

- The elimination of Indian, Pakistani, and Israeli nuclear arsenals, but with their fissile material retained on their territories under international safeguards as a hedge against a breakdown of the agreement. These three states would also agree to join the NPT as nonnuclear weapon states.

In addition, as an essential part of this process, all the nonnuclear weapon states would reaffirm their nonnuclear status and all the NPT parties would commit themselves to joint action—including force if necessary—against any violator. These levels would be the end point until the world has changed sufficiently to permit contemplation of a prohibition on nuclear weapons.

With respect to the NPT itself, the regime then would be very strong. At each five-year Review Conference, the parties could consider new measures in the context of the five-power disarmament process, which undoubtedly would take many years. These would simply be basic mileposts that the states parties would set forth in order to maintain a proper course and better ensure full participation by all the other parties in the implementation of the NPT. They would not be time-bound objectives and could carry over from Review Conference to Review Conference. The intent would be to gradually merge the nonproliferation constraint of the NPT, along with the practice of non-use of nuclear weapons into customary international law binding forever on all states. This is the direction the international community should head if the world is to be freed from the dangers of nuclear weapons in the next century.

Conclusion

No matter the direction arms control, nonproliferation, and disarmament efforts take in the coming years, they will and should remain central components of international security policy. It is clear that the practice of arms control has been multilateralized in recent years. The enhanced effectiveness of NGOs in the Information Age, increasing emphasis on nonproliferation, and the expanding role of nonnuclear weapon states have broadened the responsibility for, and conduct of, nuclear arms control beyond the nuclear weapon states. Nevertheless, unless the nuclear weapon states themselves take responsible action in the coming years, arms control as well as nonproliferation cannot be successful. By pursuing a path similar to the one described above, the international community can preserve and revitalize nuclear arms control and ensure that the next century is more secure than the last.

Notes

1. While the terms "arms control," "nonproliferation," and "disarmament" are not synonymous and differ from one another considerably, here and throughout this article the term "arms control" and the phrases "arms control," "nonproliferation," and "disarmament" are used interchangeably.
2. Jacques Chirac, Tony Blair, and Gerhard Schroder, "A Treaty We All Need," *New York Times*, October 8, 1999.

Stephen Cambone

An Inherent Lesson in Arms Control

The decision by the U.S. Senate not to ratify the Comprehensive Test Ban Treaty (CTBT) provides important lessons about arms control practices and objectives for the coming years. Those lessons fall into three broad categories. The first is political relations between the White House and Capitol Hill. The second relates to the terms of a treaty, particularly the alignment of its technical features with its purpose. The third category is the relationship between arms control and deterrence. Each offers food for thought for the pending debate over the deployment of a national missile defense system and the future of the Anti-Ballistic Missile (ABM) Treaty.

Political Relations

The first lesson is that "politics" matter. "Politics" clearly played a role in the defeat of the CTBT. It was not, as some would have it, the politics of scandal or isolationism. Rather it was politics of a simpler kind, the politics of mistrust. From its first days, the Clinton administration has had an uneasy relationship with the Congress. The administration's ill-prepared policy initiatives, its failures to consult with its congres-

Stephen Cambone is director of research for the Institute for National Strategic Studies at the National Defense University. The views expressed here are his own and do not represent those of INSS, NDU, DoD, or any other government agency.

Copyright © 2000 by The Center for Strategic and International Studies and the Massachusetts Institute of Technology
The Washington Quarterly • 23:2 pp. 207–218.

sional allies, and its willingness to abandon positions long held by its own party caused disaffection among Democrats. The deft footwork of the administration in parrying and frequently defeating the efforts of the Republicans gave rise to cries of foul play. The president frustrated the new majority by recasting their major themes or initiatives and then either capturing them as his own or denigrating them as foolish.

The mistrust between the White House and Capitol Hill, generated in domestic policy debates, also affected national security policy. It surfaced immediately over gays in the military. Events in Somalia followed by decisions to intervene in Haiti and Bosnia and the administration's justification for these actions as support for the "will of the international community" exacerbated that mistrust. Seven years into the Clinton administration, the president and Congress have agreed on relatively few national security issues beyond the expansion of the North Atlantic Treaty Organization (NATO). Secretary of State Madeleine Albright put it this way in her November 22, 1999, essay in *Time*: "Unfortunately ... the [a]dministration and Congress have not yet agreed on a common post-[C]old [W]ar strategy" for meeting the new dangers the nation faces.

In the field of arms control, the Senate's actions on two earlier treaty ratification votes revealed this mistrust. In the case of the second Strategic Arms Reduction Treaty (START II), the Senate declared in its ratification resolution that U.S. reductions called for in the treaty should not dangerously outpace those of Russia. It feared the administration would move toward START II levels before Russia ratified the treaty. A requirement to retain START I force levels was contained in successive Defense authorization acts. It has been relaxed somewhat by the current authorization act that recognizes the existing budgetary constraints on Russia's strategic forces.

Another arms control issue on which the White House and Senate have disagreed is the application of the ABM Treaty to theater missile defense (TMD). Since 1994, the majority in the Senate has held that agreements with Russia to distinguish or demarcate TMD systems from ABM systems of the type pursued and eventually obtained by the administration were unnecessary. Some argued that the ABM Treaty did not restrict TMD, while others contended that these agreements constituted a substantive change to the treaty requiring the Senate's advice and consent. Despite the clear opposition of the Senate majority, the administration concluded a demarcation agreement. This convinced many Republicans that, despite its assurances to the contrary, the administration was attempting to use the agreements to expand the authority of the ABM Treaty and to dangerously limit the capability of U.S. TMD to satisfy Russian demands.

For its part, the administration had argued that the demarcation agreements were designed to protect the integrity of the ABM Treaty by defining a difference between TMD and ABM capabilities. It insisted that the agreements did not limit theater defenses. It also insisted that the agreements did not amount to substantive changes to the ABM Treaty—specifically that they did not extend the treaty to include theater systems—and therefore did not constitute amendments to the treaty requiring the advice and consent of the Senate. Unwilling to accept these assurances, the Senate's ratification resolution amending the Conventional Forces in Europe Treaty required that the president submit to the Senate for its advice and consent the agreements he reached with Russia and other former Soviet Union states on TMD, the so-called demarcation agreements. The president accepted this condition of ratification, but he has not yet submitted the demarcation agreements to the Senate.

The administration is no more trustful of the Congress. For example, it was reluctant to consult on its negotiating approach on TMD out of fear that it would be misrepresented. And, following the passage of the Missile Defense Act of 1999, which declared it to be U.S. policy to deploy a national missile defense (NMD), the White House issued a statement declaring that the law did not, in fact, mean that the United States was committed to a deployment of missile defense. This statement was issued after the administration had failed to have the act amended to condition deployment on criteria related to cost, effectiveness, technical readiness, and its diplomatic effect. In the view of the

White House, its statement was needed to preserve executive prerogatives, to reassure U.S. allies and Russia, and to avoid a "rush to failure" in deploying missile defenses.

A deep lack of trust between the executive and legislative branches is not likely to be overcome by an appeal to the hoary traditions of bipartisanship on national security matters. In such moments, only a solid record of dealing in good faith over time on a variety of issues can assure a full and frank exchange between the two treaty-making partners. This record is especially necessary when considering a treaty, such as the CTBT, that is so highly charged.

Clearly no such record existed at the moment of the vote. Worse, even overtures of good faith had gone unrewarded. Those in a position to know say that the White House was informed in midsummer 1999 about the Senate leadership's concerns. These included the manner in which it was negotiated; the particular terms of the treaty; and deep concerns about the measures for assuring compliance, on the one hand, and the safety, security, reliability, and credibility of the U.S. nuclear stockpile, on the other. Nor were these issues raised for the first time in the summer of 1999. Hearings had been held on these and many other issues related to the CTBT during the preceding sessions of Congress. In light of these concerns, the Republican leadership warned the administration that it did not have the votes to secure ratification of the CTBT and offered to postpone a vote. It assured the White House, however, that if it came to vote, the CTBT would be defeated.

A number of Democratic senators chose to pursue the matter in any case, threatening to bring the Senate's business to halt unless the CTBT was placed on the calendar. The result, given no indication that the administration was prepared to address the substantive concerns of the leadership, was a foregone conclusion in mid-year.

Treaty Rationale, Terms, and Purpose

A second lesson drawn from the CTBT vote is that the rationale developed to guide Cold War arms-control efforts are not so easily adapted to the evolving post-Cold War strategic environment. The CTBT was a Cold War-era treaty. Its original rationale was to inhibit the proliferation of nuclear weapons by new states by prohibiting testing. For states with nuclear weapons, a CTBT would also prevent the development of new, perhaps more usable, weapons.

Additional reasons were developed over the years to support a CTBT, including the argument that it was an essential step to engage in negotiations toward general and complete disarmament, ostensibly fulfilling the Article VI pledge of the nuclear weapon states in the Nuclear Non-Proliferation Treaty (NPT). More recently, the case has been made that a CTBT, irrespective of its particular success in stemming proliferation, would establish an international norm against the acquisition and improvement of nuclear weapons.

Recollections of history and recent experience undermined the CTBT's rationale. The first two U.S. atomic weapons delivered the anticipated explosive yield the first time they were detonated in 1945. One was a relatively uncomplicated device, a gun-assembled type, called Little Boy. The other was a more sophisticated implosion type, which has become the type-design of choice.

In the years since 1945, and especially in the last decade or so, there has been a wide diffusion of the scientific and engineering knowledge related to nuclear weapon design. It has given rise to a broad consensus that first-generation nuclear weapons—unsophisticated by the contemporary standards of the United States—can be developed confidently, without nuclear testing, by a country that can acquire the fissile materials and mount a serious design effort. As a result, most are persuaded by the administration's finding that North Korea possesses one or perhaps two nuclear devices developed without testing. Many believed India and Pakistan had workable nuclear weapons prior to their tests in 1998. Recent press reports that the CIA can not rule out the possibility that Iran has acquired nuclear weapons highlights the concern of Gen. Anthony Zinni, Commander in Chief, U.S. Central Command, that Iran is likely to have a handful of nuclear weapons in its arsenal in only a few years. The likelihood is low that Iran would need to test a first-generation device. After the invasion of Kuwait, Iraq began a crash program to produce a nuclear device in six to nine months based on uranium removed from the safeguarded reactor at Tuwaitha. There is near universal agreement that Israel also possesses nuclear weapons.

Because nuclear weapons can be developed without testing, opponents of the CTBT were not persuaded it would have had a substantial effect on proliferation. Nor were they convinced that the Cold War-era techniques for monitoring and verifying the treaty were adequate to detect cheating and resolve ambiguity related to actual testing. Verification capabilities and the compliance standards associated with them were the source of fierce disagreement surrounding Soviet compliance with Strategic Arms Limitation Talks (SALT), the Intermediate-Range Nuclear Force (INF) Treaty, the ABM Treaty, and the Biological and Toxin Weapons Convention. The disagreement over the U.S. capacity to monitor and verify nuclear testing were especially contentious in the past, particularly during debates over the Threshold Test Ban Treaty's limit of 150 kilotons of explosive yield.

Proponents argued that the CTBT was, as a whole, "effectively verifiable" due to the combination of a ban on nuclear-explosive testing with the monitoring, verification, and inspection provisions of the treaty. That is, the CTBT's benefits outweighed the military risk that could be gained by surreptitious testing. Treaty proponents pointed to its requirement for 331 international monitoring stations to collect relevant data, including both natural and man-made seismic and acoustic events, to establish a data center where all collected information is available to all signatories, and to create an onsite inspection regime.

But here, too, recent experience and advances in science and engineering undermined confidence in the CTBT's monitoring and verification regime. We know, as noted above, that testing is not needed to develop a first-generation nuclear weapon. The techniques for spoofing sensors or concealing tests (e.g., through decoupling the explosion from the surrounding earth) are also well known. They are not sophisticated techniques; aspiring nuclear weapon states can employ them. Those members of the regime who are looking to use such techniques have the advantage of knowing a great deal about its monitoring, verification, and inspection because that knowledge is open to all members. That means monitoring and verification in the end depends less on the treaty's provisions than on the national technical means of signatories, particularly the United States.

The U.S. intelligence community is highly capable. But as determined actors have demonstrated repeatedly in recent years, they are capable of denying the intelligence community timely information about their actions, of deceiving and misleading it about their intentions, and, in the end, of surprising it. To be sure, some of the intelligence community's vulnerability to denial and deception practices is a result of its own shortcomings. These have been chronicled in Adm. David Jeremiah's report following India's nuclear test and the Rumsfeld Commission's "Intelligence Side Letter." The director of central intelligence has testified that the intelligence community is working hard to overcome these shortcomings.

As the Rumsfeld Commission pointed out, however, repairing the shortcomings of the intelligence community, while necessary, will not be sufficient. Espionage, demarches, press releases, unauthorized publications, and leaks as well as the inexorable march of satellite- and information-based technology have eroded the advantages once enjoyed by the U.S. intelligence community and increased the likelihood of surprise.

Even when surprise is not an issue, ambiguity is likely to reign. In the late 1970s, a flash of light was detected in the southern hemisphere, leading to speculation about its source. Some argue Israel was involved, others that it was a South African test, others that both were involved. In 1997, South African deputy foreign minister Aziz Pahad claimed that the event in the Indian Ocean on September 22, 1979, was a South African nuclear test. Shai Feldman, in a published review of arms control issues in the Middle East, concluded that Israel and South Africa have probably not cooperated in the nuclear realm.

Six months after the event, the press was reporting disagreement within the U.S. government about the characteristics of the weapons tested by Pakistan in May 1998. This, in turn, set off a dispute between the intelligence community and the Congress on the issue. Nor is ambiguity related only to events conducted by new nuclear powers. In September 1999, a senior intelligence official said "we [the intelligence community] just don't know at this point" whether an event detected earlier in the month at Russia's Novya Zemlya test site was a small nuclear blast or a conventional explosion that did not reach critical mass. The same press report asserts that intelligence agencies "also detected what is believed to have been a small Chinese underground nuclear test in June."

The debate on the CTBT revealed the difficulty of adapting Cold War technical approaches to securing contemporary arms-control objectives. It also came to a vote at a moment when the efforts to deny and deceive the U.S. intelligence community were most visible undermining confidence in the treaty's verifiability. The combination proved an insurmountable obstacle.

Deterrence and Arms Control

A third lesson drawn from the debate over the CTBT is that the fissure in thinking among U.S. policy elites on the relationship between deterrence and arms control is now exposed. The existence of this fissure in the policy elite is not new. What is new is that the debate on the CTBT may have placed majorities on both sides of the issue into irreconcilable positions.

During the Cold War, arms control evolved into a carefully orchestrated set of agreements meant to codify extant notions of nuclear deterrence and to assure deployment over time of forces in the number and with the capabilities essential to its enforcement. This was possible because most of the majority that favored arms control were fundamentally committed to deterrence. Among the majority who stressed the requirement to strengthen deterrence in every way possible, arms control agreements could be crafted that at the very least did no harm, as in the case of START I, or actually achieved long-held objectives, as in the case of START II. Hence, during the Cold War, compromise was possible on the basis of a commitment to improve deterrent capabilities and to control the growth of, reduce, or otherwise regulate the size and characteristics of the deterrent forces.

The CTBT debate seems unlikely to yield such compromise. To its proponents, the CTBT was not about deterrence as it is classically understood. To be sure, proponents assume the current and future U.S. capability to retaliate for any attack on the United States is a given, an unquestionable premise. Moreover, they argued, the CTBT would not diminish that capability for many years to come, if at all. The stockpile stewardship program is designed to assure, in a no-testing environment, the safety, reliability, and security of the weapons for the indefinite future. Beyond this, protecting the U.S. capacity to improve its capabilities was not only unnecessary but also contrary to the purposes of the treaty. The end to testing was meant to freeze capabilities where they are—both in the United States and among other states possessing or on the verge of possessing nuclear weapons.

If the CTBT was not about deterrence in the classic sense, it was about setting new standards of behavior in the international system. It was about putting arms control to new uses. The president made this clear in 1996 when he announced his intention to secure a treaty by 1999. National Security Advisor Samuel Berger, in his speech shortly after the Senate's decision, and the Secretary of State, in her *Time* essay, reiterated this rationale. Because the CTBT does not affect classic deterrence, goes the logic of their argument, the United States has the opportunity to use arms control to fashion what Berger called "global rules with global backing."

Put another way, the CTBT was represented by its proponents as arms control that related less to reinforcing the U.S. deterrent *per se* than to altering the broader strategic environment in which the United States operated. The intended effect of the treaty was to reduce both the need, and the capability, for nuclear deterrence leading over time to an end of the need for deterrence itself.

Opponents never wavered in their conviction that the CTBT would pose a threat to the deterrent capacity of the United States. The formulation offered by Senator Olympia Snowe (R-Maine) fairly well captured the view of the Senate majority that "the no-testing, unlimited duration policy [of the CTBT] would fatally undermine confidence in the reliability of our nuclear stockpile as a sturdy hedge against international aggression."

In particular, opponents expressed very little confidence in the stockpile stewardship program. A sizable number of knowledgeable scientists and engineers still believe that the program could permit current weapons to be maintained and that modest modifications might be possible. The Senate majority heeded the concern of an increasing number of scientists, however, that maintaining the weapons and making modifications to them will be difficult at best. Nearly all scientists believe that the restrictions imposed by the CTBT do not affect the United States and Russia equally.

Based on these conclusions, the Senate decided it had little reason to believe that restricting U.S. capability would appreciably affect the further proliferation of nuclear weapons. It was not persuaded that the stockpile stewardship program would successfully maintain U.S. capabilities. Some also worried that the CTBT would foreclose the U.S. option to develop new weapon designs should that be necessary to meet an evolving threat.

Looking forward, it is difficult to imagine how these positions might be reconciled within the framework of a CTBT debate. Proponents fought for a treaty that bans nuclear explosive testing. The United States interprets this to mean a zero-yield treaty, that is, literally no explosions are permitted that result in a nuclear yield. They insisted on this provision in the belief that in the end advances in nuclear weaponry required such testing. For proponents to retreat on this point, a matter of principle, is to surrender the moral high ground on which their campaign had been fought.

Proponents might seek a compromise; that is the gist of the argument of Senator Joseph Biden (D-Del.) and others that the issue be reconsidered. Advocates might consider former Secretary of Defense James Schlesinger's suggestion that the permitted yield be raised to five kilotons. This would increase the probability of detection, it would provide for greater confidence that the United States could maintain its nuclear deterrent, and it might allow development of new designs. But so long as opponents lack confidence in the administration, are unconvinced that the treaty can substantially affect proliferation, believe that the impact of the treaty may disproportionately constrain the United States, and can muster the needed 34 votes in the Senate, they are unlikely to agree to reopen the issue.

Conclusion

These lessons apply to pending national security decisions, particularly to the upcoming debate on missile defenses and the future of the ABM Treaty. The recent decision on the CTBT suggests that if the nation is to move forward successfully on missile defense, at least three conditions will need to be met:

- A reasonable level of confidence and trust is needed between the executive and legislative branches. Absent this, Congress will be reluctant to provide the president the benefit of the doubt on an issue as contentious as the ABM Treaty.

In the end, responsibility for the political relationship between the treaty-making partners rests with the executive branch, in particular the president himself. It is he who has the authority to negotiate treaties and he who is responsible for their execution. It is incumbent upon him, then, consistent with his prerogatives and his obligation to protect his communications with foreign governments, to insure that the Senate is consulted in advance on his objectives in a negotiation. The Clinton administration did consult with a Senate observer group on NATO enlargement. Past administrations have used observer groups for SALT, START, and INF. In participating in an observer group, senators do not surrender the constitutional obligation of the Senate to provide its advice and consent to ratification. But they do take on the obligation to avoid using privileged information for partisan purpose in the course of the ratification process. The Senate has reestablished an observer group for ABM negotiations. The administration might consider making more assiduous use of it, reviving a process that led to the successful ratification of START and NATO enlargement.

- The purpose and specific terms of a treaty must reflect the objective reality of today's security environment, not yesterday's.

The ABM Treaty, in the view of some, suffers from the same concerns as did the CTBT. As defensive technologies have advanced beyond those available, and in some cases envisioned, at the time the ABM Treaty was signed, the compliance rulings which govern the testing and deployment of deployment ballistic missile have become increasingly strained. These strains are the heart of the dispute between the administration and the Congress over the demarcation agreements on theater defenses cited earlier.

In addition, Russia is no longer the only nation that poses a ballistic missile threat to the United States. The logic that supported the ABM Treaty and SALT I package in 1972—stability between two superpowers—is no longer consistent with the strategic situation confronting the United States. With respect to strategic threats, the United States now lives in a multipolar environment. Fixing the U.S.-Russian relationship does not, *ipso facto*, satisfy the requirements to meet these multiple strategic threats.

The technical features of the ballistic missile threat have evolved as well. The ABM Treaty limits capability against strategic ballistic missiles. In 1972, such missiles were associated with either strategic ballistic missile submarines or land-based missiles with ranges of 5,500 kilometers or more. But what is to be made of the North Korean Tapeo Dong 1 (TD-1) launched in 1998? To our great surprise, the North Koreans placed a third stage on what we thought was a two-stage theater ballistic missile. With that they demonstrated that the TD-1 could send a small payload to strategic ballistic missile ranges. How should such capability be treated by the ABM Treaty? If the United States develops a TMD able to shoot down the TD-1, should it also be treated as a strategic missile defense given its demonstrated range? If so, then such theater ballistic missile defenses are illegal under the ABM Treaty.

If not, then it is incumbent on those who would advocate adherence to the ABM Treaty to demonstrate how meaningful distinctions can be drawn. The demarcation agreement negotiated by the administration with the Russians does not solve this problem.

Those who wish to preserve the ABM Treaty's limits on defenses will need to demonstrate how its extension reflects objective conditions, both those we see now and those that are easily foretold. For example, treaty proponents worry that a defense deployment will provoke an offensive arms race. This pressure is exacerbated by an expectation that the low level of defense currently sought by the administration will inevitably give way to still higher levels over time, in turn causing offensive forces to be raised in anticipation of those higher defense levels.

One way to approach this problem is to revise the current U.S. negotiating policy. It now calls for a minimal initial deployment, followed by later deployments should the threat evolve in unspecified ways. Among the elements of an alternative approach would be a formal notification of withdrawal from the treaty to deploy a larger, though still constrained, defense to perform a limited set of specifically declared missions. The defense deployment declaration could include a unilateral commitment not to exceed a given capability either for a particular period of time or until a specified change in the threat occurs. During the six months the treaty requires between notification to withdraw and actual withdrawal, negotiations could be conducted with Russia to reach a bilateral agreement along these lines. Such an approach is not without its own risks, but it could provide others with a clear statement of U.S. intent and observable means of calibrating that intent with U.S. capability, thus aiding stability. It could also provide the United States with clearly delineated thresholds for sizing its deployed defense forces and a rationale on which to base its defense research and development.

• Deterrence and arms control remain linked and deterrence continues to drive the purposes of arms control.

In the case of the ABM Treaty, both proponents and opponents will agree to the first half of this proposition. It is on the second half that they are likely to part company. Proponents of missile defense will argue that deployments will strengthen deterrence. They are also likely to argue that arms control, in the form of the ABM Treaty, is inhibiting defenses and undermining deterrence. Opponents will respond that if defense deployments bring down the Cold War regime of arms control, lasting damage will have been done to deterrence, in whose name that regime was constructed. Missile defense proponents will need to take this argument seriously. They will need to show how they can fashion the contemporary equivalent of the Cold War compromise between the needs of deterrence and the desired outcome of any arms control agreement.

More imagination than was shown in the CTBT debate, and has thus far been shown the ABM Treaty debate, may prove necessary. Classic arms control approaches are unlikely to garner support (and should not) from either opponents or proponents of missile defense. A unilateral commitment of the kind suggested above, coupled with the sort of political, economic, and technical agreements envisioned by the Bush administration in its Global Protection Against Limited Strikes proposals may provide a starting point. These included a willingness to create mechanisms by which the benefits of defense are more broadly shared among congenial states, to increase reliance on self-defense among these states even as they eschew offensive ballistic missile programs, and to offer appropriate technical assistance.

Finally, the United States may need to provide a broader definition both of what we seek to deter and how we intend to do so. The U.S. interest in deterrence is not limited to nuclear (or chemical and biological) attacks on the U.S. homeland. Nor can deterrence be easily enforced in the emerging environment through dependence on strategic offensive or theater and NMD forces, working alone or in concert. It also requires enhanced intelligence collection and analysis as well as conventional forces coupled to diplomatic initiatives to dampen incipient threats if possible, to reduce existing threats when opportunity presents itself, and to encourage collective action in response to aggression. There can be a place for arms control in such a strategy; the challenge is to find it.

Arms Control in a New Era

From the outset of his administration, President George W. Bush has used two principles to change dramatically the United States' conduct of its arms control policy: first, emphasize unilateral action, conducted—if possible, but not necessarily—in concert with former U.S. adversaries at the negotiating table; and second, be willing to discard arms control mechanisms that might be considered outdated or harmful to U.S. interests.

By the end of 2001, the administration had implemented both principles in U.S. policy. The president announced reductions in U.S. strategic offensive forces to a level of 1,700–2,200 deployed warheads. A short time later, Russian president Vladimir Putin announced that Russia would reduce its strategic offensive forces to 1,500–2,200 deployed warheads. Then, on December 13, 2001, Bush declared the U.S. intent to withdraw from the 1972 Anti-Ballistic Missile (ABM) Treaty within six months, stressing that the treaty is a relic of the Cold War and hampers the ability of the United States to defend itself.

These cataclysmic events took place in a policy arena that has remained fairly stable during the past 30 years. "Arms control" throughout this period has usually meant carefully negotiated agreements, whether bilateral or multilateral, with legally binding measures to

Rose Gottemoeller is a senior associate at the Carnegie Endowment for International Peace.

Copyright © 2002 by The Center for Strategic and International Studies and the Massachusetts Institute of Technology
The Washington Quarterly • 25:2 pp. 45–58.

implement them. To discard that approach, and the treaties them-selves, in favor of more informal, unilateral arms control measures gives rise to several questions. Will the change be good for the United States, and does it help the country achieve its strategic goals? Or will pitfalls and problems undo many of the advances that have been achieved in arms reduction and control? Will the policy shift prevent the emergence of a new and more positive relationship with Russia?

Consistent with the general theory that change is good, the arms control relationship has indeed become tangled in recent years and could use some shock therapy to remove the knots. Just as Bush has said, the policy still takes too many of its cues from the Cold War. At the same time, however, too much of a jolt is likely to break the thread. The particular danger is that unilateral measures will be rushed into place to supersede negotiated agreements before a high level of trust is established at all levels in Moscow and Washington. Bush and Putin enjoy a good working relationship, which cannot be said of every sector and layer in the systems that stand beneath them. Legislators, other po-litical players, civil servants, and diplomats, even the Russian and U.S. publics, have far to go before they will consider the other country a re-liable partner and ally.

Indeed, by insisting that old treaties should disappear, Bush may be undercutting his own vision of a new, more cooperative relationship with Russia. Without broad consensus in both capitals that U.S.-Rus-sian cooperation is vital, the two countries might be tempted to walk away from interaction in sensitive arenas such as nuclear arms reduc-tion, once the binding regimes are lost. In other words, an approach that depends on unilateral measures alone may remove the impetus for cooperation between Moscow and Washington, thus making the Bush vision unattainable.

To counter this problem and get the best results from the Bush shock therapy will require some careful work. Yet, the situation is not hope-less. The United States and Russia have established a number of chan-nels for joint cooperation in recent years that is unprecedented by Cold War standards and goes beyond the strict formalistic approach of negotiated arms control treaties. To fulfill the president's vision and ensure that cooperation flourishes in the long term, these new approaches should be judiciously combined with existing agreements.

Where We Have Been

The basic structure of an agreement on strategic offensive-defensive arms control has existed since the first Strategic Arms Limitation Talks (SALT I) and ABM Treaties were signed in 1972. Innovations such as on-site inspections have made the structure more complex and effective over the years, but the concept has remained the same. As long as strategic defense systems were constrained, strategic offensive forces could be reduced without the threat that effective defenses would overwhelm the ability of remaining forces to deter.

In other words, in a world where one side builds strong defenses and both sides have relatively similar numbers of offensive weapons, the environment tends toward instability. The side with the strong defenses, feeling immune from attack, might be tempted to use its offensive weapons to overwhelm its opponent. The opponent, perceiving this threat, would have an incentive to build up its own offensive forces, thus sparking an arms race involving both offensive and defensive systems.

The offensive-defensive arms control deal struck 30 years ago broke this cycle and enabled sharp reductions in strategic offensive nuclear forces over time. On its face, Bush's abrogation of the ABM Treaty threatens to renew the cycle and return to the old arms race paradigm—an outcome that has been a major source of concern and complaint from both arms control experts and the international community.

Bush has strongly asserted, however, that he is not seeking this outcome. Since his presidential campaign, he has promised to reduce U.S. strategic offensive forces steadily and, through a process of transparency and openness, to convey to the Russians that the missile defenses that the United States will deploy will not undermine the Russian strategic offensive arsenal.

Contemporary Nuclear Debates

For this reason, his plan to negotiate a new offensive-defensive deal, which he worked out with Putin at the Ljubljana and Genoa summits in June and July of 2001, came as a surprise. Bush's position seemed to contradict his and his team's long-held stance and implied that the United States and Russia would be able to retain some vestige of the extant regime, with perhaps a modified ABM Treaty accompanying sharp reductions in strategic offensive forces, linked to the structure of the Strategic Arms Reduction Treaty (START I), the 1993 successor to the SALT process.

The Bush-Putin summit held in Crawford, Texas, in November 2001 dealt a blow to these expectations. It became clear that the White House would be unwilling, after all, to retain the ABM Treaty, even on a temporary basis, no matter how it was adapted to permit testing. Putin expressed his puzzlement over this outcome shortly after the ABM withdrawal announcement:

> We were prepared for certain modifications of the treaty. We asked to be given the specific parameters that stood in the way of U.S. desires to develop defensive systems. We were fully prepared to discuss [them]. But nothing specific was given to us. ... We heard only insistent requests for bilateral withdrawal from the treaty. To this day I fail to understand that insistence.[1]

At the end of 2001, the United States and Russia were left with no offensive-defensive deal, no ABM Treaty, a U.S. national missile defense system in the making, and declarations of each side's strong intention to reduce strategic offensive weapons. At the same time, the Russian team was still intently seeking a legally binding framework for the nuclear arms control relationship. Russian experts viewed Bush's first public statement about abrogating the ABM Treaty with great significance, because they believed it invoked the two sides to create a legal document to record the new framework for strategic cooperation. They noted that the translation of Bush's remarks used the Russian verb *oformit'*, which means to draw up a legal document. The Russians considered this statement a concession—perhaps the only concession—to Putin, who had expressed a strong desire for a legally binding agreement to ensure the monitoring and verification of the reductions. One hopes this translation from English was not an error.

Thus, the Bush administration has created a new arms control era, but whether it is for good or for ill is uncertain as both sides embark on that path. What measures, if any, from previous arms reduction agreements might each side fold into the development of the "new strategic framework"? What would the ideal outcome of the current process be? Accounting for the expressed preferences of both Russia and the United States, this process will undoubtedly go through several phases before it approximates an ideal outcome. Some practical steps will be necessary to move through the phases and overcome problems that will hinder the process. What are they? Are further principles needed to guide the new arms control relationship?

A Phased Approach to an Ideal Outcome

The starting point for the transition is the present, with formal arms control agreements regulating the strategic stability relationship. The United States and Russia thus far have apparently agreed that they should preserve some aspects of the current treaty system, especially START I, in order to ensure stability during the transition to the new strategic framework. The Russians call this approach "avoiding a legal vacuum."

The end point exists in the future, when strategic nuclear deterrence and formal, negotiated arms control would have only residual importance. Under this "ideal outcome," the relationship between the United States and Russia would be similar to the relationship between the United States and France or Great Britain. Ultimately, the United States and Russia would not target nuclear weapons against each other and would engage in extensive cooperation on strategic matters. For example, in this new era of strategic cooperation, they might jointly work on missile defenses, stewardship of their nuclear weapon stockpiles, and disposition of Cold War–era nuclear weapons and materials in both countries.

This ideal outcome will not be achieved instantaneously. Many governmental and nongovernmental players in the arms control arena are uncertain about whether the result can really unfold as the two presidents have indicated, that is, by quickly shedding the vestiges of the Cold War and moving to an essentially new relationship. On both sides, for example, a number of technical, highly charged issues remain from the implementation of START I, and they hamper consideration of a new, less stringent relationship that sets aside then-President Ronald Reagan's "trust but verify" maxim.

Of necessity, therefore, the two sides are actually in a transitional period that will pass through several phases. The phases required to achieve a new strategic relationship will be important, because they will determine whether or not the process will be successful. For this reason, frankly embracing a phased approach that enables the two countries to clear old troubling issues from the agenda as they move toward new cooperation would be desirable. One version of how such phases may unfold over the next decade follows, but other variants are certainly possible.

The first phase would take place throughout 2002 and incorporate a presidential summit in Russia in the early summer, as well as several other presidential and ministerial meetings on the margins of multilateral and bilateral forums. The general design of this phase would be to set the documentary groundwork for deeper change in the coming years. Documents released at either the presidential or the ministerial level could agree to the following:

Issue a presidential joint statement declaring that each country's strategic offensive forces and missile defense systems should not threaten the strategic forces of the other country. The announcement could also state that the two countries will work together to move toward a nonthreatening relationship in phases. The first step in this direction was taken at the Crawford summit, when the two presidents released a statement declaring that neither country threatened the other.[2]

Coordinate unilateral reductions in strategic nuclear forces. Bush and Putin have announced numbers (1,700–2,200 for the United States, 1,500–2,200 for Russia) and have apparently agreed to prepare a written document including some legal characteristics, particularly regarding monitoring and verification. The exact format remains to be determined. The document might be an adaptation of an existing treaty (such as a simplified START I Verification Protocol) or a new agreement, which could be simplified in its approach (such as an abbreviated Strategic Framework Agreement).

Accelerate efforts to address worrisome practices, such as the deployment of strategic nuclear weapons on hair-trigger alert, that have remained in place since the Cold War. The deactivation of strategic systems and finalized construction of the joint early-warning center could be early successes. Particularly important would be dual steps to break up logjams that have arisen in the construction of the center in Moscow. Additional steps could be considered to enhance early-warning cooperation further and to reduce launch readiness.

Cooperate on missile defenses to build both countries' confidence that these defense systems do not threaten their strategic offensive forces. Such cooperation, growing out of the joint statement mentioned above, might continue in this first phase with joint consideration of the threat. In fact, at a NATO meeting in December 2001, Sergei Ivanov, Russia's defense minister, announced his country's intention to cooperate with NATO on theater missile defenses.

Phase two would take the United States and Russia beyond the preparation of the initial documentary groundwork to the actual implementation of certain activities. This phase might begin in 2002 and would last for several years, at least until the end of the current U.S. administration's term in 2004. Implementation, however, could take longer. The focus of this phase would be to clear away the negative underbrush left from the previous era as well as to establish mechanisms, such as those described below, to enable the new relationship to unfold.

Create a high-level venue, perhaps under the purview of special presidential representatives, to air and resolve long-standing concerns in the relationship between the two countries. Possible issues might include proliferation of weapons of mass destruction to countries such as Iran and the status of nonstrategic nuclear weapons. Each of these issues—and more—has been a persistent irritant in the U.S.-Russian relationship. The matters could continue to be handled individually, but a special high-level consultative process might create some new momentum toward finding solutions.

Establish a joint defense-military planning mechanism in order to enhance transparency on the thinking and programs of each side. Such a venue could focus on expanding the role of joint defense-military planning as well as broad exchanges on the threat, technologies, and architectures of particular programs. Both sides could consider offensive and defensive technologies in this setting.

Initiate joint projects on missile defense technology. This effort might specifically consider how an existing technology might be usefully deployed, such as the deployment of the S-300 as part of a NATO theater defense system. Alternatively, the task might involve jointly developing a technology that discussions held during the first phase found promising.

Develop expert processes to determine new measures to ensure the transparency of offensive and defensive systems. The United States and Russia may decide to retain monitoring and verification measures from previous agreements such as START I, but they also may determine that additional transparency is needed, for example, monitoring warheads once they have been removed from operational deployment. Bush and his cabinet have also promised extensive transparency in the development and deployment of missile defenses. Determining both offensive and defensive measures would require expert technical work.

The third phase would find the two sides much more comfortable in their interactions in the strategic arena, but the general approach would unfold only after the first two preparatory phases. By 2008–2012, the U.S. and Russian governments might find the following steps possible:

Further reduce strategic nuclear forces to numbers of 1,000 or less in each country. This process should include transparency measures agreed between the two sides on the steps taken to eliminate strategic as well as nonstrategic warheads and delivery systems, although a legally binding agreement might not be required at this point. Instead, industrial-contracting relationships, wherein commercial firms from the two countries would be engaged in eliminating weapon systems, may re-

place the necessity for the two governments to verify or monitor implementation of reductions formally.

*Incorporate other countries that have tested nuclear weapons into the
warhead reduction process.* China, France, Great Britain, India, and Pakistan might be engaged in discussions during the first two phases, but
actual reductions in their forces would only begin once the United
States and Russia had completed significant reductions, probably to a
level of as few as 1,000 on each side.

Continue to routinize joint defense and military planning. This step
might include joint acquisition of weapons and extensive interaction of
military industries in Russia and NATO member countries.

*Develop a large-scale joint project or projects to deploy missile defenses in
specific theaters or at national levels.* By this time, both sides should have
resolved differences over the role of missile defenses.

*Cooperate closely on threat reduction and nonproliferation of weapons of
mass destruction in different regional settings.* Drawing on the U.S.-Rus-
sian experience in the 1990s, the two countries might join forces to reduce the threat of the proliferation of nuclear, chemical, and biological
weapons produced in different regions of the world.

As the third phase unfolds, the United States and Russia would actually be entering the new era of strategic cooperation that Bush and Putin
have heralded. A rush to declare that this era is already underway, however, is a recipe for disappointment. The two sides may be willing, but
policy and structural changes will take time. Therefore, emphasizing the
need for a patient, phased approach to the transition—whether this
three-phased template proves real, or another one is devised—is important. To highlight just how different the new era would be, detailing some
of the policy requirements—for both Washington and Moscow—that are
likely to flow from the activities laid out for the third phase is helpful.

The New Era of Strategic Cooperation

Reductions in strategic nuclear forces in this new era could look much
different than they do today. Current reduction practice flows from the

legally binding and very detailed procedures laid out in START I. In the United States at least, the U.S. Congress enforces extensive reviews of treaty compliance to support the implementation of this practice. Compliance irregularities have historically led to significant problems in the U.S.-Russian relationship. A new, more informal approach might require some significant loosening of compliance requirements, which, in turn, would need congressional acquiescence.

Putin has shown greater interest in legally binding treaty implementation measures than his U.S. counterpart has, which is ironic because Russia has long been interested in reducing the expense of implementing the very precise procedures laid out in START I. To resolve this evident contradiction, the Russian side seems willing to see the emergence of a "hybrid system," retaining some START I monitoring and verification measures while streamlining or discarding others and adding new transparency measures to address new issues. In discussions in Moscow in December 2001, Russian experts specifically mentioned that they would like to see the number of START I inspections cut by 20–30 percent, but that they would like to retain all notifications, data exchanges, and related "confidence-building measures" from the treaty. The creation of such a hybrid system would lead to changes in START I that may require advice and consent from the U.S. Senate and the Russian Duma. The system would also probably require the resolution of existing disagreements within the Joint Compliance and Inspection Commission, the START implementing body. Finally, new measures to ensure transparency and build each country's confidence—perhaps in some highly sensitive areas such as monitoring of warheads—would need to be developed.

Sensitive measures relating to warheads have been anticipated for years and, in fact, were intended to be a very explicit part of the START III planned by Presidents Bill Clinton and Boris Yeltsin. These measures are likely to require special action to carry them forward, however, such as an Agreement for Cooperation under the U.S. Atomic Energy Act. In the past, these agreements have been negotiated with Great Britain and France and have enabled cooperation on matters involving nuclear weapons. Negotiating an Agreement for Cooperation with Russia would move that country toward the relationship that Great Britain and France enjoy with the United States, but the agreement would require an enormous amount of careful work and high-level attention to bring it to fruition.

Some arms reduction activities, however, could take advantage of less formal arrangements. For the past several years, for example, under the Cooperative Threat Reduction (CTR) program, U.S.-based engineering companies including Bechtel and Lockheed-Martin have been helping to eliminate START-accountable weapon platforms in Russia. U.S. contractors have helped dismantle Russian strategic strike submarines, destroy Russian intercontinental ballistic missiles, and cut up Russian heavy bombers. These "industrial partnerships" have given the United States additional confidence, beyond the START verification process, in the status of Russia's strategic forces. The arrangements represent the kind of "natural transparency" that occurs when commercial firms are intimately involved in an industrial process. If the Russians suddenly decided to reverse course and stop the destruction of weapon systems for which they had contracted, the U.S. companies involved would be the first to know, and the U.S. government would closely follow them.

These industrial partnerships have emerged as part of a U.S. assistance program, whereby the United States pays to eliminate these strategic platforms. Because the relationship is based on U.S. assistance, Russia does not have reciprocal rights to work at similar U.S. facilities. Some Russian experts have, in fact, indicated a concern that the Bush administration's new emphasis on informal transparency measures—measures not based on treaties—means that the United States intends to eschew further START verification, which is reciprocal, in favor of CTR measures, which are not.

In a new era of strategic cooperation, the United States perhaps could consider the notion of U.S.-Russian industrial partnerships at U.S. elimination facilities. In fact, the same teams of U.S. principal contractors and Russian subcontractors might be certified to work in both Russian and

U.S. facilities. Such an effort could begin with very small steps. Russian military personnel have commented that even a symbolic move in this direction—a single Russian team working with a U.S. company at a U.S. facility—could enormously impact opinions in Moscow.

Moving from strategic offense to strategic defense, cooperation on missile defense technologies is another area to consider for the new strategic era. Secretary of Defense Donald Rumsfeld has stressed that the United States should be willing to engage the Russian Federation in whatever way necessary to prove that the U.S. missile defense system is not directed against Russia.[3] From the outset, the Bush administration has considered possible cooperation on the development of missile defense technology. In fact, the Bush team has done much to renew the Russian-American Observation Satellite (RAMOS) program, a decade-long joint project to develop early-warning satellite technology that could be applied to a missile defense system.

In a new strategic era, however, such cooperation could go far beyond a single project and would involve very close interaction among military developmental and manufacturing industries in Russia, the United States, and other NATO countries. Currently, such cooperation seems difficult to imagine, but a model already exists: the joint project that has unfolded during the past eight years to develop and build the International Space Station (ISS). The ISS project and its predecessor, the U.S. Space Shuttle-Mir joint missions, involved an essential marriage between U.S. and Russian hybrid military-civilian industries that produce missiles for military purposes and space-launch vehicles for peaceful purposes.

U.S.-Russian cooperation in space has successfully emphasized the nonmilitary side of the industry by developing joint arrangements that regularly result in Russian space experts working in Houston and other NASA facilities and their U.S. counterparts working at Star City near Moscow. The two manned space programs are now essentially intertwined—a process that did not occur without tension. Nevertheless, the ISS experience has shown that extensive cooperation between both countries' military and industrial sectors not only is feasible but also can be mutually beneficial. The program has also led to additional voluntary arrangements among aerospace companies on each side. Boeing, for example, has signed contracts with a number of Russian aerospace institutes and enterprises for the services of talented engineers and software specialists, who provide Boeing with engineering services from their offices in Moscow. This venture has enabled Boeing to undertake successful efforts to redesign aircraft, and the results have led to significant reductions in the manufacturing costs for Boeing's airplanes.

Thus, substantial interaction has already occurred on the nonmilitary side of U.S. and Russian aerospace industries. Although moving to the military side to pursue cooperation on missile defense technologies would raise complications in terms of sensitive information, developing sufficient procedures to enable close cooperation should be possible, given the extensive practice already developed in civilian projects. This effort would constitute another form of natural transparency, this time in the area of strategic defense.

Undoubtedly, developing such cooperation for national missile defense systems would take time. Cooperation in the civilian aerospace sector has taken the better part of a decade to reach its current stage of deep interaction. The United States and the Russian Federation may therefore wish to pursue parallel tracks in other arenas early in the relationship, in order to lay the groundwork for joint work at the national level.

The area of theater missile defenses may be promising. A number of statements expressing this sentiment preceded Minister of Defense Sergei Ivanov's recent announcement at NATO of cooperation in this area. For example, as early as the Clinton-Putin Moscow summit in June 2000, Putin stated that Russia was ready to offer its theater missile defense technologies for consideration in the NATO context. One NATO country, Greece, has already been deploying some Russian-built air defense systems, demonstrating the experience—although not always easy—of working together in this area. (The Russian media have highlighted the difficulties that Greek officers have encountered in their training with the Russian air defense systems, including drunkenness among Russian experts at the training facility. Despite the difficulties, the Greeks were nevertheless complimentary of the technology.)[4] In short, rapid engagement on theater defenses in the NATO context may provide valuable and early precedents for working together on missile defenses at the national level.

These examples have been presented to convey a sense of how different U.S.-Russian cooperation would be in a new era of strategic cooperation and how much change in extant policy and practice is required on the part of both countries. Unless each side confronts these complications at the outset, the new approach to arms control policy that Bush has outlined will flounder, and the new strategic relationship between the United States and Russia will fail to materialize. Consequently, explicitly defining the principles that will guide arms control policy as the relationship moves forward, thereby laying the groundwork for the new era, is necessary.

New Principles for Arms Control Policy

Bush's two principles for nuclear arms control policy—emphasizing unilateral action with or without the participation of former adversaries and discarding arms control mechanisms deemed outdated or harmful to U.S. interests willingly—are alone insufficient to usher in a new era of strategic cooperation. This approach may generate change and accelerate action but cannot create by itself the conditions under which the United States and Russia will develop a new and more closely knit strategic relationship. Thus, the Bush administration has set in motion both abrogation of the ABM Treaty and new, deep reductions in strategic offensive forces, but the new strategic relationship is probably many years and several phases of interaction away.

In order to achieve a new era of strategic cooperation, the two countries will need to present and embrace several additional principles for U.S.-Russian interaction. Otherwise, existing barriers to cooperation throughout the U.S. and Russian systems will continue to undermine the relationship, and the two countries will face disappointment and perhaps even new tensions. A basic list of additional principles should include the following:

- emphasizing partnerships rather than dependent relationships;
- adapting existing precedents to advance the new trend toward cooperation; and
- depending explicitly on natural interactions, such as in the business sector, to provide confidence in the relationship on the part of both countries.

The emphasis on partnership is straightforward but bears repeating. During the past decade, the United States and Russia have interacted frequently in a dependent relationship based on assistance, and the experience has taken a toll on the bilateral relationship. The United States has often assumed a dominant role because it has been financing the assistance, creating resentment and prompting negative reactions on the Russian side. One way to counteract this effect as the two countries move toward a new era requires Russia to bring more resources to the table in the joint relationship; this contribution is indeed possible as the health of the Russian economy improves. Searching for areas of cooperation where Russia can offer its own unique capabilities is another option; the laboratory-to-laboratory cooperation involving weapons labs in the United States and Russia is one successful example. Russian concepts, ideas, and technologies can genuinely contribute to resolving problems, such as cleaning up nuclear waste in both countries. By searching out such areas for cooperation, the United States and Russia would create a realistic, unforced agenda for a partnership beneficial to both sides.

The previously cited example also highlights the second principle: the adaptation of existing precedents to advance the new cooperation. The United States and Russia were thrown together 10 years ago, after the breakup of the Soviet Union, to protect the old Soviet weapons complex from neglect and theft. Under the auspices of the CTR and other related programs, both countries developed wide-ranging industrial relationships inside the former Soviet complex. These relationships have not only enabled implementation of the two countries' cooperative programs but have also added a useful, less formal layer to the strategic arms control process. The venture is widely heralded as a model for the new era of strategic cooperation.

The model will not fulfill that promise, however, unless it can be applied in both countries. Because the industrial relationships flowed from an assistance program, they have not developed reciprocally on U.S. soil. Recognizing the importance of that precedent, both sides need to adapt the model—not slavishly but carefully, in a step-by-step manner—before the experience of CTR and its sister programs will have a role in the future arms control relationship. Even a symbolic measure would be valuable.

In turn, both the United States and the Russian Federation will be able to take advantage of the natural transparency that results from industrial and commercial relationships. In fact, the third principle underlying the new era should be that neither side will have to strive to develop confidence in the implementation of agreements; each will see such confidence emerge as the natural result of working closely together. Implementation of agreements, in effect, will take place as a cooperative venture rather than a matter of actions by an individual nation, verified or monitored by another.

Such outcomes are many years away. When they are realized, they will truly herald a new era of strategic cooperation. We should not delude ourselves, however, that this new era will emerge as a kind of perfect system existing without any legal arrangements or agreements between governments. Even with our closest allies, the British, we are unlikely to do away with, as a matter of our national law, the U.S. Atomic Energy Act, the Agreement for Cooperation that governs our cooperation on sensitive nuclear matters. We can dispense with Cold War excesses in the nuclear treaty world, but even the closest of relationships with the Russian Federation, as with our closest allies, will require some continuing legal mechanisms.

Yet, assuming we are patient, we can do much to simplify and improve the U.S.-Russian relationship. We must carefully consider the phases that we will need to traverse to arrive at a new era of strategic cooperation. The first phases will be preparatory, making it possible to determine what is useful to keep for the future and what should be discarded from the past. The initial phases will also enable both sides to examine the barriers to a more cooperative relationship that exist in each country and to decide how to address them. In particular, the preparatory phases will facilitate the resolution of long-standing issues, such as the proliferation of nuclear technologies to Iran by some Russian firms. Throughout all these stages in the new relationship, both governments should be prepared not to hurry, for the emergence of the new era will take time, effort, and care.

Notes

1. Andrew Gowers, Robert Cottrell, and Andrew Jack, "Putin under Pressure," *Financial Times*, December 17, 2001.

2. "Remarks by U.S. Defense Secretary Donald Rumsfeld at a Roundtable with Russian Political Scientists," Itar-Tass, August 13, 2001, distributed by the Federal News Service.

3. "Joint Statement by President George W. Bush and President Vladimir V. Putin on a New Relationship Between the United States and Russia," White House, Office of the Press Secretary, November 13, 2001, www.whitehouse.gov/news/releases/2001/11/20011113-4.html (accessed November 13, 2001).

4. See Vladimir Malyshev, "Perfect Missiles," *Sankt-Peterburgskie vedomosti*, September 1, 2000, translated in WPS (R ussian Media Monitoring Agency) Defense and Security Digest, September 18, 2000.

John Steinbruner

Renovating Arms Control through Reassurance

Security policy has traditionally focused on the threat of deliberate aggression with a clarity and emotional intensity that presumably derives from the far recesses of time. For most of history, it was appropriate to be primarily concerned with intentional aggression since the destruction human beings could inflict on one another had to be consciously organized if it was to occur on a major scale. It is increasingly evident, however, that advanced technology and the sheer magnitude of human activity are generating a different form of threat. Today, an unanticipated chain of spontaneous effects might rival or exceed the destructiveness of intentional war. This sort of accidental war might erupt, ironically, from the military operations designed to protect against the risk of classic aggression itself.

The danger of accidental war was demonstrated in World War I and was recognized in its aftermath. The experience of World War II, however, obscured the lesson and powerfully reinforced the traditional concern of intentional aggression. Over the ensuing decades, as the instruments of warfare acquired capacities for rapid and massive destruction, the military forces that wielded them were configured to deter or to defeat deliberate

John Steinbruner is a professor at the University of Maryland School of Public Affairs. This article is based on his book, *Principles of Global Security* (Brookings Institution Press, forthcoming).

Copyright © 2000 by The Center for Strategic and International Studies and the Massachusetts Institute of Technology
The Washington Quarterly • 23:2 pp. 197–206.

attack. Precautions were taken to assure that their enormously destructive power would not be employed without legitimate authorization, but those precautions were clearly subordinated to the purpose of deterrence. That effect was achieved and is plausibly credited with preventing at least the largest forms of deliberate aggression, but the accomplishment has enabled a massive accident to occur. Overwhelming deterrence entails some inherent risk of inadvertent catastrophe.

The political consciousness of the Cold War that inspired the commitment to overwhelming deterrence is distant history, but its major legacy has survived essentially intact and largely uncontested. The main protagonists—the United States and Russia—are now attempting to work out an amicable relationship, but each still maintains thousands of nuclear weapons continuously prepared to initiate a massive assault on the other within a few minutes. The destructive capacity of these forces poses the greatest physical threat to both societies and to the rest of the world. In the absence of an ideological quarrel, however, there is such abiding faith in deterrence that the risk of potential destruction is accepted as assuring protection rather than as presenting an imminent danger. There has been no serious attempt to terminate mass deterrent operations. Even reducing forces to levels that have been provisionally agreed upon will not remove the ability to inflict damage far beyond any historical experience.

By contrast, the arms control process designed to contain the capacity for destruction has been subjected to a barrage of querulous objection. The Russian Duma has not ratified the second Strategic Arms Reduction Treaty (START II), even though the ceilings it imposes are substantially higher than the deployment level Russia is likely to be able to sustain over the long term. The U.S. Senate has voted against ratification of the Comprehensive Test Ban Treaty (CTBT) even though it would lock in a large technical advantage for the United States and is considered by much of the world to be an established obligation essential for the prevention of proliferation. In both instances, it appears overwhelmingly obvious that the two countries are far better off with the spurned treaties than without them, but vigorous arguments to the contrary have been advanced as an apparent extension of domestic politics.

In the case of the CTBT, U.S. opponents claimed that the treaty could not be verified. The range of plausible uncertainty, however, is well below the minimum explosive yield for any test that could be expected to produce useful weapons-design information.[1] Similarly, opponents argued that the reliability of the U.S. weapons stockpile could not be assured over the longer term, even though all nonnuclear components of the weapons could and would be tested under the terms of the treaty. Any suspected problem with the fissionable material could be resolved by remanufacturing them to their original specifications.[2] The fact that central provisions of legal restraint can be held hostage to such arguments advanced at the extreme edge of rational judgment is a symptom of pathology in the arms control process.

Although it is difficult to determine at this point just how serious the apparent pathology might be, it is certainly prudent to be concerned. It is unlikely that ratification of START II or of the CTBT will be accomplished before new presidents take office in Russia and the United States. Meanwhile zealous advocates of national missile defense in the United States can be expected to stage an assault on the ABM Treaty, which they would like to declare obsolete, and there is a substantial chance that the effort will succeed. The Clinton administration has promised to make a specific deployment decision in July 2000. It has proposed amendments to the treaty that would legalize the limited deployment immediately intended, but Russia has stated quite firmly that it will not accept those amendments or any variation that would validate the U.S. program. If the United States proceeds with a deployment effort in admitted violation of the treaty, as it has threatened to do, then the Russians have promised to declare all offensive force limitations invalid and might choose to violate agreed restrictions on multiple warhead deployments. At that point, with India and Pakistan on the verge of overtly deploying nuclear weapons, a reverberating series of potential reactions could conceivably shatter the Nuclear Non-Proliferation

Treaty (NPT) and collapse the entire framework of legal restraint on nuclear weapons deployment.

Since the basic principle of legal restraint is widely considered to be indispensable, the acknowledged failure of major treaties would presumably generate a protective political reaction. It is questionable, however, whether the existing agreements could be restored once they had been violated by authorized deployment programs. It is even more questionable whether they could be replaced through the tedious and largely unproductive process of adversarial negotiation that has prevailed over the past decade. In fact, the current arms control regime is likely to require major renovation, responding to dramatically changed circumstances, regardless of whether there is an acute crisis over U.S. national missile defense.

The Argument for Renovation

In considering what a major renovation might attempt to do, it is natural to begin by rehearsing the familiar characteristics of the existing arrangements and the basic reasons why they developed as they did. The principal legal restrictions on nuclear weapons deployments evolved through bilateral negotiations between the United States and the Soviet Union. The central agreements were formulated to impose, first, ceilings and, then, a schedule of reductions on the deployment of delivery vehicles capable of carrying nuclear weapons over relatively long ranges. The intent was to distinguish a strategic level of threat, where the common interest in mutual restraint was judged to be stronger, from other, more localized forms of military engagement considered to be more contentious. The focus of control on delivery vehicles was chosen since they were more easily verifiable by remote means of observation. The underlying presumption was that the two countries would continue to be hostile adversaries. The basic purpose of establishing formal agreements was to regulate the balance of opposing capability in order to render it less burdensome and less dangerous to both sides.

From the outset, both governments and military establishments understood that the agreements would protect the deterrent capacities of both parties. Offensive and defensive forces would be regulated in relation to each other. Similarly, the 1963 Limited Test Ban Treaty, a multilateral document imposing comprehensive restrictions on nuclear weapons testing, and the NPT, imposing selective restrictions on the development of nuclear weapons by other military establishments, were understood to be supplemental to the bilateral treaties and contingent upon their further development. Although segmented into separate legal documents, the overall arrangement has been, in effect, a global bargain to regulate use of the world's most destructive technology. Without these agreements, the 44 countries that operate nuclear reactors today could theoretically deploy nuclear weapons. All these agreements are intertwined and the underlying logic is a simple and virtually inevitable rule: if anyone is to be constrained in the application of this technology, then everyone must be.

The surrounding circumstances have changed substantially, of course, since the original arms-control treaties were formulated. Quite apart from questions of ideology and political intention, Russia is not, and is never likely to be, a replacement for the Soviet Union as the balancing correspondent to the United States in the core bilateral arrangement. Russia does not have the economic capacity to assume that role and cannot plausibly develop it anytime soon. Moreover, Russia has fundamentally different strategic imperatives. The society is undergoing extensive internal regeneration, the urgent purpose of which is to connect productively to the globalizing international economy. Its considerable importance to the outside world is contingent upon the outcome of that regeneration. The fate of its military establishment is also entangled in that process, but the central question is not the capacity for strategic bombardment, but rather its internal managerial coherence.

Russia must exercise responsible control over what is believed to be the largest nuclear-weapons inventory. It must also preserve the basic elements of civil order on its own territory. The ability of a beleaguered government caught up in internal transformation to do these things cannot be presumed. What can be presumed is that Russia will need substantial reassurance if it is to manage its inherited nuclear arsenal safely. That reassurance will have to be extended to all the legitimate missions its military is responsible for performing, not merely those considered strategic by the outside world.

Although the internal transformation of Russia is proving to be especially difficult, the international security implications are not unique. With the military predominance of the U. S. alliance system now arguably the greatest in history, all countries outside of that system suffer a corresponding disadvantage. Hegemonic power often imagined in popular rhetoric does not automatically come with that military strength, but military preponderance does create issues of inequity. For those countries concerned about a potential military confrontation with the U.S. alliance system for reasons not necessarily under their control, this is a major security problem. Since it is not feasible for any country or group of countries to match the military capacity of the U.S. alliance system for the foreseeable future, there is a strong incentive to pursue asymmetrical deterrent strategies. In other words, these countries are being driven to identify vulnerable hostages they could threaten in order to fend off intimidation. If advanced technologies are adapted for that purpose and critical assets targeted, the resulting arrangement would be very dangerous indeed. The priority for the United States and acknowledged friends is to reassure the disadvantaged to prevent these asymmetrical deterrent strategies. The central purpose of arms control in the new situation, then, is not to deter but to reassure. Deterrence has become too large and too inequitably distributed for its own good.

As the word implies, a renovation of this sort would not eliminate but rather reconfigure the existing international security structure. So, presumably, nuclear weapons would continue to be deployed for an indefinite period and would exercise their inherent deterrent effect. Limitations on deployed numbers and on development testing would be preserved, a schedule of judicious reductions would be set, and proliferation controls would be maintained. The main emphasis would shift, however, from restrictions on the number of deployed weapons to restrictions on their operational practices. Because adequate deterrence is more easily achieved in today's international security environment, formal agreements would be designed to maximize reassurance by establishing high standards of operational safety. The purpose would be to prevent accidental, unauthorized, or inadvertent use of the deployed weapons more reliably.

In advanced form, such an arrangement would remove all weapons from an alert status in which they are immediately available for use, and would verify that condition by collaborative monitoring techniques that could not be bypassed, blinded, or fooled. Official doctrines of nuclear weapons use would be restricted by legal agreement exclusively to "no-first-use," meaning retaliation only against attack by another nuclear weapon and only then in proportion to the original attack itself. Corresponding restrictions would be imposed on the first use of conventional weapons as well in order to regulate their use for purposes of retribution as in Iraq, Afghanistan, and Sudan recently. It is not only the imposing nuclear deterrent of the United States that creates a need for reassurance, but its increasingly intrusive and inherently more usable capacity for precise conventional attack as well.

Admittedly these provisions would be a major extension of existing arms control arrangements and would probably incite even more vehement objection from the traditional critics. Since they respond more directly to the emerging problems of international security, however, that greater relevance might generate more robust support from others. At any rate, the stark imbalance in capacity that has developed today will assuredly not be accepted as equitable, and the implications of inequity are likely to be relentless.

Exploratory Applications

The arms control regime does not have a reigning architect in the sense that a building does. As a matter of practical politics, it is unlikely that anyone who would want to redesign arms control based on the principle of reassurance would ever be granted the authority to do so. Major adjustments of that sort usually occur in a series of seemingly incremental steps, with a shift in organizing principle recognized only after the fact. The fate of legal restraint will predictably turn on specific issues, the most important and immediate instance being the impending collision of policy over the U.S. national missile defense (NMD) program. As with any incipient crisis, that situation offers opportunity as well as danger; the practical question is how the opportunity might be used to begin to apply the principles of renovation.

The tendency to gloss over, or obfuscate, disagreements is the first problem that should be addressed. Despite rising nationalist resentment on the Russian side—a reaction that a truly objective observer presumably would find understandable under the circumstances—the two governments are clearly not eager for a full-blown confrontation on the NMD issue. They will probably strain to put an accommodating spin on whatever decisions they make. On the whole, of course, that reflects a constructive attitude necessary for any desirable outcome, but it makes it difficult to bring the sharp contradiction in underlying policy into focus.

The hard fact is that Russia cannot responsibly accept the current U.S. position. The limited NMD deployment being projected would establish the foundation for a much more extensive and more capable system over time. Since relative offensive capabilities can be expected to diverge under even the most advanced treaty limitations that have been officially discussed, the net result would pose an extreme threat to the viability of the Russian deterrent force. The United States would gradually acquire a potentially decisive capacity to destroy the Russian force without suffering significant retaliation. The United States has not offered or even seriously contemplated the drastic offensive force restrictions that would be necessary to preclude that development. It will not be possible to address this problem until it is admitted.

There is a corresponding problem with China that is even less visible. China has deployed only about 20 ballistic missile launchers that could reach the United States and does not routinely operate them on alert status. On any normal day, the United States could destroy those launchers in a preemptive attack. China, long aware of this, has chosen to tolerate the risk. The Chinese deterrent force directed against the United States could have been made larger and more robust long ago if

China wanted to. Beijing has apparently judged the overall risk of a deliberate first strike by the United States to be less than the risk inherent in the high-alert deployments long maintained by Russia and the United States. A completely renovated arms control arrangement based on reassurance would follow that example.

China has warned, however, that it would reconsider its posture if the United States were to deploy either an NMD or a theater missile defense (TMD) system designed for broad-area protection in Asia. Because the Anti-Ballistic Missile (ABM) Treaty is strictly bilateral between the United States and Russia, China does not have legal standing to raise its concerns. In real strategic terms, however, Beijing's concerns are as legitimate as Moscow's and comparably important as well, although the specific implications may be somewhat different. This problem will also not be addressed until it is acknowledged.

What might be done, then, if both these problems were to be admitted? A natural first step is to address the surveillance of ballistic missile trajectories, a major operational problem that links the traditional arms-control agenda with a renovated one. Under existing security practices, which are designed principally to deter, continuous surveillance combined with highly alert force operations provides a principal method of protection against preemptive destruction. But it also provides a critical element of reassurance necessary to prevent the practice of deterrence from becoming a self-defeating provocation to war. By continuously observing the missile trajectories that the opponent would use to conduct an attack, Russia and the United States continuously demonstrate to themselves that a major attack is not immediately underway and that retaliation is not immediately required. It is vital to the United States that Russia never make any misjudgment in that regard and similarly for Russia that the United States not do so.

Unfortunately, although their interests are symmetrical, the capacities to prevent a catastrophic misjudgment are not. The U.S. surveillance system has comprehensive, state-of-the-art coverage of possible attack corridors, which protects Washington from falsely concluding a Russian attack has been launched. The Russian surveillance system, in contrast, has major gaps in coverage, both in space and in time, and is believed to be slipping in quality. That creates a risk that an attack will be falsely attributed to the United States.

At a summit meeting in September 1998, Russia and the United States agreed in principle to establish a joint center for missile surveillance. Implementation of that initiative is probably the single most effective step that might immediately be taken both to stabilize the traditional deterrent relationship and to introduce the broader concept of reassurance. If the United States provided missile flight information upon which Russia was willing to rely, it would be a much more advanced form of security collaboration than any during the Cold War. Presidents Bill Clinton and Boris Yeltsin proposed this initiative at a time when neither enjoyed commanding political authority, and the idea had not been developed by the U.S. and Russian security bureaucracies in sufficient detail. Subsequent efforts to implement this idea were suspended by the Russians in reaction to the Kosovo crisis.

To assure reliance on such a vital matter and to prevent suspicion that would only compound the problem, Russia would have to be deeply and irreversibly integrated into the U.S. missile-tracking system—so deeply, in fact, that Russia would have to be treated as nearly a coequal partner. That would require revising attitudes on both sides to an extent not currently considered feasible. Nonetheless, if a constructive breakthrough is to occur in the shadow of an incipient NMD crisis, then joint missile surveillance is one of the more prominent possibilities. In principle it could even be extended to China.

Broader Ideas

For venturesome souls, joint missile surveillance can also be seen as a leading item on a much broader agenda involving how information would be gathered and disseminated under a renovated security arrangement. In the Cold War practice of verification, reassuring information is exchanged under strictly limited and exhaustively negotiated terms designed to demonstrate compliance with specified agreements.

Under the START agreements, for example, the parties declare their ballistic missile inventories and promise not to interfere beyond specified limits with the national surveillance systems used to independently observe those inventories.

A renovated arrangement would exchange information more openly, conceivably including daily operational practices, in order to demonstrate not only legal compliance but much broader intent. Thus, in addition to documenting basic weapons inventories, the parties would assertively seek to demonstrate the integrity of their managerial control systems and would begin to harmonize and ultimately integrate the operations of those systems. A common accounting and physical security system would be devised for exercising strict control over fabricated warheads and fissionable materials, and discussion of joint operation would begin. More accurate accounting than is currently possible under traditional rules of verification will be required to reduce active deployment to levels ranging in the hundreds of weapons. Joint operation of the system would probably be necessary to establish high-quality reassurance about the state of nuclear weapons inventories.

In anticipation of that eventual requirement, all of the nuclear weapons states should be involved in the design of such an arrangement. As yet, however, such a system does not appear to have been seriously discussed in bilateral terms, let alone as the multilateral arrangement it would ultimately have to be. Since it is likely to take several decades to develop such a system with high standards of accuracy and protection, it is important to begin the design immediately. Similarly, the notion of bilateral cooperation between Russia and the United States on missile surveillance could include joint military-air-traffic control. That seems categorically unacceptable if the dominant purpose is to prepare for imminent war. It is desirable, however, if the dominant purpose is to reassure others that war is not imminent and cannot be rapidly prepared.

If reassurance were to be the guiding spirit, as it largely is among the members of the U.S. alliance system, then a great deal of operational information currently considered sensitive presumably would be shared among those accepting the terms of exchange. That could include budget projections, investment plans, training schedules, and deployment exercises. Undoubtedly, there would still be prudent limits to such exchanges, but in a renovated arrangement, those limits would be much narrower than under current practice.

In the latter stages of the Cold War, the stabilizing effect of voluntarily disclosed information came to be recognized, and a number of confidence-building measures were formally introduced. In the aftermath of the Cold War, it is important to extend that tradition and upgrade its priority. Since it is unlikely that equitable force balances can be established anytime soon, it is all the more important that the idea of confidence and the underlying principle of reassurance be elevated from subordinate status to the main priority. That is how arms control should be renovated.

Notes

1. It is generally accepted that weapons tests with nuclear explosive yields of ten tons TNT equivalent up to a few hundred tons might evade reliable verification. Not even the United States, with the most extensive store of test data at its disposal, would rely on tests in that range for the design of weapons in the much higher yield ranges used for the deterrent forces. All other countries would be very substantially less able to do so. Moreover, the enhanced verification provisions that would be enabled by the Comprehensive Test Ban Treaty (CTBT) would make it increasingly difficult to conduct a test series in the very low range of uncertainty without eventually being detected.

2. See Sidney Drell, *The JASON'S Report on Nuclear Testing: Summary and Conclusions*, August 1, 1995, available at http://www.stimson.org/rd-table/jasons.htm.